MATH
ECONOMICS
IN

MATH
ECONOMICS

Susheng Wang

Hong Kong University of Science and Technology

 **World Scientific**

NEW JERSEY • LONDON • SINGAPORE • BEIJING • SHANGHAI • HONG KONG • TAIPEI • CHENNAI

Published by

World Scientific Publishing Co. Pte. Ltd.

5 Toh Tuck Link, Singapore 596224

USA office: 27 Warren Street, Suite 401-402, Hackensack, NJ 07601

UK office: 57 Shelton Street, Covent Garden, London WC2H 9HE

Library of Congress Cataloging-in-Publication Data

Wang, Susheng.

   Math in economics / Susheng Wang (Hong Kong University of Science and Technology, Hong Kong). -- 2nd Edition.

      pages cm

   Includes bibliographical references and index.

   ISBN 978-9814663212 (alk. paper) -- ISBN 978-9814663816 (alk. paper)

   1. Economics--Mathematical models. I. Title.

   HB135.W364 2015

   510--dc23

                                                 2015009299

British Library Cataloguing-in-Publication Data

A catalogue record for this book is available from the British Library.

In-house Editors: Dipasri Sardar/Philly Lim

Typeset by Stallion Press

Email: enquiries@stallionpress.com

Printed in Singapore

Contents

Preface

The target audience. This book covers math at the senior undergraduate, Master's and Ph.D. levels for students in business schools and economics departments. It concisely covers the main math knowledge and tools useful for business and economics studies, including matrix analysis, basic math concepts, general optimization, dynamic optimization, ordinary differential equations, difference equations, and probability theory. Basic math tools, particularly optimization tools, are essential for students in a business school, especially for students majoring in economics, accounting, finance, management, and marketing. Nowadays most graduate programs in business schools require their students to take a short and intense course in math just before or shortly after commencing their studies. This book is designed to be used in such a course.

The coverage. Chapter 1 focuses on the part of linear algebra that is essential for business studies — matrix analysis. Chapter 2 covers the basic concepts underlying real analysis, including set, sequence, convergence, continuity, differentiation, homogeneity, inverse functions, and fixed points. Chapter 3 discusses general topics in optimization, including definite matrices, concavity, quasiconcavity, unconstrained and constrained optimization, the Lagrange theorem, the Kuhn–Tucker theorem, and the envelope theorem. Chapter 4 explains the concept of dynamic optimization, with a particular emphasis on discrete-time stochastic optimization and continuous-time deterministic optimization. It describes several popular approaches to dynamic optimization, including backward induction, the Lagrange method, the Hamilton method, the Bellman equation, the Euler equation, transversality conditions, and the phase diagram. Chapter 5 covers first-order differential equations and linear equation systems. It introduces various ways of solving first-order differential equations — the standard method of solving linear equations, and the Laplace transformation. Chapter 6 details first-order difference equations and linear difference equations. It introduces the iterative method and z-transformation. Finally, Chapter 7 covers probability theory, including probability space, conditional probability, random variables, distribution functions, conditional distributions, and convergence.

Special features of this book. There is no shortage of math books for business studies. This book covers all the necessary topics but places a special emphasis on optimization as it is an essential topic for business students. Many details are deliberately left out for conciseness. Thus, this book is suitable for those students who will be picking up most of the details in class. It will also appeal to those instructors who prefer to fill in the details themselves. This book can also serve as a handy reference for those who have already learned much of the materials.

Supporting materials. Exercises and solutions are available at www.bm.ust.hk/~sswang/math-book/. Errors are inevitable and corrections will be posted there. Interested readers will also find additional materials such as new sections and chapters at the website.

Chapter 1

Linear Algebra

We will focus on the part of linear algebra that is most useful for business studies — matrices. Basic knowledge of linear algebra is assumed.

1. Vector

A scalar is either a real number $a \in \mathbb{R}$ or a complex number $z \in \mathbb{C}$, where $\mathbb{R}$ is the set of all real numbers and $\mathbb{C}$ is the set of all complex numbers. A vector is an ordered sequence of numbers:

$$x = \begin{pmatrix} x_1 \\ x_2 \\ \vdots \\ x_n \end{pmatrix}. \tag{1.1}$$

The numbers x_i are called entries, coefficients or elements. The entries can generally be complex numbers. However, except when eigenvalues are involved, we assume real entries and denote an n-dimensional vector by $x \in \mathbb{R}^n$. For convenience, we sometimes write it as (x_i) or $(x_i)_n$. In business studies, for example, a vector can represent a financial asset, with its entries representing features of the financial asset.

A special vector is the zero vector: $0 \in \mathbb{R}^n$. Given a vector in (1.1), we can define its transpose and denote it by x' or x^T, with

$$x' = x^T \equiv (x_1, x_2, \ldots, x_n).$$

We typically write a vector as a vertical/column vector; its horizontal/row version is x'. For a vector $x \in \mathbb{R}^n$, we can define its length as $\|x\|$, where

$$\|x\| \equiv \sqrt{x_1^2 + \cdots + x_n^2},$$

and call it the norm. Then we can define the distance between any two points x and y in $\mathbb{R}^n$ by the norm $\|x - y\|$.

Given two vectors $a = (a_i)_n$ and $b = (b_i)_n$, we can define their summation $a + b$, subtraction $a - b$, and multiplication $a'b$, $\langle a, b \rangle$ or $a \cdot b$ respectively by

$$a + b = \begin{pmatrix} a_1 + b_1 \\ \vdots \\ a_n + b_n \end{pmatrix}, \quad a - b = \begin{pmatrix} a_1 - b_1 \\ \vdots \\ a_n - b_n \end{pmatrix}, \quad a \cdot b = \sum_{i=1}^{n} a_i b_i.$$

We can also multiply a vector $a \in \mathbb{R}^n$ by a number $\lambda \in \mathbb{R}$:

$$\lambda a \equiv \begin{pmatrix} \lambda a_1 \\ \vdots \\ \lambda a_n \end{pmatrix}.$$

These operations are intuitively shown in Figure 1.1, and, if θ is the angle between vectors a and b, we have

$$a \cdot b = \|a\| \cdot \|b\| \cdot \cos(\theta).$$

Proposition 1.1. *For vectors $a, b, c \in \mathbb{R}^n$, we have*

(a) *The associative law of summation:* $(a + b) + c = a + (b + c)$.
(b) *The commutative law of summation:* $a + b = b + a$.
(c) *The commutative law of multiplication:* $a \cdot b = b \cdot a$.
(d) *The distributive law:* $a \cdot (b + c) = a \cdot b + a \cdot c$. ∎

A vector $\beta \in \mathbb{R}^n$ is a linear combination of vectors $\alpha_1, \ldots, \alpha_m \in \mathbb{R}^n$, if there exist $\lambda_1, \ldots, \lambda_m \in \mathbb{R}$ such that

$$\beta = \lambda_1 \alpha_1 + \cdots + \lambda_m \alpha_m.$$

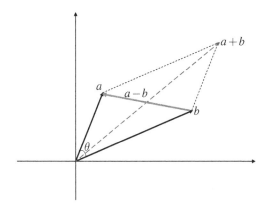

Figure 1.1. Graphical Illustration of Vector Operations

For example, a mutual fund is a linear combination of some basic assets. Define the span of a few vectors $\alpha_1, \ldots, \alpha_m$ as

$$span(\alpha_1, \ldots, \alpha_m) = \{\text{all linear combinations of vectors } \alpha_1, \ldots, \alpha_m\}.$$

We call $\alpha_1, \ldots, \alpha_m$ the generating vectors of the span. For example, a financial market can be considered as the span of some basic financial assets.

A few vectors $\alpha_1, \alpha_2, \ldots, \alpha_m \in \mathbb{R}^n$ are linearly dependent if there exist numbers $\lambda_1, \lambda_2, \ldots, \lambda_m \in \mathbb{R}$, not all such that

$$\lambda_1 \alpha_1 + \lambda_2 \alpha_2 + \cdots + \lambda_m \alpha_m = 0.$$

Vectors that are not linearly dependent are linearly independent. Hence, vectors $\alpha_1, \alpha_2, \ldots, \alpha_m$ are linearly independent if the equation $c_1 \alpha_1 + c_2 \alpha_2 + \cdots + c_m \alpha_m = 0$ occurs only if $c_1 = c_2 = \cdots = c_m = 0$. Linear independence means that none of the vectors can be a linear combination of the rest. In $span(\alpha_1, \ldots, \alpha_m)$, if one of the generating vectors, say α_m, is a linear combination of the rest of the generating vectors, then

$$span(\alpha_1, \ldots, \alpha_m) = span(\alpha_1, \ldots, \alpha_{m-1}).$$

That is, if a generating vector is a linear combination of other generating vectors, this generating vector is redundant. If we can find a set of linearly independent generating vectors for a space (which we can always do), then the number of such vectors is the minimum possible number of any set of generating vectors for this space.

Example 1.1. Any two linearly independent vectors in $\mathbb{R}^2$ can span the whole space $\mathbb{R}^2$ this can be shown graphically. In general, $\mathbb{R}^n$ can be spanned by n linearly independent vectors. ■

2. Matrix

A matrix is an ordered sequence of column vectors or row vectors, which can be written in the following form:

$$A = \begin{pmatrix} a_{11} & \cdots & a_{1n} \\ \vdots & & \vdots \\ a_{m1} & \cdots & a_{mn} \end{pmatrix}. \tag{1.2}$$

The numbers a_{ij} are called entries, coefficients or elements. The entries can generally be complex numbers. However, except when eigenvalues are involved, we assume real entries. We say that matrix A in (1.2) is of dimension $m \times n$ and denote $A \in \mathbb{R}^{m \times n}$. For convenience, we sometimes write it as (a_{ij}) or $(a_{ij})_{m \times n}$. In business, a matrix can represent a set of data of a few economic variables.

Example 1.2. The following is a linear equation system for variables $x_1, \ldots, x_n$:

$$a_{11}x_1 + a_{12}x_2 + \cdots + a_{1n}x_n = d_1,$$
$$a_{21}x_1 + a_{22}x_2 + \cdots + a_{2n}x_n = d_2,$$
$$\vdots$$
$$a_{m1}x_1 + a_{m2}x_2 + \cdots + a_{mn}x_n = d_m.$$

This linear equation system can be written as $Ax = d$, where A is defined in (1.2) and $d = (d_i)_m$. ■

A special matrix is the zero matrix: $0 \in \mathbb{R}^{m \times n}$, in which all the entries are zero. When $m = n$, we have a square matrix. A special square matrix is the identity matrix: $I_n \in \mathbb{R}^{n \times n}$, in which all the diagonal entries are 1 and the rest are zero.

Given two matrices A and B, we can define their summation $A + B$, subtraction $A - B$, and multiplication AB. A requirement for the operations is to have matching dimensions as shown in the following:

$$A_{m \times n} + B_{m \times n}, \quad A_{m \times n} - B_{m \times n}, \quad A_{m \times n} B_{n \times k}.$$

For $A = (a_{ij})$ and $B = (b_{ij})$, with matching dimensions, the operations are defined by

$$A \pm B = \begin{pmatrix} a_{11} \pm b_{11} & \cdots & a_{1n} \pm b_{1n} \\ \vdots & & \vdots \\ a_{m1} \pm b_{m1} & \cdots & a_{mn} \pm b_{mn} \end{pmatrix},$$

$$AB = \begin{pmatrix} \sum_{t=1}^{n} a_{1t} b_{t1} & \cdots & \sum_{k=1}^{n} a_{1t} b_{tk} \\ \vdots & & \vdots \\ \sum_{t=1}^{n} a_{mt} b_{t1} & \cdots & \sum_{t=1}^{n} a_{mt} b_{tk} \end{pmatrix}.$$

We can also multiply a matrix $A = (a_{ij})_{m \times n}$ by a number $\lambda \in \mathbb{R}$:

$$\lambda A \equiv \begin{pmatrix} \lambda a_{11} & \cdots & \lambda a_{1n} \\ \vdots & & \vdots \\ \lambda a_{m1} & \cdots & \lambda a_{mn} \end{pmatrix}.$$

Vectors can be treated as one-column matrices, and so the definition of matrix operations applies to vectors too. That is, the operations for one-column matrices are consistent with those defined for vectors.

Example 1.3. Given two vectors $a \in \mathbb{R}^m$ and $b \in \mathbb{R}^n$, derive ab'. ∎

Why do we define such matrix operations? The reason is that these definitions turn out to be very convenient in many applications. Take a multiplication operation as an example. Suppose that a vector $x \in \mathbb{R}^n$ is mapped linearly to another vector $y \in \mathbb{R}^n$ by $y = Ax$, where $A \in \mathbb{R}^{n \times n}$, and suppose that the vector y is further mapped to $z \in \mathbb{R}^n$ by $z = By$, where $B \in \mathbb{R}^{n \times n}$. The question is: how can we map x directly to z? The answer is: we can find a matrix $C \in \mathbb{R}^{n \times n}$ such that $z = Cx$ and this matrix C turns out to be $C = BA$, where the multiplication operation is defined above.

Theorem 1.1. *Whenever the matrix operations are feasible, we have*

(a) *The associative law of summation:* $(A + B) + C = A + (B + C)$.
(b) *The associative law of multiplication:* $A(BC) = (AB)C$.
(c) *The commutative law of summation:* $A + B = B + A$.
(d) *The distributive law:* $A(B + C) = AB + AC, (B + C)A = BA + CA$. ∎

Denote the determinant of a square matrix A by $|A|$. Why do we denote the determinant this way? The reason is that, for the case of a 3×3 matrix $A = (\alpha_1, \alpha_2, \alpha_3)$ the absolute value of the determinant is the size of the object (called parallelepiped) defined by the column vectors of the matrix (see Figure 1.2).

Theorem 1.2. *For any $A, B \in R^{n \times n}$, we have $|AB| = |A||B|$.* ∎

Each n-dimensional vector x can be treated as an $n \times 1$ matrix. If so, all the rules for and properties of vectors can be derived from the rules for and properties of matrices. That is, vectors are special matrices.

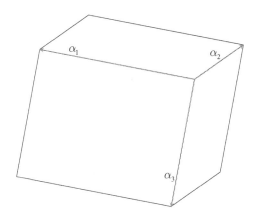

Figure 1.2. The Volume of a Parallelepiped

For $A \in \mathbb{R}^{n \times n}$, if there is another $B \in \mathbb{R}^{n \times n}$ such that $AB = BA = I$, A is said to be invertible or non-singular. Then denoting B by A^{-1}, A^{-1} is called the inverse matrix of A. The inverse is unique.

How to find the inverse matrix? For this, we need minors. Given a square matrix $A = (a_{ij})_{n \times n}$, we call the following determinant the minor of a_{ij}:

$$M_{ij} \equiv \begin{vmatrix} a_{11} & \cdots & a_{1,j-1} & a_{1,j+1} & \cdots & a_{1,n} \\ \vdots & & \vdots & \vdots & & \vdots \\ a_{i-1,1} & \cdots & a_{i-1,j-1} & a_{i-1,j+1} & \cdots & a_{i-1,n} \\ a_{i+1,1} & \cdots & a_{i+1,j-1} & a_{i+1,j+1} & \cdots & a_{i+1,n} \\ \vdots & & \vdots & \vdots & & \vdots \\ a_{n1} & \cdots & a_{n,j-1} & a_{n,j+1} & \cdots & a_{n,n} \end{vmatrix},$$

and call the following value the cofactor of a_{ij}:

$$C_{ij} \equiv (-1)^{i+j} M_{ij}.$$

Denote

$$A^* \equiv \begin{pmatrix} C_{11} & \cdots & C_{1n} \\ \vdots & & \vdots \\ C_{n1} & \cdots & C_{nn} \end{pmatrix}^T,$$

and call it the adjoint of A.

Theorem 1.3. *For any square matrix $A = (a_{ij}) \in \mathbb{R}^{n \times n}$, we have*

(1) $\displaystyle\sum_{k=1}^{n} a_{ik} C_{ik} = \sum_{k=1}^{n} a_{kj} C_{kj} = |A|, \quad$ *for any i, j;*

(2) $\displaystyle\sum_{k=1}^{n} a_{ik} C_{jk} = \sum_{k=1}^{n} a_{ki} C_{kj} = 0, \quad$ *for any $i, j, i \neq j$.* ∎

The first result in Theorem 1.3 comes directly from the definition of determinant and the second result can be easily derived from the first result.

Theorem 1.4. *For* $A \in \mathbb{R}^{n \times n}$, A *is invertible if and only if* $(iff)|A| \neq 0$. *When* A *is invertible, the inverse is*

$$A^{-1} = \frac{1}{|A|}A^*. \quad \blacksquare$$

Corollary 1.1. *For a square matrix* A,

(1) *Its inverse matrix is unique;*
(2) *If there is a matrix* B *such that* $AB = I$ *or* $BA = I$, *then* A *is invertible and* $B = A^{-1}$. $\quad \blacksquare$

Example 1.4. Find the inverse of

$$A = \begin{pmatrix} a & b \\ c & d \end{pmatrix}.$$

We have $C_{11} = d, C_{12} = -c, C_{21} = -b, C_{22} = a$. Thus,

$$A^{-1} = \frac{1}{ad - bc} \begin{pmatrix} d & -b \\ -c & a \end{pmatrix}. \quad \blacksquare$$

Theorem 1.5. *If* $A, B \in \mathbb{R}^{n \times n}$ *are invertible, then*

- $(A^{-1})^{-1} = A$,
- $(AB)^{-1} = B^{-1}A^{-1}$. $\quad \blacksquare$

Given matrix

$$A = \begin{pmatrix} a_{11} & a_{12} & \cdots & a_{1n} \\ a_{21} & a_{22} & \cdots & a_{2n} \\ \vdots & \vdots & & \vdots \\ a_{m1} & a_{m2} & \cdots & a_{mn} \end{pmatrix},$$

denote the transpose of A by A' or A^T, where

$$A' = \begin{pmatrix} a_{11} & a_{12} & \cdots & a_{m1} \\ a_{21} & a_{22} & \cdots & a_{m2} \\ \vdots & \vdots & & \vdots \\ a_{1n} & a_{2n} & \cdots & a_{mn} \end{pmatrix}.$$

That is, $(a_{i,j})'_{m \times n} = (a_{ji})_{n \times m}$. We denote the entry of matrix A at position (ij) by A_{ij} i.e., $A_{ij} = a_{ij}$. Then

$$A'_{ij} = A_{ji}.$$

A matrix A is symmetric if $A' = A$. A symmetric matrix must be a square matrix.

The following theorem presents the key properties of the transpose operation.

Theorem 1.6. *For the transpose operation, we have*

- $(A')' = A$.
- $(A + B)' = A' + B'$.
- $(AB)' = B'A'$.
- $(cA)' = cA'$, *for any* $c \in \mathbb{R}$.
- $(A')^{-1} = (A^{-1})'$.

Proof. We prove the third property. We have

$$(AB)'_{ij} = (AB)_{ji} = \sum_k A_{jk} B_{ki} = \sum_k A'_{kj} B'_{ik}$$

$$= \sum_k B'_{ik} A'_{kj} = (B'A')_{ij}.$$

Hence, we have $(AB)' = B'A'$.

We also prove the last property. Since $A^{-1}A = I$, if we take the transpose of both sides, we have $A'(A^{-1})' = I$. This means that $(A^{-1})'$ is the inverse of A', i.e., $(A^{-1})' = (A')^{-1}$ which is the last property. ∎

For a square matrix $A \in \mathbb{R}^{n \times n}$, denote

$$tr(A) \equiv a_{11} + a_{22} + \cdots + a_{nn},$$

and call it the trace of A. The trace applies only to square matrices. The trace is the second key number of a matrix, following the determinant. The third key number is the rank of a matrix, which will be defined later. The following theorem presents the key properties of the trace.

Theorem 1.7.

- $tr(cA) = c \cdot tr(A)$, *for any* $c \in \mathbb{R}$.
- $tr(A') = tr(A)$.
- $tr(A + B) = tr(A) + tr(B)$.
- $tr(AB) = tr(BA)$.
- $tr(T^{-1}AT) = tr(A)$.

Proof. We prove the fourth property only. We have

$$tr(AB) = \sum_i (AB)_{ii} = \sum_i \sum_k A_{ik}B_{ki} = \sum_k \sum_i A_{ik}B_{ki}$$

$$= \sum_k \sum_i B_{ki}A_{ik} = \sum_k (BA)_{kk} = tr(BA).$$

The last property comes from the fourth property:

$$tr(T^{-1}AT) = tr(TT^{-1}A) = tr(IA) = tr(A). \quad \blacksquare$$

For a matrix $A \in \mathbb{R}^{m \times n}$, if the maximum number of linearly independent row vectors of A is r, then A is said to have rank r and is denoted by $rank(A) = r$. A submatrix of a given matrix consists of a rectangular array of entries in specified rows and columns of the given matrix. These rows and columns need not be adjacent.

Theorem 1.8. *For any* $A \in \mathbb{R}^{n \times n}$,

$$rank(A) = \text{the maximum number of independent row vectors}$$
$$= \text{the maximum number of independent column vectors}$$
$$= \text{the size of the largest invertible}$$
$$\text{square submatrix of } A. \quad \blacksquare$$

Example 1.5. Consider matrix $A = \begin{pmatrix} 2 & -1 & 3 \\ 4 & -2 & 5 \\ 2 & -1 & 4 \end{pmatrix}$. Since the first two column are proportional to each other, there are at most two linearly independent columns. Hence, $rank(A) \leq 2$. We can easily find a non-singular submatrix.

$$\begin{vmatrix} 2 & 3 \\ 4 & 5 \end{vmatrix} = -2 \neq 0,$$

indicating that the first and third columns are linearly independent. Hence, $rank(A) \geq 2$. Therefore, we must have $rank(A) = 2$. ∎

The following proposition presents some useful properties of the rank.

Proposition 1.2.

- *For $A \in \mathbb{R}^{m \times n}, B \in \mathbb{R}^{n \times k}$,*

  $$rank(A) + rank(B) - n \leq rank(AB) \leq min[rank(A), rank(B)].$$

- *For $A \in \mathbb{R}^{m \times n}, B \in \mathbb{R}^{m \times n}$,*

  $$rank(A + B) \leq rank(A) + rank(B). \quad ∎$$

Another definition of a matrix product is sometimes useful too. Given two matrices A and B, the Kronecker product is

$$A \otimes B = \begin{pmatrix} a_{11}B & \cdots & a_{1n}B \\ \vdots & & \vdots \\ a_{m1}B & \cdots & a_{mn}B \end{pmatrix}, \quad \text{where } A = \begin{pmatrix} a_{11} & \cdots & a_{1n} \\ \vdots & & \vdots \\ a_{m1} & \cdots & a_{mn} \end{pmatrix}.$$

Example 1.6.

$$\begin{pmatrix} 3 & 0 \\ 5 & 2 \end{pmatrix} \otimes \begin{pmatrix} 1 & 4 \\ 4 & 7 \end{pmatrix} = \begin{pmatrix} 3\begin{pmatrix} 1 & 4 \\ 4 & 7 \end{pmatrix} & 0\begin{pmatrix} 1 & 4 \\ 4 & 7 \end{pmatrix} \\ 5\begin{pmatrix} 1 & 4 \\ 4 & 7 \end{pmatrix} & 7\begin{pmatrix} 1 & 4 \\ 4 & 7 \end{pmatrix} \end{pmatrix}$$

$$= \begin{pmatrix} 3 & 12 & 0 & 0 \\ 12 & 21 & 0 & 0 \\ 5 & 20 & 7 & 28 \\ 20 & 35 & 28 & 49 \end{pmatrix}. \quad ∎$$

The following theorem presents the key properties of the Kronecker product.

Theorem 1.9.

- $(A \otimes B)^{-1} = A^{-1} \otimes B^{-1}$.
- $(A \otimes B)' = A' \otimes B'$.
- $|A \otimes B| = |A|^m |B|^n$, *if* $A \in \mathbb{R}^{n \times n}$ *and* $B \in \mathbb{R}^{m \times m}$.
- $tr(A \otimes B) = tr(A) \cdot tr(B)$. $\blacksquare$

3. Linear Equation Systems

For a matrix $A \in \mathbb{R}^{m \times n}$ and a vector $d \in \mathbb{R}^m$, the following m equation for the vector $x \in \mathbb{R}^n$ is called a linear equation system:

$$Ax = d. \tag{1.3}$$

We call the following equation the homogeneous linear system of (1.3):

$$Ax = 0. \tag{1.4}$$

The following theorem finds a condition for its existence.

Theorem 1.10. *Equation* (1.3) *has a solution iff* $rank(A) = rank(A, d)$.

Theorem 1.11 (Cramer's Rule). *Given a square matrix* $A \in \mathbb{R}^{n \times n}$ *and writing A as a sequence of column vectors* $A = (a_1, a_2, \ldots, a_n)$, *if A is non-singular, then* (1.3) *has a unique solution and it is* $\bar{x} = (\bar{x}_1, \ldots, \bar{x}_n)'$, *where*

$$\bar{x}_i = \frac{|a_1, a_2, \ldots, a_{i-1}, d, a_{i+1}, \ldots, a_n|}{|A|}, \quad i = 1, 2, \ldots, n. \quad \blacksquare$$

Example 1.7. Solve the following equation system:

$$\begin{cases} 2x_1 + 3x_2 = 4, \\ 3x_1 - 5x_2 = 1. \end{cases}$$

By Cramer's Rule, we can quickly find the solution:

$$x_1 = \frac{\begin{vmatrix} 4 & 3 \\ 1 & -5 \end{vmatrix}}{\begin{vmatrix} 2 & 3 \\ 3 & -5 \end{vmatrix}} = \frac{23}{19}, \quad x_2 = \frac{\begin{vmatrix} 2 & 4 \\ 3 & 1 \end{vmatrix}}{\begin{vmatrix} 2 & 3 \\ 3 & -5 \end{vmatrix}} = \frac{10}{19}. \quad \blacksquare$$

Let $N(A)$ be the set of all solutions of (1.4). Call $N(A)$ the null space of A or the solution set of (1.4).

Theorem 1.12. *If $rank(A) = r$,*

- *And if $r = n$, then (1.4) has a unique solution and (1.3) has either a unique solution or no solution.*
- *There exist $n - r$ linearly independent solutions $\alpha_1, \ldots, \alpha_{n-r}$ of (1.4) such that $N(A) = span(\alpha_1, \ldots, \alpha_{n-r})$.*
- *Suppose that x^* is a solution of (1.3). Then x is a solution of (1.3) iff there is $x_0 \in N(A)$ such that $x = x^* + x_0$.* $\blacksquare$

The rank indicates the number of independent equations in (1.4). Theorem 1.12 is intuitive, and indicates that if r equations in (1.4) are independent, the equation system in (1.4) has $n - r$ degrees of freedom. Further, if a solution of (1.3) exists, then this degree of freedom applies to (1.3) as well.

4. Pseudo Inverse

A matrix $A \in \mathbb{R}^{m \times n}$ is a tall matrix if $m > n$. A matrix $A \in \mathbb{R}^{m \times n}$ has full rank if it has the largest possible rank: $rank(A) = \min(n, m)$.

The inverse matrix is defined only for a non-singular square matrix. The pseudo inverse extends the existence of an inverse matrix to any matrix. Specifically, for an arbitrary matrix $A \in \mathbb{R}^{m \times n}$, a matrix A^+ is called the pseudo inverse of A if

- $AA^+A = A$ and $A^+AA^+ = A^+$, and
- A^+A and AA^+ are symmetric.

Theorem 1.13.

(a) *For any matrix A, there is a unique pseudo inverse A^+.*
(b) *If A is non-singular, then $A^+ = A^{-1}$.*
(c) *If A is a tall matrix with full rank, then $A^+ = (A'A)^{-1}A'$.* ∎

Part (a) of Theorem 1.13 indicates that every matrix has a pseudo inverse. See Greene (1993, p. 37) for the construction of A^+. Parts (b) and (c) can be easily verified.

Consider an over-determined system of equations:

$$Ax = d,$$

where A is a tall matrix. If A has full rank, then the solution is $x = A^+d$. We can see this easily. Since $A'Ax = A'd$ we immediately have $x = A^+d$. This solution is the so-called least-squares solution.

5. Elementary Operations

Elementary operations are excellent for manipulating matrices. Elementary row operations on a matrix A include:

1. Multiplying a row of A by a non-zero scalar k:

$$\text{e.g.,} \quad \begin{pmatrix} a_{11} & a_{12} \\ a_{21} & a_{22} \end{pmatrix} \rightarrow \begin{pmatrix} ka_{11} & ka_{12} \\ a_{21} & a_{22} \end{pmatrix}.$$

2. Multiplying a row of A by a scalar k and adding it to another row:

$$\text{e.g.,} \quad \begin{pmatrix} a_{11} & a_{12} \\ a_{21} & a_{22} \end{pmatrix} \rightarrow \begin{pmatrix} a_{11} & a_{12} \\ a_{21} + ka_{11} & a_{22} + ka_{12} \end{pmatrix}.$$

3. Interchanging two rows of A:

$$\text{e.g.,} \quad \begin{pmatrix} a_{11} & a_{12} \\ a_{21} & a_{22} \end{pmatrix} \rightarrow \begin{pmatrix} a_{21} & a_{22} \\ a_{11} & a_{12} \end{pmatrix}.$$

Elementary column operations are similarly defined. An elementary operation is either an elementary row operation or an elementary column operation. Two matrices A and B are row-equivalent if one can be obtained from the other by a finite sequence of elementary row operations.

Elementary operations have many applications. One of them is to solve a linear equation system. The following theorem outlines the method.

Theorem 1.14. *For $A, B \in \mathbb{R}^{m \times n}$ and $c, d \in \mathbb{R}^m$, if (A, d) and (B, c) are row-equivalent, then the linear systems $Ax = d$ and $Bx = c$ have the same solutions.* ∎

The proof of the above theorem is straightforward. The theorem, however, provides a convenient way to solve linear systems. The following three examples show the method.

Example 1.8. For a system of equations,

$$\begin{pmatrix} 1 & -2 & 3 & -4 \\ 0 & 1 & -1 & 1 \\ 1 & 3 & 0 & 1 \\ 0 & -7 & 3 & 1 \end{pmatrix} x = \begin{pmatrix} -4 \\ -3 \\ 1 \\ -3 \end{pmatrix},$$

we do the following elementary row operations:

$$\begin{pmatrix} 1 & -2 & 3 & -4 & 4 \\ 0 & 1 & -1 & 1 & -3 \\ 1 & 3 & 0 & 1 & 1 \\ 0 & -7 & 3 & 1 & -3 \end{pmatrix}$$

$$\rightarrow \begin{pmatrix} 1 & -2 & 3 & -4 & 4 \\ 0 & 1 & -1 & 1 & -3 \\ 0 & 5 & -3 & 5 & -3 \\ 0 & -7 & 3 & 1 & -3 \end{pmatrix} \rightarrow \begin{pmatrix} 1 & -2 & 3 & -4 & 4 \\ 0 & 1 & -1 & 1 & -3 \\ 0 & 0 & 2 & 0 & 12 \\ 0 & 0 & -4 & 8 & -24 \end{pmatrix}$$

$$\rightarrow \begin{pmatrix} 1 & -2 & 3 & -4 & 4 \\ 0 & 1 & -1 & 1 & -3 \\ 0 & 0 & 1 & 0 & 6 \\ 0 & 0 & -1 & 2 & -6 \end{pmatrix} \rightarrow \begin{pmatrix} 1 & -2 & 3 & -4 & 4 \\ 0 & 1 & -1 & 1 & -3 \\ 0 & 0 & 1 & 0 & 6 \\ 0 & 0 & 0 & 2 & 0 \end{pmatrix}$$

$$\rightarrow \begin{pmatrix} 1 & -2 & 3 & -4 & 4 \\ 0 & 1 & -1 & 1 & -3 \\ 0 & 0 & 1 & 0 & 6 \\ 0 & 0 & 0 & 1 & 0 \end{pmatrix} \rightarrow \begin{pmatrix} 1 & -2 & 3 & 0 & 4 \\ 0 & 1 & -1 & 0 & -3 \\ 0 & 0 & 1 & 0 & 6 \\ 0 & 0 & 0 & 1 & 0 \end{pmatrix}$$

$$\rightarrow \begin{pmatrix} 1 & -2 & 0 & 0 & -14 \\ 0 & 1 & 0 & 0 & 3 \\ 0 & 0 & 1 & 0 & 6 \\ 0 & 0 & 0 & 1 & 0 \end{pmatrix} \rightarrow \begin{pmatrix} 1 & 0 & 0 & 0 & -8 \\ 0 & 1 & 0 & 0 & 3 \\ 0 & 0 & 1 & 0 & 6 \\ 0 & 0 & 0 & 1 & 0 \end{pmatrix}.$$

Hence, the solution is

$$x_1 = -8, \quad x_2 = 3, \quad x_3 = 6, \quad x_4 = 0. \quad \blacksquare$$

Example 1.9. Consider

$$Ax = 0,$$

where

$$A = \begin{pmatrix} 2 & -1 & 3 \\ 4 & -2 & 5 \\ 2 & -1 & 4 \end{pmatrix}.$$

Do the following elementary row operations:

$$\begin{pmatrix} 2 & -1 & 3 \\ 4 & -2 & 5 \\ 2 & -1 & 4 \end{pmatrix} \rightarrow \begin{pmatrix} 2 & -1 & 3 \\ 0 & 0 & -1 \\ 0 & 0 & 1 \end{pmatrix} \rightarrow \begin{pmatrix} 2 & -1 & 0 \\ 0 & 0 & 0 \\ 0 & 0 & 1 \end{pmatrix}.$$

That is, the original system of equations is equivalent to

$$\begin{cases} 2x_1 - x_2 = 0 \\ \qquad x_3 = 0. \end{cases}$$

The solution is therefore

$$\begin{cases} x_1 = \dfrac{1}{2}x_2, \\ x_3 = 0, \end{cases}$$

where x_2 is arbitrary. This means that the null space $N(A)$ has one degree of freedom or the dimension of $N(A)$ is 1. More precisely,

$$N(A) = \left\{ k \begin{pmatrix} 1 \\ 2 \\ 0 \end{pmatrix} k \in \mathbb{R} \right\}, \tag{1.5}$$

which is a one-dimensional subspace generated by the vector $(1, 2, 0)'$. Example 1.5 has shown that matrix A has rank 2. By Theorem 1.12, we expect its solution set $N(A)$ to be of dimension one, which is consistent with our solution in (1.5). ∎

Example 1.10. Consider

$$Ax = 0,$$

where

$$A = \begin{pmatrix} 2 & -1 & 1 \\ 4 & -2 & 2 \\ 2 & -1 & 1 \end{pmatrix}.$$

This matrix can be transformed into the following matrix by elementary row operations:

$$\begin{pmatrix} 2 & -1 & 1 \\ 0 & 0 & 0 \\ 0 & 0 & 0 \end{pmatrix}.$$

We can easily find two solutions,

$$\alpha_1 = \begin{pmatrix} 0 \\ 1 \\ 1 \end{pmatrix}, \quad \alpha_2 = \begin{pmatrix} 1 \\ 2 \\ 0 \end{pmatrix}.$$

We have intentionally found two linearly independent solutions. Hence, by Theorem 1.12, we have $N(A) = span(\alpha_1, \alpha_2)$. ∎

Example 1.11. We now solve the following equations system:

$$\begin{pmatrix} 2 & -1 & 3 \\ 4 & -2 & 5 \\ 2 & -1 & 4 \end{pmatrix} x = \begin{pmatrix} 1 \\ 1 \\ 2 \end{pmatrix}. \tag{1.6}$$

Using elementary row operations, we have

$$\begin{pmatrix} 2 & -1 & 3 & 1 \\ 4 & -2 & 5 & 1 \\ 2 & -1 & 4 & 2 \end{pmatrix} \rightarrow \begin{pmatrix} 2 & -1 & 3 & 1 \\ 0 & 0 & -1 & -1 \\ 0 & 0 & 1 & 1 \end{pmatrix} \rightarrow \begin{pmatrix} 2 & -1 & 0 & -2 \\ 0 & 0 & 0 & 0 \\ 0 & 0 & 1 & 1 \end{pmatrix},$$

which implies the following equation system:

$$\begin{cases} 2x_1 - x_2 = -2, \\ \quad\quad x_3 = 1. \end{cases}$$

One solution of this equation is $x^* \equiv (-1, 0, 1)$, which is one particular solution of (1.6). The solution set of the homogeneous equation of (1.6) is $N(A)$ defined in (1.5). Hence, the general solution of (1.6) is $x = x^* + x_0$, where $x_0 \in N(A)$. ∎

Let e be an elementary operation. Denote the resulting matrix after the operation e on A by $e(A)$. For the identity matrix, we call $e(I)$ an elementary matrix. We can easily verify the following proposition.

Theorem 1.15.

- *Elementary matrices are invertible.*
- *If e is an elementary row operation, then $e(A) = e(I)A$.*
- *If e is an elementary column operation, then $e(A) = Ae(I)$.* ∎

We verify Theorem 1.15 in the following example.

Example 1.12. Suppose that e_2 is a second type of row operation that multiplies the first row by k and adds it to the second row:

$$e_2 \left[\begin{pmatrix} a_{11} & a_{12} \\ a_{21} & a_{22} \end{pmatrix} \right] = \begin{pmatrix} a_{11} & a_{12} \\ a_{21} + ka_{11} & a_{22} + ka_{12} \end{pmatrix}.$$

We have

$$e_2(I) = \begin{pmatrix} 1 & 0 \\ k & 1 \end{pmatrix},$$

and

$$e_2(I) \begin{pmatrix} a_{11} & a_{12} \\ a_{21} & a_{22} \end{pmatrix} = \begin{pmatrix} a_{11} & a_{12} \\ a_{21} + ka_{11} & a_{22} + ka_{12} \end{pmatrix}.$$

Therefore,

$$e_2 \left[\begin{pmatrix} a_{11} & a_{12} \\ a_{21} & a_{22} \end{pmatrix} \right] = e_2(I) \begin{pmatrix} a_{11} & a_{12} \\ a_{21} & a_{22} \end{pmatrix}.$$

This verifies Theorem 1.15 for this special case. ∎

The inverse operation of an elementary operation is an elementary operation that brings the matrix back to its original state.

Proposition 1.3. *The inverse operation of an elementary row operation exists and is an elementary row operation of the same type.* ∎

We show Proposition 1.3 by the following example.

Example 1.13. Let us now see if an inverse operation of e_2 in Example 1.12 exists. Define an elementary row operation $\tilde{e}_2$ by

$$\tilde{e}_2(I) \equiv \begin{pmatrix} 1 & 0 \\ -k & 1 \end{pmatrix}.$$

We have

$$\tilde{e}_2(I) \begin{pmatrix} a_{11} & a_{12} \\ a_{21} + ka_{11} & a_{22} + ka_{12} \end{pmatrix} = \begin{pmatrix} a_{11} & a_{12} \\ a_{21} & a_{22} \end{pmatrix}.$$

That is, $\tilde{e}_2$ is an inverse operation of e_2. We can see that $\tilde{e}_2$ is also a second type of row operation. This verifies Proposition 1.3 for this special case. Notice that

$$\tilde{e}_2(I)e_2(I) = I,$$

implying $\tilde{e}_2(I) = [e_2(I)]^{-1}$. ∎

Elementary operations can also be used to find an inverse matrix. The following theorem outlines the method.

Theorem 1.16. *For $A, B \in \mathbb{R}^{m \times n}$, if there is a sequence of elementary row operations row operations converting (A, I) to (I, B), then $B = A^{-1}$.* ∎

With Theorem 1.16, we demonstrate the second application of elementary operations: We can use row elementary operations to find an inverse matrix.

Example 1.14. Find the inverse matrix of the following matrix:

$$A = \begin{pmatrix} 0 & 1 & 2 \\ 1 & 1 & 4 \\ 2 & -1 & 0 \end{pmatrix}.$$

Do the following elementary row operations:

$$\begin{pmatrix} 0 & 1 & 2 & 1 & & \\ 1 & 1 & 4 & & 1 & \\ 2 & -1 & 0 & & & 1 \end{pmatrix}$$

$$\rightarrow \begin{pmatrix} 1 & 1 & 4 & 0 & 1 & 0 \\ 0 & 1 & 2 & 1 & 0 & 0 \\ 2 & -1 & 0 & 0 & 0 & 1 \end{pmatrix} \rightarrow \begin{pmatrix} 1 & 1 & 4 & 0 & 1 & 0 \\ 0 & 1 & 2 & 1 & 0 & 0 \\ 0 & -3 & -8 & 0 & -2 & 1 \end{pmatrix}$$

$$\rightarrow \begin{pmatrix} 1 & 1 & 4 & 0 & 1 & 0 \\ 0 & 1 & 2 & 1 & 0 & 0 \\ 0 & 0 & -2 & 3 & -2 & 1 \end{pmatrix} \rightarrow \begin{pmatrix} 1 & 1 & 0 & 6 & -3 & 2 \\ 0 & 1 & 0 & 4 & -2 & 1 \\ 0 & 0 & -2 & 3 & -2 & 1 \end{pmatrix}$$

$$\rightarrow \begin{pmatrix} 1 & 0 & 0 & 2 & -1 & 1 \\ 0 & 1 & 0 & 4 & -2 & 1 \\ 0 & 0 & -2 & 3 & -2 & 1 \end{pmatrix}.$$

Therefore,

$$A^{-1} = \begin{pmatrix} 2 & -1 & 1 \\ 4 & -2 & 1 \\ -\dfrac{3}{2} & 1 & -\dfrac{1}{2} \end{pmatrix}. \quad ∎$$

The above derivation suggests how to prove the following theorem.

Theorem 1.17. *Any invertible matrix $A \in \mathbb{R}^{n \times n}$ is row-equivalent to the identity matrix.* ■

Theorem 1.17 guarantees that the method of finding an inverse matrix using elementary operations will always work as long as the inverse matrix exists.

The third application of elementary operations is to find the rank of a matrix. For this purpose, we present the following theorem.

Theorem 1.18. *The rank of any matrix will not change when multiplied by a non-singular matrix. That is, for $A \in \mathbb{R}^{m \times n}$, $P \in \mathbb{R}^{m \times m}$, and $Q \in \mathbb{R}^{n \times n}$, if P and Q are invertible, then*

$$rank(A) = rank(PA) = rank(AQ). \quad ■$$

The above theorem shows that elementary operations will not change the rank. Thus, we can use elementary operations to simplify a matrix first and then use Theorem 1.18 to find the rank.

Example 1.15. Find the rank of matrix A in Example 1.5. We do few column and row elementary operations to obtain

$$\begin{pmatrix} 2 & -1 & 3 \\ 4 & -2 & 5 \\ 2 & -1 & 4 \end{pmatrix} \rightarrow \begin{pmatrix} 0 & 1 & 3 \\ 0 & 2 & 5 \\ 0 & 1 & 4 \end{pmatrix} \rightarrow \begin{pmatrix} 0 & 1 & 3 \\ 0 & 0 & -1 \\ 0 & 0 & 1 \end{pmatrix} \rightarrow \begin{pmatrix} 0 & 1 & 0 \\ 0 & 0 & 0 \\ 0 & 0 & 1 \end{pmatrix}.$$

By Theorem 1.18, we can easily show that the rank of the last matrix above is 2. Hence, the rank of A is 2. ■

6. Block Matrix

We can divide a matrix into blocks of submatrices. For example,

$$A = \begin{pmatrix} 1 & 0 & 0 & 0 \\ 0 & 1 & 0 & 0 \\ -1 & 2 & 1 & 0 \\ 1 & 1 & 0 & 1 \end{pmatrix} = \left(\begin{array}{cc:cc} 1 & 0 & 0 & 0 \\ 0 & 1 & 0 & 0 \\ \hdashline -1 & 2 & 1 & 0 \\ 1 & 1 & 0 & 1 \end{array} \right) = \begin{pmatrix} I_2 & 0 \\ A_1 & I_2 \end{pmatrix},$$

where $A_1 \equiv \begin{pmatrix} -1 & 2 \\ 1 & 1 \end{pmatrix}$. Similarly, the following matrix is also divided into four blocks:

$$B = \begin{pmatrix} 1 & 0 & \vdots & 3 & 2 \\ -1 & 2 & \vdots & 0 & 1 \\ \cdots & \cdots & \cdots & \cdots & \cdots \\ 1 & 0 & \vdots & 4 & 1 \\ -1 & -1 & \vdots & 2 & 0 \end{pmatrix} = \begin{pmatrix} B_{11} & B_{12} \\ B_{21} & B_{22} \end{pmatrix}.$$

The advantage of this is that, in matrix manipulation, we can treat the blocks as numbers. In this example, we can treat A and B as 2×2 matrices. When all the matrix operations are feasible, the matrix operations can be applied directly to the blocks. In the above example, one can easily verify that

$$AB = \begin{pmatrix} B_{11} & B_{12} \\ A_1 B_{11} + B_{21} & A_1 B_{12} + B_{22} \end{pmatrix}.$$

That is, by treating A_1, I_2, and B_{ij} as numbers, we have

$$\begin{pmatrix} I_2 & 0 \\ A_1 & I_2 \end{pmatrix} \begin{pmatrix} B_{11} & B_{12} \\ B_{21} & B_{22} \end{pmatrix} = \begin{pmatrix} B_{11} & B_{12} \\ A_1 B_{11} + B_{21} & A_1 B_{12} + B_{22} \end{pmatrix}.$$

In general,

$$\begin{pmatrix} A_{11} & \cdots & A_{1l} \\ \vdots & & \vdots \\ A_{n1} & \cdots & A_{nl} \end{pmatrix} \begin{pmatrix} B_{11} & \cdots & B_{1r} \\ \vdots & & \vdots \\ B_{l1} & \cdots & B_{lr} \end{pmatrix}$$

$$= \begin{pmatrix} \sum_k A_{1k} B_{k1} & \cdots & \sum_k A_{1k} B_{kr} \\ \vdots & & \vdots \\ \sum_k A_{nk} B_{k1} & \cdots & \sum_k A_{nk} B_{kr} \end{pmatrix},$$

where all $A_{ik} B_{kj}$ are feasible matrix multiplications. We, however, should not treat $A_{ik} B_{kj}$ as $B_{kj} A_{ik}$. That is, in matrix manipulation, we can treat matrix blocks as numbers as long as all the matrix multiplications are valid, but the order of the matrices must be kept in each multiplication.

Example 1.16. Let

$$D \equiv \begin{pmatrix} a_{11} & \cdots & a_{1k} & 0 & \cdots & 0 \\ \vdots & & \vdots & \vdots & & \vdots \\ a_{k1} & \cdots & a_{kk} & 0 & \cdots & 0 \\ c_{11} & \cdots & c_{1k} & b_{11} & \cdots & b_{1r} \\ \vdots & & \vdots & \vdots & & \vdots \\ c_{r1} & \cdots & c_{rk} & b_{r1} & \cdots & b_{rr} \end{pmatrix} = \begin{pmatrix} A & 0 \\ C & B \end{pmatrix}.$$

Assume that A and B are invertible. Let us find D^{-1}. Let

$$D^{-1} = \begin{pmatrix} X_{11} & X_{12} \\ X_{21} & X_{22} \end{pmatrix}.$$

Then

$$\begin{pmatrix} I_k & 0 \\ C & I_r \end{pmatrix} = \begin{pmatrix} A & 0 \\ C & B \end{pmatrix} \begin{pmatrix} X_{11} & X_{12} \\ X_{21} & X_{22} \end{pmatrix}$$

$$= \begin{pmatrix} AX_{11} & AX_{12} \\ CX_{11} + BX_{21} & CX_{12} + BX_{22} \end{pmatrix},$$

which implies

$$\begin{cases} I = AX_{11}, \\ AX_{12} = 0, \\ CX_{11} + BX_{11} = 0, \\ CX_{12} + BX_{22} = I. \end{cases}$$

We then find $X_{11} = A^{-1}$, $X_{12} = 0$, $X_{22} = B^{-1}$, and $X_{21} = -B^{-1}CA^{-1}$. That is,

$$\begin{pmatrix} A & 0 \\ C & B \end{pmatrix}^{-1} = \begin{pmatrix} A^{-1} & 0 \\ -B^{-1}CA^{-1} & B^{-1} \end{pmatrix}.$$

In particular, when $C = 0$, we have

$$\begin{pmatrix} A & 0 \\ C & B \end{pmatrix}^{-1} = \begin{pmatrix} A^{-1} & 0 \\ 0 & B^{-1} \end{pmatrix}.$$

We can alternatively use Theorem 1.16 to find the inverse matrix. We have

$$
\begin{pmatrix} A & 0 & I & 0 \\ C & B & 0 & I \end{pmatrix} \rightarrow \begin{pmatrix} A & 0 & I & 0 \\ 0 & B & -CA^{-1} & I \end{pmatrix}
$$

$$
\rightarrow \begin{pmatrix} I & 0 & A^{-1} & 0 \\ 0 & I & -B^{-1}CA^{-1} & B^{-1} \end{pmatrix}.
$$

Hence, the inverse matrix is

$$
\begin{pmatrix} A & 0 \\ C & B \end{pmatrix}^{-1} = \begin{pmatrix} A^{-1} & 0 \\ -B^{-1}CA^{-1} & B^{-1} \end{pmatrix}. \quad \blacksquare
$$

7. Eigenvalue and Diagonalization

One important application of eigenvalues is to transform a matrix into a simple matrix. Consider transforming a square matrix $A \in \mathbb{R}^{n \times n}$ into a diagonal matrix as follows: there is a matrix T such that

$$
T^{-1}AT = D,
$$

where $D = diag\{d_1, \ldots, d_n\}$ is a diagonal matrix with diagonal entries $d_i, i = 1, 2, \ldots, n$ and zero elsewhere. Express T as a sequence of column vectors $T = (\xi_1, \ldots, \xi_n)$. Then

$$
A(\xi_1, \ldots, \xi_n) = (\xi_1, \ldots, \xi_n) \begin{pmatrix} d_1 & & \\ & \ddots & \\ & & d_n \end{pmatrix},
$$

implying

$$
(A\xi_1, \ldots, A\xi_n) = (d_1\xi_1, \ldots, d_n\xi_n),
$$

in turn implying

$$
A\xi_i = d_i\xi_i, \quad \text{for all } i.
$$

Hence, this expression is the key to identifying the diagonal matrix if it exists. Therefore, this expression is used to define eigenvalues.

For a square matrix $A \in \mathbb{R}^{n \times n}$, if there is a non-zero vector $x \in \mathbb{R}^n$ and a scalar λ such that

$$Ax = \lambda x,$$

then λ is called a characteristic root or eigenvalue, and x is called a characteristic vector or eigenvector. Call the following equation the characteristic equation of A:

$$|\lambda I - A| = 0,$$

and $|\lambda I - A|$ the characteristic polynomial. It turns out that this equation defines all the eigenvalues of A.

Theorem 1.19. λ *is an eigenvalue iff it satisfies the characteristic equation.* ∎

We have

$$|\lambda I - A| = \lambda^n - (a_{11} + a_{22} + \cdots + a_{nn})\lambda^{n-1} + \cdots + (-1)^n A. \quad (1.7)$$

Example 1.17. For $A = \begin{pmatrix} a & b \\ c & d \end{pmatrix}$, we have

$$\begin{aligned}
|\lambda I - A| &= \begin{vmatrix} \lambda - a & -b \\ -c & \lambda - d \end{vmatrix} = (\lambda - a)(\lambda - d) - bc \\
&= \lambda^2 - (a + d)\lambda + ad - bc \\
&= \lambda^2 - tr(A)\lambda + |A|.
\end{aligned}$$

This confirms the formula in (1.7). ∎

Suppose that the eigenvalues of A are $\lambda_1, \lambda_2, \ldots, \lambda_n$ which may repeat. Then

$$\begin{aligned}
|\lambda I - A| &= (\lambda - \lambda_1) \cdots (\lambda - \lambda_n) \\
&= \lambda^n - (\lambda_1 + \cdots + \lambda_n)\lambda^{n-1} + \cdots + (-1)^n \lambda_1 \cdots \lambda_n.
\end{aligned}$$

By comparing this with (1.7), we find

$$tr(A) = \lambda_1 + \cdots + \lambda_n, \quad |A| = \lambda_1, \ldots, \lambda_n.$$

Example 1.18. Given a matrix

$$A = \begin{pmatrix} 1 & 0 \\ 1 & 2 \end{pmatrix},$$

let us use eigenvalues to simplify it (hopefully to a diagonal matrix). From the characteristic equation

$$|\lambda I - A| = \begin{vmatrix} \lambda - 1 & 0 \\ -1 & \lambda - 2 \end{vmatrix} = (\lambda - 1)(\lambda - 2) = 0,$$

we find two eigenvalues $\lambda_1 = 1$ and $\lambda_2 = 2$. For $\lambda_1 = 1$, from

$$(\lambda_1 I - A)x = \begin{pmatrix} \lambda - 1 & 0 \\ -1 & \lambda - 2 \end{pmatrix} x = \begin{pmatrix} 0 & 0 \\ -1 & -1 \end{pmatrix} x = 0,$$

we find an eigenvector

$$x_1 = \begin{pmatrix} 1 \\ -1 \end{pmatrix}.$$

For $\lambda_2 = 2$, from

$$(\lambda_2 I - A)x = \begin{pmatrix} \lambda_2 - 1 & 0 \\ -1 & \lambda_2 - 2 \end{pmatrix} x = \begin{pmatrix} 1 & 0 \\ -1 & 0 \end{pmatrix} x = 0,$$

we find another eigenvector

$$x_2 = \begin{pmatrix} 0 \\ 1 \end{pmatrix}.$$

Let

$$T \equiv (x_1, x_2) = \begin{pmatrix} 1 & 0 \\ -1 & 1 \end{pmatrix}.$$

Then

$$A(x_1, x_2) = (Ax_1, Ax_2) = (\lambda_1 x_1, \lambda_2 x_2) = (x_1, x_2) \begin{pmatrix} \lambda_1 & 0 \\ 0 & \lambda_2 \end{pmatrix}.$$

That is,

$$AT = T \begin{pmatrix} \lambda_1 & 0 \\ 0 & \lambda_2 \end{pmatrix}.$$

We therefore have

$$T^{-1}AT = \begin{pmatrix} \lambda_1 & 0 \\ 0 & \lambda_2 \end{pmatrix} = \begin{pmatrix} 1 & 0 \\ 0 & 2 \end{pmatrix}. \quad \blacksquare$$

The transformation in the above example leads to a general theory of matrix transformation. Two square matrices $A, B \in \mathbb{R}^{n \times n}$ are similar if there is a square matrix $T \in \mathbb{R}^{n \times n}$ such that $T^{-1}AT = B$. We call this a similarity transformation. Such a transformation will not change the key characteristics of a matrix, including the determinant, rank, trace, and eigenvalues. A matrix A is said to be diagonalizable if it is similar to a diagonal matrix.

Theorem 1.20. *Eigenvectors belonging to different eigenvalues are linearly independent.* $\blacksquare$

Theorem 1.21. *A square matrix $A \in \mathbb{R}^{n \times n}$ is diagonalizable iff it has n linearly independent eigenvectors.* $\blacksquare$

Example 1.19. Given a matrix

$$A = \begin{pmatrix} 1 & 0 & 0 \\ -2 & 1 & 1 \\ -2 & 0 & 2 \end{pmatrix},$$

let us try to diagonalize it. From the characteristic equation

$$|\lambda I - AI| = \begin{vmatrix} \lambda - 1 & 0 & 0 \\ 2 & \lambda - 1 & -1 \\ 2 & 0 & \lambda - 2 \end{vmatrix} = (\lambda - 1)^2 (\lambda - 2) = 0,$$

we find two eigenvalues $\lambda_1 = 1$ and $\lambda_2 = 2$. For $\lambda_1 = 1$, from

$$(\lambda_1 I - A)x = \begin{pmatrix} \lambda_2 - 1 & 0 & 0 \\ 2 & \lambda_2 - 1 & -1 \\ 2 & 0 & \lambda_2 - 2 \end{pmatrix} x = \begin{pmatrix} 0 & 0 & 0 \\ 2 & 0 & -1 \\ 2 & 0 & -1 \end{pmatrix} x = 0,$$

we find two linearly independent eigenvectors

$$x_1 = \begin{pmatrix} 0 \\ 1 \\ 0 \end{pmatrix}, \quad x_2 = \begin{pmatrix} 1 \\ 0 \\ 2 \end{pmatrix}.$$

We have deliberately chosen two orthogonal vectors. Orthogonal vectors must be linearly independent. For $\lambda_2 = 2$, from

$$(\lambda_2 I - A)x = \begin{pmatrix} \lambda_2 - 1 & 0 & 0 \\ 2 & \lambda_2 - 1 & -1 \\ 2 & 0 & \lambda_2 - 2 \end{pmatrix} x = \begin{pmatrix} 1 & 0 & 0 \\ 2 & 1 & -1 \\ 2 & 0 & 0 \end{pmatrix} x = 0,$$

we find another eigenvector

$$x_3 = \begin{pmatrix} 0 \\ 1 \\ 1 \end{pmatrix}.$$

Let

$$T \equiv (x_1, x_2, x_3) = \begin{pmatrix} 0 & 1 & 0 \\ 1 & 0 & 1 \\ 0 & 2 & 1 \end{pmatrix}.$$

Then

$$A(x_1, x_2, x_3) = (Ax_1, Ax_2, Ax_3) = (\lambda_1 x_1, \lambda_1 x_2, \lambda_2 x_3)$$

$$= (x_1, x_2, x_3) \begin{pmatrix} \lambda_1 & 0 & 0 \\ 0 & \lambda_1 & 0 \\ 0 & 0 & \lambda_2 \end{pmatrix}.$$

That is,

$$AT = T \cdot diag\{\lambda_1, \lambda_1, \lambda_2\}.$$

We therefore have

$$T^{-1}AT = diag\{\lambda_1, \lambda_1, \lambda_2\} = diag\{1, 1, 2\}. \quad \blacksquare$$

In general, if

$$|\lambda I - A| = (\lambda - \lambda_1)^{n_1} \cdots (\lambda - \lambda_k)^{n_k},$$

where $\lambda_i, i = 1, \ldots, k$, are all the distinct eigenvalues of A and $n_1 + \cdots + n_k = n$, then we should try to find n_i linearly independent eigenvectors for each λ_i. If we succeed in doing so, this matrix is diagonalizable; otherwise it is not.

8. Symmetric Matrix

A complex number can be written as $z = a + bi$, where $a, b \in \mathbb{R}$ and $i \equiv \sqrt{-1}$. For each complex number $z = a + bi$, define its conjugate as $\bar{z} \equiv a - bi$. For any two complex numbers x and y, we have

$$\overline{x \cdot y} = \bar{x} \cdot \bar{y}$$

For a matrix $A = (a_{ij})_{m \times n}$, define its conjugate as $\bar{A} = (\bar{a}_{ij})_{m \times n}$. Then the above property also holds for matrix multiplication. That is, for any two matrices A and B, we have

$$\overline{AB} = \bar{A}\bar{B},$$

as long as the matrix multiplication is valid.

A matrix A is symmetric if $A' = A$. A matrix A is a real matrix if all its entries are real numbers.

Proposition 1.4. *The eigenvalues of any real symmetric matrix are all real.* ■

Two vectors $\alpha, \beta \in \mathbb{R}^n$ are orthogonal if $\alpha \cdot \beta = 0$. A square matrix T is orthogonal if $T'T = I$, i.e., $T^{-1} = T'$. A vector α is a unit vector if $\|\alpha\| = 1$.

Proposition 1.5. $T \in \mathbb{R}^{n \times n}$ *is orthogonal* $\Leftrightarrow$ *its column vectors are orthogonal unit vectors* $\Leftrightarrow$ *its row vectors are orthogonal unit vectors.* ■

Proposition 1.6. *If A is a real symmetric matrix, then any two eigenvectors of different eigenvalues are orthogonal to each other.* ■

Proposition 1.7. *A collection of non-zero orthogonal vectors must be linearly independent.* ■

Theorem 1.22. *For any real symmetric matrix A, there exists an orthogonal matrix T such that $T^{-1}AT$ is diagonal.* ■

In the above theorem, the diagonal entries of $D \equiv T^{-1}AT$ are eigenvalues (not necessarily all distinct), and the column vectors of T are the corresponding eigenvectors.

Example 1.20. Consider the following second-degree equation:

$$a_{11}x_1^2 + 2a_{12}x_1x_2 + a_{22}x_2^2 + a_1x_1 + a_2x_2 + c = 0. \qquad (1.8)$$

Let

$$A \equiv \begin{pmatrix} a_{11} & a_{12} \\ a_{21} & a_{22} \end{pmatrix}, \quad a \equiv \begin{pmatrix} a_1 \\ a_2 \end{pmatrix}, \quad x \equiv \begin{pmatrix} x_1 \\ x_2 \end{pmatrix}.$$

By Theorem 1.22, there exists an orthogonal matrix T and a diagonal matrix $D = diag\{\lambda_1\lambda_2\}$ such that $T^{-1}AT = D$. Let

$$z \equiv \begin{pmatrix} z_1 \\ z_2 \end{pmatrix} \equiv T^{-1}\begin{pmatrix} x_1 \\ x_2 \end{pmatrix}, \quad \beta \equiv \begin{pmatrix} \beta_1 \\ \beta_2 \end{pmatrix} \equiv Ta.$$

Then if both $\lambda_1 \neq 0$ and $\lambda_2 \neq 0$,

$$x'Ax + a'x + c = x'TT^{-1}ATT^{-1}x + a'TT^{-1}x + c = z'DZ + \beta'z + c$$
$$= \lambda_1 z_1^2 + \lambda_2 z_2^2 + \beta_1 z_1 + \beta_2 z_2 + c$$
$$= \lambda_1\left(z_1 + \frac{\beta_1}{2\lambda_1}\right)^2 + \lambda_2\left(z_2 + \frac{\beta_2}{2\lambda_2}\right)^2 + d, \qquad (1.9)$$

where d is some constant. Let

$$y_i \equiv z_i + \frac{\beta_i}{2\lambda_i}, \quad i = 1, 2.$$

Then

$$x'Ax + a'x + c = \lambda_1 y_1^2 + \lambda_2 y_2^2 + d = 0. \qquad (1.10)$$

By Proposition 1.4, we know that both λ_1 and λ_2 are real numbers. Hence, there are three possibilities: (1) λ_1 and λ_2 have the same sign; (2) λ_1 and λ_2 have different signs; and (3) either λ_1 or λ_2 is zero. By (1.10), the first two possibilities give the first two standard forms in the following:

$$\text{Ellipse:} \quad \frac{y_1^2}{b_1^2} + \frac{y_2^2}{b_2^2} = 1,$$

$$\text{Parabola:} \quad \frac{y_1^2}{b_1^2} - \frac{y_2^2}{b_2^2} = 1 \quad \text{or} \quad \frac{y_2^2}{b_2^2} - \frac{y_1^2}{b_1^2} = 1,$$

$$\text{Hyperbola:} \quad y_1^2 = b_2 y_2 \quad \text{or} \quad y_2^2 = b_1 y_1. \qquad (1.11)$$

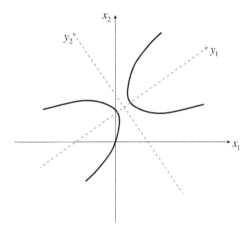

Figure 1.3. A Second-Degree Equation under Different Axis Systems

If one of λ_1 and λ_2 is zero, say $\lambda_2 = 0$, by the same derivation as in (1.9), we have

$$x'Ax + \alpha'x + c = \lambda_1 \left(z_1 + \frac{\beta_1}{2\lambda_1} \right)^2 + \beta_2(z_2 + b),$$

where b is some constant. Let

$$y_1 \equiv z_1 + \frac{\beta_1}{2\lambda_1}, \quad y_2 \equiv z_2 + b.$$

Then we have the third standard form in (1.11).[1] In Figure 1.3, using the axis system for (x_1, x_2), the two curves are represented by the equation in (1.8); but when the axis system for (y_1, y_2) is used, the two curves are represented by $\frac{y_1^2}{b_1^2} - \frac{y_2^2}{b_2^2} = 1$, which is much simpler. Changing the axis system corresponds precisely to a similarity transformation. ■

9. Idempotent Matrix

A real symmetric matrix A is called an idempotent matrix if $A^2 = A$.

Example 1.21. Given a full-rank tall matrix H, matrix $A \equiv H(H'H)^{-1} H'$ is symmetric and idempotent. ■

---

[1]See Matthews (1998, p. 129) for details.

Theorem 1.23.

(1) *The eigenvalues of an idempotent matrix are either* 0 *or* 1.
(2) *The only full-rank idempotent matrix is the identity matrix.*
(3) *The rank of an idempotent matrix is equal to its trace.*
(4) *Any idempotent matrix is positive semi-definite.* ∎

Notes

Good references include Sydsæter *et al.* (2005, Chapter 1), Chiang (1984, Chapters 4 and 5), and Greene (1993, Chapter 2).

Appendix

A.1. *Proof of Theorem 1.4*

If A is invertible, by definition, there exists a matrix B such that $AB = I$. Hence,

$$1 = |I| = |AB| = |A| \cdot |B|,$$

implying $|A| \neq 0$.

Conversely, if $|A| \neq 0$, we can construct a matrix B by

$$B \equiv \frac{1}{|A|} A^*.$$

For the matrix A, denote

$$A_{ij} \equiv \text{the entry of } A \text{ at the } i\text{th row and } j\text{th column.}$$

By Theorem 1.3, we find

$$(AA^*)_{ii} = \sum_{k=1}^{n} a_{ik} C_{ik} = |A|,$$

and, for any i and j, $i \neq j$, we find

$$(AA^*)_{ij} = \sum_{k=1}^{n} a_{ik} C_{jk} = 0.$$

Hence, $AA^* = |A| \cdot I_n$, implying that $A^*/|A|$ is the inverse matrix and thus A is invertible.

A.2. *Proof of Corollary 1.1*

(1) If $AB = I$ and $CA = I$, then $C = CAB = IB = B$. That is, the inverse matrix is unique.
(2) For a square matrix A, if there is a matrix B such that $AB = I$ or $BA = I$, we have $|A| \neq 0$ and hence, by Theorem 1.4, A is invertible. By the uniqueness of an inverse matrix, we have $B = A^{-1}$.

A.3. *Proof of Theorem 1.5*

By the definition of an inverse matrix, $AA^{-1} = I$ implies $A = (A^{-1})^{-1}$ and $(AB)(B^{-1}A^{-1}) = I$ implies $(AB)^{-1} = B^{-1}A^{-1}$.

A.4. *Proof of Theorem 1.6*

We prove only the third and fifth properties. The rest are obvious. To prove the third property, for a matrix C denote

$$C_{ij} \equiv \text{the entry of } C \text{ at the } i\text{th row and } j\text{th column.}$$

We have

$$(AB)'_{ij} = (AB)_{ji} = \sum_k A_{jk} B_{ki} = \sum_k B_{ki} A_{jk} = \sum_k B'_{ik} A'_{kj} = (B'A')_{ij}.$$

Thus, $(AB)' = B'A'$.

To prove the fifth property, since $AA^{-1} = I$, we have $(A^{-1})'A' = I$, implying $(A^{-1})' = (A')^{-1}$.

A.5. *Proof of Theorem 1.7*

We prove only the most important property: $tr(AB) = tr(BA)$. Since the entry at the ith row and jth column of AB is $\sum_k a_{ik} b_{kj}$,

we have

$$tr(AB) = \sum_i (AB)_{ii} = \sum_i \sum_k a_{ik}b_{ki}$$

$$= \sum_i \sum_k b_{ki}a_{ik} = \sum_k \sum_i b_{ki}a_{ik} = \sum_k (BA)_{kk} = tr(BA).$$

A.6. *Proof of Theorem 1.10*

Denote by A a sequence of column vectors $A = (\alpha_1, \ldots, \alpha_n)$. The equation in (1.3) has a solution iff d is a linear combination $\alpha_1, \ldots, \alpha_n$. Hence, if (1.3) has a solution, we have $rank(Ad) \leq rank(A)$, implying $rank(A) = rank(A, d)$. Conversely, if $rank(A) = rank(A, d)$, then d must be a linear combination $\alpha_1, \ldots, \alpha_n$, implying that (1.3) has a solution.

A.7. *Proof of Theorem 1.16*

Suppose that there are elementary row operations $e_1, e_2, \ldots, e_k$ such that

$$e_1(I) \cdot e_2(I) \cdots e_k(I)(A, I) = (I, B).$$

Then

$$(e_1(I) \cdot e_2(I) \cdots e_k(I)A, \; e_1(I) \cdot e_2(I) \cdots e_k(I)I) = (I, B),$$

implying

$$e_1(I) \cdot e_2(I) \cdots e_k(I)A = I, e_1(I) \cdot e_2(I) \cdots e_k(I)I = B.$$

These in turn imply

$$A^{-1} = e_1(I) \cdot e_2(I) \cdots e_k(I) = B.$$

A.8. *Proof of Theorem 1.17*

We apply the method of mathematical induction. First, this theorem is obviously true if $n = 1$. Further, for any $n > 1$, assume that any $(n-1) \times (n-1)$ invertible matrix is row-equivalent to the identity matrix. Given an invertible matrix $A = (a_{ij})_{n \times n}$, at least one entry in the first column must be non-zero. We can move this non-zero entry a_{i1} to the first row by a third type of row operation. Since we can do this, we will simply assume $a_{11} \neq 0$. We can then use this non-zero entry to eliminate other entries in the first column using the second type of operations. That is, after some row operations, we are guaranteed to obtain

$$A \rightarrow \begin{pmatrix} 1 & b_{12} & \cdots & b_{1n} \\ 0 & b_{22} & \cdots & b_{2n} \\ \vdots & \vdots & & \vdots \\ 0 & b_{n2} & \cdots & b_{nn} \end{pmatrix}.$$

Since A is invertible, B must also be invertible, where

$$B = \begin{pmatrix} b_{22} & \cdots & b_{2n} \\ \vdots & & \vdots \\ b_{n2} & \cdots & b_{nn} \end{pmatrix}.$$

Since B is invertible, by assumption, B is row-equivalent to I_{n-1}, meaning that there is a matrix P that is the product of a few elementary matrices such that $PB = I_{n-1}$. We have

$$\begin{pmatrix} 1 & 0 & \cdots & 0 \\ 0 & & & \\ \vdots & & P & \\ 0 & & & \end{pmatrix} \begin{pmatrix} 1 & b_{11} & \cdots & b_{1n} \\ 0 & & & \\ \vdots & & B & \\ 0 & & & \end{pmatrix} = \begin{pmatrix} 1 & b_{12} & \cdots & b_{1n} \\ 0 & & & \\ \vdots & & PB & \\ 0 & & & \end{pmatrix}$$

$$= \begin{pmatrix} 1 & b_{12} & \cdots & b_{1n} \\ 0 & & & \\ \vdots & & I_{n-1} & \\ 0 & & & \end{pmatrix}.$$

The last matrix in (1.12) is obviously row-equivalent to the identity matrix. Also, since, for any two square matrices E_1 and E_2, we have

$$\begin{pmatrix} 1 & 0 \\ 0 & E_1 \end{pmatrix} \begin{pmatrix} 1 & 0 \\ 0 & E_2 \end{pmatrix} = \begin{pmatrix} 1 & 0 \\ 0 & E_1 E_2 \end{pmatrix},$$

$\begin{pmatrix} 1 & 0 \\ 0 & P \end{pmatrix}$ must be the product of a few elementary matrices. Hence, we have proven that any $n \times n$ invertible matrix is row-equivalent to the identity matrix. Therefore, by mathematical induction, any invertible matrix is row-equivalent to the identity matrix.

A.9. *Proof of Theorem 1.19*

If λ is an eigenvalue, then there exists an eigenvector x such that $Ax = \lambda x$, which implies $(\lambda I - A)x = 0$. Thus, $|\lambda I - A| = 0$. Conversely, if $|\lambda I - A| = 0$, then there exists a non-zero x such that $(\lambda I - A)x = 0$, which implies $Ax = \lambda x$.

A.10. *Proof of Theorem 1.21*

If there are n independent eigenvectors $\alpha_1, \ldots, \alpha_n$ with corresponding eigenvalues $\lambda_1, \ldots, \lambda_n$, then

$$(A\alpha_1, \ldots, A\alpha_n) = (\alpha_1, \ldots, \alpha_n) \begin{pmatrix} \lambda_1 & & \\ & \ddots & \\ & & \lambda_n \end{pmatrix}.$$

If we take $T \equiv (\alpha_1, \ldots, \alpha_n)$, we have

$$T^{-1}AT = diag\{\lambda_1, \ldots, \lambda_n\}.$$

Thus, A is diagonalizable.

Conversely, if A is diagonalizable to the matrix $D = diag\{\lambda_1, \ldots, \lambda_n\}$ with $T^{-1}AT = D$ and $\alpha_1, \ldots, \alpha_n$ being the column vectors of T then $\alpha_1, \ldots, \alpha_n$ are linearly independent and $AT = TD$, which implies $A\alpha_i = \lambda_i \alpha_i$ for all i. That is, $\alpha_1, \ldots, \alpha_n$ are eigenvectors.

A.11. *Proof of Proposition 1.4*

Let $A\xi = \lambda\xi$. Since $A = \bar{A}$ and $A = A'$, we find

$$\bar{\xi}'A\xi = \lambda\bar{\xi}'\xi \quad \text{and} \quad \bar{\xi}'A\xi = \overline{(A\xi)'}\xi = \overline{(\lambda\xi)'}\xi = \bar{\lambda}\bar{\xi}'\xi,$$

implying $\bar{\lambda} = \lambda$.

A.12. *Proof of Proposition 1.5*

Express T as a sequence of column vectors: $T = (\alpha_1, \ldots, \alpha_n)$. Then

$$T'T = \begin{pmatrix} \alpha_1' \\ \vdots \\ \alpha_n' \end{pmatrix} (\alpha_1, \ldots, \alpha_n) = \begin{pmatrix} \alpha_1'\alpha_1 & \cdots & \alpha_1'\alpha_n \\ \vdots & & \vdots \\ \alpha_n'\alpha_1 & \cdots & \alpha_n'\alpha_n \end{pmatrix}.$$

Hence, $T'T = I$ iff $\alpha_i'\alpha_i = 1$ for all i and $\alpha_i'\alpha_j = 0$ for any $i \neq j$. That is, the column vectors of T are orthogonal unit vectors.

Further, define the matrix B as the transpose of T i.e., $B \equiv T'$. Since $T'T = I$, we have $B'B = I$, which by the above proof implies that the column vectors of B are orthogonal unit vectors. The column vectors of B are the row vectors of T.

A.13. *Proof of Proposition 1.6*

Given $A\xi = \lambda\xi$ and $A\eta = \delta\eta$ with $\lambda \neq \delta$, we have

$$\eta' A\xi = \lambda\eta'\xi \quad \text{and} \quad \eta' A\xi = (A\eta)'\xi = \delta\eta'\xi.$$

Hence, $\eta'\xi = 0$.

A.14. *Proof of Proposition 1.7*

Given a list of non-zero orthogonal vectors $\alpha_1, \ldots, \alpha_n$ consider

$$\lambda_1\alpha_1 + \cdots + \lambda_n\alpha_n = 0.$$

If we multiply the above equation by α_i, we get $\lambda_i\alpha_i \cdot \alpha_i = 0$, implying $\lambda_i = 0$. Hence, the above equation implies $\lambda_1 = \cdots = \lambda_n = 0$. Therefore, $\alpha_1, \ldots, \alpha_n$ are linearly independent.

A.15. *Proof of Theorem 1.23*

(1) By Theorem 1.22, there exists a diagonal matrix D and an orthogonal matrix T such that $T^{-1}AT = D$, where the diagonal entries of D are the eigenvalues of A. Since $T^{-1}AT = D$ implies $T^{-1}A^2T = D^2$, we have $D = D^2$. Hence, any eigenvalue λ must satisfy $\lambda = \lambda^2$, implying $\lambda = 0$ or 1.

Alternatively, since $A\xi = \lambda\xi$ and $A^2\xi = A(\lambda\xi) = \lambda^2\xi$ for the non-zero vector ξ, we must have $\lambda = \lambda^2$.

(2) If A has full rank, since the rank does not change after a transformation, D must have full rank too, implying $D = I$. Hence, $A = TDT^{-1} = I$.

(3) Since the rank and trace do not change after a transformation, we have

$$rank(A) = rank(D) \quad \text{and} \quad trace(A) = trace(D).$$

Further, since $rank(D) = trace(D)$, we have $rank(A) = trace(A)$.

(4) Since D is positive semi-definite and semi-definiteness remains after a transformation, matrix A must be positive semi-definite. Alternatively, for any vector $x \in \mathbb{R}^n$, letting $y \equiv T'x$ and $D = diag\{d_1, \ldots, d_n\}$, we have

$$x'Ax = x'(TDT^{-1})x = x'(TDT')x = (T'x)'D(T'x) = y'Dy$$

$$= \sum_{i=1}^{n} d_i y_i^2 \geq 0.$$

Hence, A is positive semi-definite.

Chapter 2

Basic Real Analysis

1. Set

A set is a primitive concept of mathematics. A set is defined as[1]

$$A \equiv \{x \,|\, \text{conditions}\}.$$

Here, x denotes a typical item, member, element or point in the set. For an item to be in the set, it has to satisfy certain conditions. It is possible that there is no item in a set, in which case we say that the set is an empty set and denote it by $\emptyset$. If a set A has finite items, we say that A is finite; otherwise it is infinite. If the elements of a set can be indexed (i.e., counted one by one) by the sequence of natural numbers (i.e., $1, 2, 3, \ldots$), we say that it is countable. A finite set is countable, but an infinite set may or may not be.

Example 2.1. The set of all fractions is infinite and countable. A fraction can be expressed as m/n, where m and n are natural numbers (Figure 2.1).

Example 2.2. The set of all real numbers is denoted by

$$\mathbb{R} \equiv \{x \,|\, x \text{ is a real number}\},$$

and

$$\mathbb{R}_+ \equiv \{x \in \mathbb{R} \,|\, x \geq 0\}.$$

---

[1]We need to exclude some senseless statements of 'conditions' in the definition in order to avoid such a set as $\{A \,|\, A \text{ is not in } A\}$.

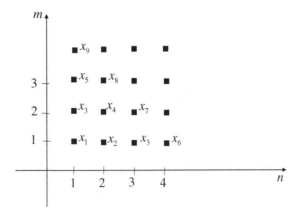

Figure 2.1. A Countable Infinite Set

The set of natural numbers is

$$\mathbb{N} = \{1, 2, 3, \ldots, n, \ldots\}.$$

The set of all points on the unit circle is

$$S^1 \equiv \{(x, y) \mid x^2 + y^2 = 1, x, y \in \mathbb{R}\}.$$

For any two numbers a, $b \in \mathbb{R}$, $a < b$, we call the following set an open interval:

$$(a, b) \equiv \{x \mid a < x < b, x \in \mathbb{R}\}.$$

Similarly, the following set is a closed interval:

$$[a, b] \equiv \{x \mid a \leq x \leq b, x \in \mathbb{R}\},$$

and the following set is a half-open half-closed interval:

$$(a, b] \equiv \{x \mid a < x \leq b, x \in \mathbb{R}\}.$$

We can also extend the definition of intervals to allow a and b to be infinities. ∎

Given two sets A and B, if $x \in A$ implies $x \in B$, then we say that A is a subset of B, and denote $A \subset B$, or $B \supset A$. If both $A \subset B$ and $B \subset A$ are true, then we say that A and B are equal, and denote $A = B$. This means that $\{1, 1, 2\} = \{1, 2\}$, for example.

Similar to vectors and matrices, we now define some operations for sets. The intersection of two sets A and B is defined as the following set:

$$A \cap B \equiv \{x \mid x \in A \text{ and } x \in B\}.$$

The union of two sets A and B is defined as the following set:

$$A \cup B \equiv \{x \mid x \in A \text{ or } x \in B\}.$$

The difference between two sets A and B is defined as the following set:

$$A \backslash B \equiv \{x \mid x \in A \text{ and } x \notin B\}.$$

These operations are shown in Figure 2.2.

When two sets A and B have an empty intersection, $A \cap B = \emptyset$, we say that these two sets are disjoint. Given two sets A and X, if $A \subset X$, we denote $A^c \equiv X \backslash A$ and call it the complement of A (see Figure 2.3).

Example 2.3. For $A = \{2, 3, 5, 7\}$ and $B = \{3, 8, 9\}$, we have

$$A \cap B = \{3\}, \quad A \cup B = \{2, 3, 5, 7, 8, 9\}, \quad A \backslash B = \{2, 5, 7\}.$$

In $\mathbb{R}$, for $A = (a, b]$, we have $A^c = (-\infty, a] \cup (b, \infty)$. ∎

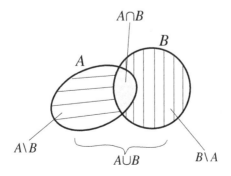

Figure 2.2. Operations of Sets

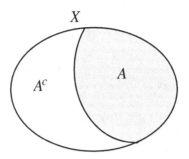

Figure 2.3. The Complement Set

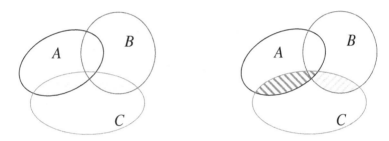

Figure 2.4. Illustration of Theorem 2.1(a)

The following theorem lists a few essential properties of set operations.

Theorem 2.1.

(a) *The commutative law:* $A \cup B = B \cup A$, $A \cap B = B \cap A$.

(b) *The associative law:* $(A \cup B) \cup C = A \cup (B \cup C)$, $(A \cap B) \cap C = A \cap (B \cap C)$.

(c) *The distributive law:* $(A \cup B) \cap C = (A \cap C) \cup (B \cap C)$, $(A \cap B) \cup C = (A \cup C) \cap (B \cup C)$.

(d) $(A \cup B)^c = A^c \cap B^c$, $(A \cap B)^c = A^c \cup B^c$.

(e) $(A \backslash B) \cap C = (A \cap C) \backslash (B \cap C) = (A \cap C) \backslash B$.

(f) $A \backslash B = A \cap B^c$. ∎

This theorem can be illustrated by diagrams. For example, the first property in (c) is shown in Figure 2.4.

The union operation is not limited to two sets. For sets $S_1, S_2, \ldots, S_n, \ldots$, we define

$$\bigcup_{i=1}^{n} S_i \equiv \{x \mid \exists i \in \{1, \ldots, n\} \text{ s.t. } x \in S_i\},$$

$$\bigcup_{i=1}^{\infty} S_i \equiv \{x \mid \exists i \in \{1, \ldots, n, \ldots\} \text{ s.t. } x \in S_i\}.$$

In fact, the index i need not be countable. For any set I, we define

$$\bigcup_{i \in I} S_i \equiv \{x \mid \exists i \in I \text{ s.t. } x \in S_i\}.$$

The set I is called the index set. Analogously, we define

$$\bigcap_{i \in I} S_i \equiv \{x \mid \forall i \in I, x \in S_i\}.$$

Given two sets X and Y, for $x \in X$ and $y \in Y$, we have an ordered pair (x, y). The Cartesian product of X and Y is a set defined by

$$X \times Y \equiv \{(x, y) \mid x \in X, y \in Y\}.$$

In general, for an index set I, we denote the Cartesian product of sets X_i by $\otimes_{i \in I} X_i$. For example, the n-dimensional Euclidean space is defined by

$$\mathbb{R}^n \equiv \{(x_1, x_2, \ldots, x_n) \mid x_i \in \mathbb{R}, \ \forall i\} = \overset{n}{\underset{i=1}{\otimes}} \mathbb{R},$$

and the positive cone of $\mathbb{R}^n$ is denoted by

$$\mathbb{R}^n_+ \equiv \{x \in \mathbb{R}^n \mid x_i \geq 0, \ \forall i\} = \overset{n}{\underset{i=1}{\otimes}} \mathbb{R}_+.$$

A point or element x in $\mathbb{R}^n$ is called a vector, more specifically an n-dimensional vector or simply an n-vector.

Example 2.4. For the two sets A and B defined in Example 2.2, we have

$$A \times B = \{(2,3), (2,8), (2,9), (3,3), (3,8), (3,9),$$
$$(5,3), (5,8), (5,9), (7,3), (7,8), (7,9)\}. \quad \blacksquare$$

2. Logical Statements

Let P and Q be two statements. The notation "$P \Rightarrow Q$" means that P implies Q. In other words, if P is true, then Q is true. We call "$Q \Rightarrow P$" the converse of "$P \Rightarrow Q$". When both "$P \Rightarrow Q$" and "$Q \Rightarrow P$" are true, we denote "$P \Leftrightarrow Q$" or "P iff Q". We say in this case that P and Q are (logically) equivalent.

If $P \Rightarrow Q$, we call P a sufficient condition for Q and Q a necessary condition for P, or P is sufficient for Q and Q is necessary for P. If $P \Leftrightarrow Q$, we say that P is a necessary and sufficient condition for Q, or Q is a necessary and sufficient condition for P.

The following two statements are logically equivalent:

$$\text{``}P \Rightarrow Q\text{''} \Leftrightarrow \text{``}Q \text{ is false} \Rightarrow P \text{ is false''}.$$

This property is very useful. If the right-hand side is easy to prove, we can prove it instead of tackling "$P \Rightarrow Q$" directly. We call such a proof a counter proof.

Example 2.5. Let

$$P = \text{``}f \text{ is differentiable''}, \quad Q = \text{``}f \text{ is continuous''}.$$

"f is differentiable at x_0" means

$$\lim_{x \to x_0} \frac{f(x) - f(x_0)}{x - x_0} \text{ exists and is finite.} \tag{2.1}$$

"f is continuous at x_0" means

$$\lim_{x \to x_0} [f(x) - f(x_0)] = 0. \tag{2.2}$$

To prove "$P \Rightarrow Q$", using (2.1), we show (2.2) is true by the fact that

$$\lim_{x \to x_0} [f(x) - f(x_0)] = \lim_{x \to x_0} \frac{f(x) - f(x_0)}{x - x_0}(x - x_0) = 0.$$

To prove "Q is false $\Rightarrow P$ is false", if (2.2) is false, i.e., $\lim_{x \to x_0}[f(x) - f(x_0)] \neq 0$, then $\lim_{x \to x_0} \frac{f(x)-f(x_0)}{x-x_0}$ does not exist or is not finite, implying that (2.1) is false. ∎

3. Mappings

Given two sets X and Y, if each point in X is associated with a unique point in Y, then such an association is called a mapping from X to Y, and is denoted by $f: X \to Y$. That is, for each $x \in X$, its associated $y \in Y$ is $y = f(x)$. In this case, X is called the domain of f and is denoted by $X = D(f)$, and Y is called the value space. The set of all values $f(x)$ for $x \in X$ is called the range of f and is denoted by

$$f(X) \equiv \{f(x) \,|\, x \in X\}.$$

When $Y \subset \mathbb{R}$, the mappings are called real-valued functions. When $Y \subset \mathbb{R}^n$, the mappings are called vector-valued functions.

When $Y = f(X)$, we say that f is onto. When $x_1 \neq x_2$ implies $f(x_1) \neq f(x_2)$, we say that f is 1-1. If $f: X \to Y$ is 1-1, then we can define an inverse of f as

$$f^{-1}: f(X) \to X, \quad \text{where } x = f^{-1}(y) \text{ iff } y = f(x).$$

Example 2.6. Consider three popular functions $f_i: \mathbb{R} \to \mathbb{R}$,

$$f_1(x) = x^3, \quad f_2(x) = e^x, \quad f_3(x) = \sin(x).$$

f_1 is 1-1 and onto. The inverse of f_1 is $f_1^{-1}: \mathbb{R} \to \mathbb{R}$, $f_1^{-1}(y) = y^{1/3}$. f_2 is also 1-1, but is not onto. The range of f_2 is $f_2(\mathbb{R}) = (0, \infty)$. The inverse of f_2 is $f_2^{-1}: (0, \infty) \to \mathbb{R}$, where $f_2^{-1}(y) = \ln(y)$. f_3 is neither 1-1 nor onto. Its range is $f_3(\mathbb{R}) = [-1, 1]$. ■

Given two sets X and Y and a mapping $f: X \to Y$ define the inverse image of a subset $S \subset Y$ as

$$f^{-1}(S) \equiv \{x \in X \,|\, f(x) \in S\}.$$

Example 2.7. For $f: \mathbb{R} \to \mathbb{R}$, $f(x) = x^3$, let $S = [-8, 8]$. Then, $f^{-1}(S) = [-2, 2]$. ■

For $x, y \in \mathbb{R}^n$, denote

$$
\begin{aligned}
x \geq y &\quad \text{if } x_i \geq y_i, \ \forall i, \\
x > y &\quad \text{if } x \geq y, \ x \neq y, \\
x \gg y &\quad \text{if } x_i > y_i, \ \forall i.
\end{aligned}
$$

A mapping $f \colon \mathbb{R}^m \to \mathbb{R}^n$ is said to be increasing if $f(x) \geq f(y)$ whenever $x \geq y$. A mapping f is decreasing if $-f$ is increasing.

Example 2.8. The following function $f \colon \mathbb{R}^2 \to \mathbb{R}^3$ is increasing:

$$
f(x_1, x_2) = \begin{pmatrix} x_1^3 + x_2 \\ e^{x_1} - 2 \\ 2x_1 + 3x_2 \end{pmatrix}.
$$

We can verify its increasingness by the fact that each of the following functions is increasing in (x_1, x_2):

$$
f_1(x_1, x_2) \equiv x_1^3 + x_2, \quad f_2(x_1, x_2) \equiv e^{x_1} - 2,
$$
$$
f_3(x_1, x_2) \equiv 2x_1 + 3x_2. \quad \blacksquare
$$

4. Sequence

Given a set S, a sequence in S is a set of ordered countable points $x^1, \ldots x^m, \ldots$, in S. This sequence can also be written as $\{x^k\}_{k=1}^\infty$ or simply $\{x^k\}$. Given a sequence $\{x^k\}_{k=1}^\infty$, a different sequence $\{x^{k_n}\}$, whose members are $\{x^k\}$ and $\{k_n\}$ is a strictly increasing sequence of natural numbers, is a subsequence of $\{x^k\}$. That is, a subsequence is formed by removing some of the members from the original sequence.

Example 2.9. $\{1, 2, \ldots, k, \ldots\}$ is a sequence and $\{1, 3, \ldots, 2k - 1, \ldots\}$ is a subsequence. $\quad \blacksquare$

For $x = (x_1, \ldots, x_n)$, $y = (y_1, \ldots, y_n) \in \mathbb{R}^m$, let $\|x\| = \sqrt{x_1^2 + \cdots + x_n^2}$ and $\langle x, y \rangle = x \cdot y$. We say that a sequence $\{x^k\}$ converges to a point x^0, denoted by $x^k \to x^0$ or $\lim_{k \to \infty} x^k = x^0$, if

$$
\forall \varepsilon > 0, \ \exists K \in \mathbb{R}_+ \text{ s.t. } \|x^k - x^0\| < \varepsilon, \text{ for all } k \geq K. \tag{2.3}
$$

This point x^0 is called the limit of $\{x^k\}$. Any sequence in S that has a limit point is called a convergent sequence in S. The limit point must be unique, but it may or may not be in S.

Example 2.10. In $S = (0, 1]$, the sequence $x^k = \frac{1}{k}$ is convergent, but the limit 0 does not belong to S. ∎

Example 2.11. Let us use the definition in (2.3) to prove that the sequence $x^k = \frac{1}{k+k^2}$ converges to 0. For any $\varepsilon > 0$, we need $|x^k - 0| = \frac{1}{k+k^2} < \varepsilon$, which is equivalent to $k + k^2 > \frac{1}{\varepsilon}$ or $k > \sqrt{\frac{1}{\varepsilon} + \frac{1}{4}} - \frac{1}{2}$. That is, for any $\varepsilon > 0$, when $k > \sqrt{\frac{1}{\varepsilon} + \frac{1}{4}} - \frac{1}{2}$, we have $|x^k - 0| < \varepsilon$. Therefore, $x^k \to 0$. ∎

Example 2.12. Let us use the definition in (2.3) to prove that the sequence $x^k = e^{\frac{1}{k}}$ converges to 1. For any $\varepsilon > 0$, we need $|x^k - 1| = e^{\frac{1}{k}} - 1 < \varepsilon$, which is equivalent to $\frac{1}{k} < \ln(1 + \varepsilon)$ or $k > \frac{1}{\ln(1+\varepsilon)}$. That is, for any $\varepsilon > 0$, when $k > \frac{1}{\ln(1+\varepsilon)}$, we have $|x^k - 1| < \varepsilon$. Therefore, $x^k \to 1$. ∎

Proposition 2.1. *A sequence is convergent if and only if all its subsequences are convergent to the same point.* ∎

The border of a set A is defined as the set of points that are not in the interior of A but are arbitrarily close to A, where closeness is defined by the existence of a convergent sequence from A. A border point of A may or may not be in A. A set that contains its own border is a closed set. Specifically, a set is said to be closed if it contains all its limit points.

For a sequence $\{x^k\}$ of real numbers, we can also discuss its convergence to infinity. We say that the sequence $\{x^k\}$ converges to $+\infty$, if

$$\forall M > 0, \quad \exists K > 0 \text{ s.t. } x^k > M, \text{ for all } k \geq K.$$

Similarly, we say that the sequence $\{x^k\}$ converges to $-\infty$, if

$$\forall M < 0, \quad \exists K > 0 \text{ s.t. } x^k < M, \text{ for all } k \geq K.$$

For example, the sequence $x^k = k^2$ converges to $+\infty$, and the sequence $x^k = -\sqrt{k}$ converges to $-\infty$. With the definition of convergence to infinity, a convergent sequence in $\mathbb{R}$ may be converted to either a finite number or infinity.

Example 2.13. Let us show that the sequence $x^k = e^k$ converges to $+\infty$. $\forall M > 0$, we need $x^k > M$, which is equivalent to $e^k > M$ or $k > \ln(M)$. That is, $\forall M > 0$, when $k > \ln(M)$, we have $x^k > M$. Therefore, $x^k \to +\infty$. ■

Theorem 2.2 (Convergence Properties).

1. $x^k \to x^0 \Rightarrow \lambda x^k \to \lambda x^0$, *where* $\lambda \in \mathbb{R}$.
2. $x^k \to x^0$ *and* $y^k \to y^0 \Rightarrow x^k + y^k \to x^0 + y^0$.
3. $x^k \to x^0 \Rightarrow \|x^k\| \to \|x^0\|$.
4. $x^k \to x^0$ *and* $y^k \to y^0 \Rightarrow \langle x^k, y^k \rangle \to \langle x^0, y^0 \rangle$. ■

A sequence $\{x^k\}$ is bounded if there is a number λ such that $\|x^k\| \leq \lambda$, for all k. A set S is bounded if there is a number λ such that $\|x\| \leq \lambda$, for all $x \in S$. A compact set in $\mathbb{R}^n$ is a set that is bounded and closed.[2]

Example 2.14. $[a, b]$ and $[a, b] \cup [c, d]$ are compact sets, but (a, b) and $[a, \infty)$ are not compact sets. ■

Proposition 2.2 (Triangular Property). *In* $\mathbb{R}^n$, *for any* x, $y \in \mathbb{R}^n$, *we always have*

$$\|x + y\| \leq \|x\| + \|y\|.$$

Proposition 2.3 (Characterization of Convergence).

(1) *Any convergent sequence with a finite limit must be bounded.*
(2) *Any monotonic sequence in* $\mathbb{R}$ *must be convergent.* ■

Proposition 2.3(2) implies that any monotonic sequence in $\mathbb{R}^n$ must be convergent, possibly to infinity in some directions.

---

[2]In an infinite-dimensional space, compactness is defined in a different way and a bounded and closed set may not be compact.

5. Continuity

The continuity of a mapping means that the function curve or surface has no break point. We use the convergence of sequences to define continuity. We first define the convergence of a function at a point and then define continuity.

Given a set $X \subset \mathbb{R}^n$ and a mapping $f \colon X \to \mathbb{R}^m$, we say that $f(x)$ converges to y^0 as $x \to x^0$ if

$$\forall \varepsilon > 0, \quad \exists \delta > 0 \text{ s.t. } 0 < \|x - x^0\| < \delta \text{ implies } \|f(x) - y^0\| < \varepsilon.$$

We denote this by

$$f(x) \to y^0 \text{ as } x \to x^0 \quad \text{or} \quad \lim_{x \to x^0} f(x) = y^0.$$

Further, if it so happens that $y^0 = f(x^0)$, then we say that f is continuous at x^0. We say that f is continuous in X if it is continuous at every point in X.

Example 2.15. Let us show that $f(x) = x^2$ is continuous at $x^0 = 0$. For any $\varepsilon > 0$, we have $|f(x) - f(0)| < \varepsilon$ if and only if $x^2 < \varepsilon$, i.e., $|x| < \sqrt{\varepsilon}$. Thus,

$$\forall \varepsilon > 0, \quad \exists \delta = \sqrt{\varepsilon} > 0 \text{ s.t. } 0 < |x - 0| < \delta \text{ implies } |f(x) - f(0)| < \varepsilon.$$

Hence, $\lim_{x \to 0} f(x) = f(0)$, i.e., $f(x)$ is continuous at $x^0 = 0$. ∎

Proposition 2.4. *If mappings f and g are continuous at a point x_0, then*

$$f + g, \quad f - g, \quad \lambda f, \quad f \cdot g, \quad f/g, \quad f \circ g, \quad \|f\|$$

are all continuous at that point, where $\lambda \in \mathbb{R}$, and $g(x_0) \neq 0$ for f/g.

6. Differentiation

Let X be a subset of $\mathbb{R}$: $X \subset \mathbb{R}$. Given a real-valued function $f \colon X \to \mathbb{R}$, where X is called the domain of f, if the following limit exists and is finite:

$$\lim_{x \to x_0} \frac{f(x) - f(x_0)}{x - x_0},$$

then it is defined as the derivative of f at point $x_0 \in X$ and is denoted by $f'(x_0)$, or $f_x(x_0)$, or $\frac{\partial f(x_0)}{\partial x}$, or $\frac{\partial f(x)}{\partial x}\Big|_{x=x_0}$. When f has a derivative at any point of $x \in X$, we say that f is differentiable on X.

Proposition 2.5. *A differentiable function must be continuous.*

Given two real-valued functions $f: X \to \mathbb{R}$ and $g: X \to \mathbb{R}$, call $h(x) \equiv f(x)g(x)$ a product function of f and g, and denote it by $h = f \cdot g$. We have the following product rule:

$$\frac{d}{dx}[f(x)g(x)] = f'(x)g(x) + f(x)g'(x).$$

Example 2.16. Given three differentiable functions $f_1(x)$, $f_2(x)$ and $f_3(x)$, by the product rule, we have

$$[f_1(x)f_2(x)f_3(x)]'$$
$$= [f_1(x)f_2(x)]'f_3(x) + f_1(x)f_2(x)f_3'(x)$$
$$= [f_1'(x)f_2(x) + f_1(x)f_2'(x)]f_3(x) + f_1(x)f_2(x)f_3'(x)$$
$$= f_1'(x)f_2(x)f_3(x) + f_1(x)f_2'(x)f_3(x) + f_1(x)f_2(x)f_3'(x). \quad \blacksquare$$

Let $f: X \to Y$ and $g: Y \to \mathbb{R}$, where $X \subset \mathbb{R}$ and $Y \subset \mathbb{R}$. We call $h(x) \equiv g[f(x)]$ a compound function of f and g, and denote it by $h = f \circ g$ or $h(x) = f \circ g(x)$. If both $f(x)$ and $g(x)$ are differentiable, then their compound function $h(x)$ is also differentiable and the compound rule holds:

$$\frac{d}{dx}f[g(x)] = f'[g(x)]g'(x).$$

Example 2.17. Given an invertible function $f: R \to R$, let us find $\frac{d}{dy}f^{-1}(y)$. Since $f[f^{-1}(y)] = y$, we have

$$f'[f^{-1}(y)]\frac{d}{dy}f^{-1}(y) = 1,$$

implying

$$\frac{d}{dy}f^{-1}(y) = \frac{1}{f'[f^{-1}(y)]}. \quad \blacksquare$$

Example 2.18. Let us find $\frac{d}{dx}\left(\frac{1}{f(x)}\right)$. Let $g(y) \equiv \frac{1}{y}$. By the fact that $\frac{1}{f(x)} = g[f(x)]$, we immediately have

$$\frac{d}{dx}\left(\frac{1}{f(x)}\right) = g'[f(x)]f'(x) = -\frac{f'(x)}{f(x)^2}.$$

Alternatively, we can also use the fact that $f(x)\frac{1}{f(x)} = 1$ to find the derivative. $\quad \blacksquare$

Theorem 2.3 (Mean-Value Theorem). *If $f\colon R \to R$ is differentiable, then for any a and b in $\mathbb{R}$, there exists $\xi \in (a,b)$ such that*

$$f(a) - f(b) = f'(\xi)(a - b). \quad \blacksquare$$

The mean-value theorem is shown graphically in Figure 2.5.

For $X \subset \mathbb{R}$, consider a vector-valued function $f\colon X \to \mathbb{R}^n$. We can write f as $f(x) = (f_1(x),\ldots,f_n(x))^T$, where $f_i\colon X \to \mathbb{R}$. For each $f_i(x)$, we have defined the derivative $f_i'(x)$. We can now define

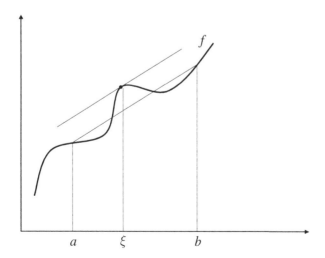

Figure 2.5. The Mean-Value Theorem

the derivative of $f(x)$ as

$$f'(x) \equiv \begin{pmatrix} f_1'(x) \\ \vdots \\ f_n'(x) \end{pmatrix}.$$

If $X \subset \mathbb{R}^n$, then a real-valued function $f\colon X \to \mathbb{R}$ is called a multi-variable function. Taking other variables $x_2, \ldots, x_n$ as constants, we can treat $f(x_1, x_2, \ldots, x_n)$ as a function of x_1 and its derivative is called the partial derivative of f w.r.t. x_1, and we can denote it by $f_{x_1}(x)$, or $f_1(x)$, or $\frac{\partial f(x)}{\partial x_1}$, where $x \equiv (x_1, x_2, \ldots, x_n)$. We can similarly define other partial derivatives of f w.r.t. other variables.

Given a multi-variable function $f(x_1, \ldots, x_n)$, at a point $\bar{x} = (\bar{x}_1, \ldots, \bar{x}_n)$, when all or some of the variables $x_1, \ldots, x_n$ change slightly, f typically changes slightly. We denote the change in x_i by dx_i and denote the change in $f(x)$ by $df(\bar{x})$. We call $df(\bar{x})$ the total derivative of f at $\bar{x}$. We have

$$df(\bar{x}) = f_{x_1}(\bar{x})dx_1 + \cdots + f_{x_n}(\bar{x})dx_n.$$

Example 2.19. Suppose that $G[x, f(x)] = 0$. Let us find $f'(x)$. We have

$$0 = G_x[x, f(x)]dx + G_y[x, f(x)]df(x)$$
$$= G_x[x, f(x)]dx + G_y[x, f(x)]f'(x)dx,$$

implying

$$f'(x) = -\frac{G_x[x, f(x)]}{G_y[x, f(x)]}. \quad \blacksquare \tag{2.4}$$

Example 2.20. Suppose that the demand and supply functions are respectively $D(p, x)$ and $S(p, x)$, where p is the price and x is some exogenous factor. Let $p^*(x)$ be the equilibrium price. Let us find the effect of x on $p^*(x)$. The equilibrium condition is

$$D[p^*(x), x] = S[p^*(x), x],$$

which determines the equilibrium price. By Equation (2.4), we immediately find

$$\frac{d}{dx}p^*(x) = -\frac{D_x[p^*(x), x] - S_x[p^*(x), x]}{D_p[p^*(x), x] - S_p[p^*(x), x]}. \quad \blacksquare$$

7. Directional Differentiation

We have learned the differentiation for a real-valued function $f\colon \mathbb{R}^m \to \mathbb{R}$. This section introduces a more general differentiation for a vector-valued function $f\colon \mathbb{R}^m \to \mathbb{R}^n$.

For $f\colon \mathbb{R}^m \to \mathbb{R}^n$, given x_0, define

$$\psi(h) = \frac{d}{dt}f(x_0 + th)|_{t=0}, \quad \forall h \in \mathbb{R}^m.$$

It turns out that ψ is linear in h. That is, there is a matrix $A \in \mathbb{R}^{n \times m}$ such that $\psi(h) = Ah$ for any $h \in \mathbb{R}^m$. We call this matrix A the directional derivative of f w.r.t. x at x_0, denoted by $f'(x_0)$ or $\frac{\partial f(x_0)}{\partial x}$. That is,

$$f'(x_0)h \equiv \frac{d}{dt}f(x_0 + th)|_{t=0}, \quad \forall h \in \mathbb{R}^m.$$

It turns out (by Gateaux) that, if all the partial derivatives of f exist, then

$$f'(x_0) = \begin{pmatrix} \dfrac{\partial f_1(x_0)}{\partial x_1} & \dfrac{\partial f_1(x_0)}{\partial x_2} & \cdots & \dfrac{\partial f_1(x_0)}{\partial x_m} \\[2ex] \dfrac{\partial f_2(x_0)}{\partial x_1} & \dfrac{\partial f_2(x_0)}{\partial x_2} & \cdots & \dfrac{\partial f_2(x_0)}{\partial x_m} \\[2ex] \vdots & \vdots & & \vdots \\[2ex] \dfrac{\partial f_n(x_0)}{\partial x_1} & \dfrac{\partial f_n(x_0)}{\partial x_2} & \cdots & \dfrac{\partial f_n(x_0)}{\partial x_m} \end{pmatrix}_{n \times m},$$

which is the so-called Jacobian matrix in economics.

For $f\colon \mathbb{R}^m \to \mathbb{R}$, its directional derivative is

$$f'(x_0) = \begin{pmatrix} \dfrac{\partial f(x_0)}{\partial x_1} & \dfrac{\partial f(x_0)}{\partial x_2} & \cdots & \dfrac{\partial f(x_0)}{\partial x_m} \end{pmatrix},$$

which is the so-called gradient in engineering. The derivative $f'(x)$ is a function $f'\colon \mathbb{R}^m \to \mathbb{R}^m$ and its directional derivative is defined as the second-order derivative of f. Denote the second-order directional derivative of f w.r.t. x at x_0 by $f''(x_0)$. As explained above, if all the second-order partial derivatives of f exist, then

$$f''(x_0) = \left(\frac{\partial^2 f(x_0)}{\partial x_i \partial x_j} \right)$$

$$\equiv \begin{pmatrix} \dfrac{\partial^2 f(x_0)}{\partial x_1 \partial x_1} & \dfrac{\partial^2 f(x_0)}{\partial x_1 \partial x_2} & \cdots & \dfrac{\partial^2 f(x_0)}{\partial x_1 \partial x_m} \\[2ex] \dfrac{\partial^2 f(x_0)}{\partial x_2 \partial x_1} & \dfrac{\partial^2 f(x_0)}{\partial x_2 \partial x_2} & \cdots & \dfrac{\partial^2 f(x_0)}{\partial x_2 \partial x_m} \\[2ex] \vdots & \vdots & & \vdots \\[2ex] \dfrac{\partial^2 f(x_0)}{\partial x_m \partial x_1} & \dfrac{\partial^2 f(x_0)}{\partial x_m \partial x_2} & \cdots & \dfrac{\partial^2 f(x_0)}{\partial x_m \partial x_m} \end{pmatrix}_{m \times m},$$

which is the so-called Hessian matrix in economics.

Theorem 2.4 (Composite Mapping Theorem). *Given two open sets $X \subset \mathbb{R}^n$ and $Y \subset \mathbb{R}^m$ and two mappings $f\colon X \to Y$ and $g\colon Y \to \mathbb{R}^k$ differentiable at $x^0 \in X$ and $y^0 \equiv f(x^0)$, respectively, the mapping $h \equiv g \circ f\colon X \to \mathbb{R}^k$ is also differentiable at x^0, and the compound rule holds*

$$\frac{\partial}{\partial x} g[f(x)]|_{x=x^0} = g'(y^0) f'(x^0),$$

where $g'(y^0) f'(x^0)$ is a matrix product.

Some useful formulas for directional derivatives are given in the following proposition.

Proposition 2.6. *Writing vectors as column vectors, we have*

(a) *For any vector α, $\frac{\partial(\alpha' x)}{\partial x} = \alpha'$.*

(b) *For any matrix A, $\frac{\partial(Ax)}{\partial x} = A$.*

(c) *For any matrix A, $\frac{\partial(x'Ax)}{\partial x} = x'(A + A')$.*

Theorem 2.5 (Taylor Expansion). *Given a set $X \subset R^n$ and a function $f\colon X \to R$, if f is twice continuously differentiable (a smooth function), then, for any two points x_0 and $x \in X$, there exists $\theta \in (0,1)$ such that*

$$f(x) = f(x_0) + f'(x_0) \cdot (x - x_0)$$
$$+ \frac{1}{2}(x - x_0)^T f''[\theta x_0 + (1 - \theta)x](x - x_0). \quad \blacksquare$$

8. Homogeneous Function

Besides concave and convex functions, homogeneous functions are of special interest to economists. A function $f\colon \mathbb{R}^n_+ \to \mathbb{R}$ is homogeneous if there is $\alpha \in \mathbb{R}$ such that

$$f(\lambda x) = \lambda^\alpha f(x), \quad \forall x \in \mathbb{R}^n_+, \ \lambda > 0.$$

In this case, we say that α is the degree of homogeneity and f is homogeneous of degree α. When $\alpha = 1$, we say that f is linearly homogeneous. When $\alpha = 0$, we say that f is zero homogeneous.

Example 2.21. The Cobb–Douglas function $f(x, y) = x^\alpha y^\beta$ is homogeneous of degree $\alpha + \beta$. $\quad \blacksquare$

Example 2.22. The CES function $f(x, y) = (\alpha x^\rho + \beta y^\rho)^{1/\rho}$ is linearly homogeneous. It has a constant elasticity of substitution $\sigma = (1 - \rho)^{-1}$ between x and y. $\quad \blacksquare$

Proposition 2.7 (Euler's Law). *If $f\colon R^n_+ \to R$ is linearly homogeneous, then*

$$f(x) = \sum_{i=1}^{n} f_{x_i}(x)x_i.$$

Proposition 2.8 (Homogeneity). *If $f(x)$ is homogeneous of degree α, then $f_{x_i}(x)$ is homogeneous of degree $\alpha - 1$, for any i.*

9. Fundamental Theorems

For a set $X \subset \mathbb{R}^n$, $x^0 \in X$ and $r > 0$, a neighborhood of x^0 is defined by

$$N_r(x^0) \equiv \{x \in X \,|\, \|x - x^0\| < r\}.$$

Here, r is the radius of the sphere $N_r(x^0)$ surrounding x^0.

Theorem 2.6 (Inverse Function Theorem). *For an open set $X \subset \mathbb{R}^n$ and a continuously differentiable function $f: X \to \mathbb{R}^n$, if $f'(x^0)$ is non-singular, there exist neighborhoods $N_a(x^0)$ and $N_b(y^0)$, where $y^0 \equiv f(x^0)$, and a unique continuously differentiable mapping $g: N_b(y^0) \to N_a(x^0)$ such that*

$$f(x) = y, \quad \text{for } x \in N_a(x^0),$$

$$y \in N_b(y^0) \Leftrightarrow x = g(y), \quad \text{for } y \in N_b(y^0). \quad \blacksquare$$

The function g in the inverse function theorem is the inverse function f^{-1}, defined in a neighborhood of y^0. In other words, a continuously differentiable function is locally invertible in a neighborhood of x^0 where the Jacobian matrix $f'(x^0)$ is non-singular.

As an example, Figure 2.6 illustrates a local inverse function for the equation $f(x) = x^2$ in a neighborhood of (x_0, y_0).

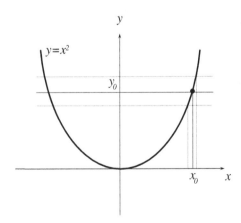

Figure 2.6. A Local Inverse Function

Notice that, when $x_0 = 0$, we have $f'(x_0) = 0$. From the diagram, we can see that it is impossible to find a local inverse function for f in this case. This shows the necessity of imposing the non-singularity condition on $f'(x^0)$ in Theorem 2.6.

Theorem 2.7 (Implicit Function Theorem). *For open sets $X \subset \mathbb{R}^n$ and $Y \subset \mathbb{R}^m$, a continuously differentiable function $f: X \times Y \to \mathbb{R}^m$, and $f(x^0, y^0) = 0$ at a point (x^0, y^0), if $f'_y(x^0, y^0)$ is non-singular, there exist neighborhoods $N_a(x^0)$ and $N_b(y^0)$ and a unique continuously differentiable mapping $h: N_a(x^0) \to N_b(y^0)$ such that*

$$f(x, y) = 0, \quad \text{for } x \in N_a(x^0),$$
$$y \in N_b(y^0) \Leftrightarrow y = h(x), \quad \text{for } x \in N_a(x^0). \quad \blacksquare$$

The function $h(x)$ in the implicit function theorem is the solution to the equation $f(x, y) = 0$ in a neighborhood of x^0. This solution is called an implicit function for $x \in N_a(x^0)$. In other words, an equation defined by a continuously differentiable function defines a solution implicitly in a neighborhood of (x^0, y^0) where the Jacobian matrix $f'_y(x^0, y^0)$ is non-singular.

As an example, Figure 2.7 illustrates a local implicit function for the equation $x^2 + y^2 - 1 = 0$ in a neighborhood of (x_0, y_0).

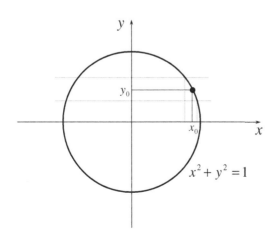

Figure 2.7. Local Implicit Function

Notice that, for $f(x,y) = x^2 + y^2 - 1$, when $y_0 = 0$, we have $f_y'(x_0, y_0) = 0$. From the diagram, we can see that it is impossible to find a local solution function for $f(x,y) = 0$ in this case. This shows the necessity of imposing the non-singularity condition on $f_y'(x^0, y^0)$ in Theorem 2.7.

The inverse function theorem and the implicit function theorem are actually equivalent and imply each other.

Call the set $H \equiv \{x \in \mathbb{R}^n | \alpha \cdot x = b\}$ a hyperplane, where α is an n-vector and b is a constant. It is a straight line in $\mathbb{R}^2$ and a straight plane in $\mathbb{R}^3$. When the dimension is higher than 3, we have a high-dimensional plane or a hyperplane.

Theorem 2.8 (Separation of Convex Sets). *Any two non-empty disjoint convex sets S and T in $\mathbb{R}^n$ can be separated by a hyperplane. That is, $\exists \alpha \in \mathbb{R}^n, \alpha \neq 0$, and $b \in \mathbb{R}$, such that*

$$\alpha \cdot x \geq b, \quad \alpha \cdot y \leq b$$

for all $x \in S$, $y \in T$. ∎

This separation theorem is graphically illustrated in Figure 2.8.

What is the use of this theorem in economics? In Figure 2.9, the production possibility set and the preferred consumption set are two convex sets, tangent at the optimal point x^*. By the separation theorem, we can find a straight line separating them. The straight line

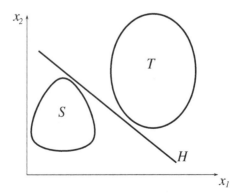

Figure 2.8. Separation of Convex Sets

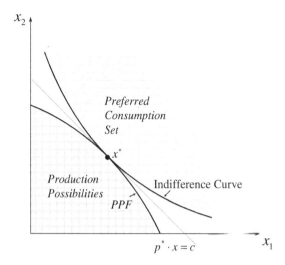

Figure 2.9. Efficiency of the Market

represents the market by which the efficient solution can be implemented. The vector p^* that defines the straight line is the equilibrium price.

Finally, we present two well-known fixed-point theorems. We say that the point x^* is a fixed point of the mapping $f: \mathbb{R}^n \to \mathbb{R}^n$ if $x^* = f(x^*)$. We are interested in a fixed point because quite often we need to prove the existence of a solution in an equation such as $g(x) = 0$. It is easy to see that this problem is equivalent to finding a fixed point for the mapping $f(x) = x + g(x)$. Therefore, the existence of a solution is the same as the existence of a fixed point. The following theorem guarantees the existence of a fixed point.

Theorem 2.9 (Brouwer Fixed-Point Theorem). *Any continuous mapping $f: S \to S$ on a compact convex set $S \subset \mathbb{R}^n$ has a fixed point.* ■

The Brouwer fixed-point theorem is graphically illustrated in Figure 2.10. Consider a compact convex set $S = [0, 1]$ and a continuous function $f: S \to S$. By continuity, as shown in Figure 2.10, the function curve has to cut the 45° line at least once, resulting in a fixed point.

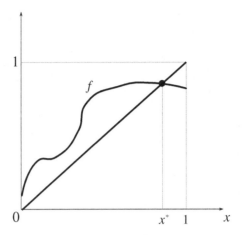

Figure 2.10. Brouwer Fixed-Point Theorem

Given a set $X \subset \mathbb{R}^n$, a function $f\colon X \rightarrow X$ is a contraction mapping if there exists $\lambda \in (0, 1)$ such that

$$\|f(x) - f(y)\| \le \lambda\|x - y\|, \quad \forall x, y \in X.$$

Notice that, if $n = 1$ and f is continuously differentiable, then the above condition is equivalent to $|f'(x)| \le \lambda$, $\forall x$. The Brouwer fixed-point theorem does not guarantee the uniqueness of fixed points. The following theorem imposes a stronger condition to guarantee the uniqueness of a fixed point.

Theorem 2.10 (Contraction Mapping Theorem[3]). *For $X \subset R^n$, any contraction mapping $f\colon X \rightarrow X$ has a unique fixed point.* ∎

The contraction mapping theorem is graphically illustrated in Figure 2.11. Consider a compact convex set $S = [0, 1]$ and a function $f\colon S \rightarrow S$ with $|f'(x)| \le \lambda$ for some $\lambda \in (0, 1)$ and for all $x \in S$. Since the slope of the function curve is bounded by $\pm 45°$, as shown in Figure 2.11, the function curve has to cut the $45°$ line once but at most once, resulting in a unique fixed point.

---

[3]X can be a complete metric space (X, d). The Euclidean space $\mathbb{R}^n$ with norm $\|\cdot\|$ is a complete metric space.

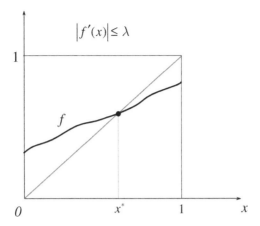

Figure 2.11. Contracting Mapping Theorem

Notes

Good references include Chiang (1984, Chapters 2, 6–8) and Sydsæter *et al.* (2005, Chapters 2, 13, 14).

Appendix

A.1. *Proof of Theorem 2.1*

We prove Property (a) only; the rest are similar. We have

$$x \in (A \cup B) \cap C \Leftrightarrow x \in A \cup B, x \in C \Leftrightarrow x \in A \quad \text{or} \quad x \in B, \ x \in C$$
$$\Leftrightarrow x \in A \cap C \quad \text{or} \quad x \in B \cap C$$
$$\Leftrightarrow x \in (A \cap C) \cup (B \cap C).$$

Hence, Property (a) holds.

A.2. *Proof of Proposition 2.3*

(1) For $\varepsilon = 1$, there exists N such that when $k > N$ we have $\|x^k - x^0\| < 1$. Then, for $k > N$, we have

$$\|x^k\| = \|x^k - x^0 + x^0\| \le \|x^k - x^0\| + \|x^0\| < 1 + \|x^0\|.$$

Hence,

$$\|x^k\| \leq \max\left\{\|x^1\|, \ldots, \|x^N\|, \ 1 + \|x^0\|\right\}.$$

(2) This is actually an axiom in real analysis, not a conclusion. It is the so-called fundamental axiom of analysis, which states that a monotonic sequence in $\mathbb{R}$ converges either to infinity or $\sup\{x^k\}$.

A.3. *Proof of Proposition 2.6*

We prove (c) only. Define $\phi(x, y) = x'Ay$. Then, $\phi(x, x) = x'Ax$ and

$$\frac{\partial(x'Ax)}{\partial x} = \phi'_x(x, x) + \phi'_y(x, x).$$

By (a), we have $\phi'_y(x, x) = x'A$. Since $\phi(x, y) = y'A'x$, again by (a), we have $\phi'_x(x, x) = x'A'$. Hence, we have (c).

A.4. *Proof of Proposition 2.7*

Taking the derivative of the equation $f(\lambda x) = \lambda f(x)$ w.r.t. λ yields

$$\sum_{i=1}^{n} f_{x_i}(\lambda x)x_i = f(x).$$

Letting $\lambda = 1$, the above implies Euler's law.

A.5. *Proof of Proposition 2.8*

Taking the derivative of the equation $f(\lambda x) = \lambda^\alpha f(x)$ w.r.t. x_i gives $\lambda f_{x_i}(\lambda x) = \lambda^\alpha f_{x_i}(x)$, which implies

$$f_{x_i}(\lambda x) = \lambda^{\alpha-1} f_{x_i}(x), \quad \forall x \in \mathbb{R}^n_+, \ \lambda > 0.$$

Hence, f_{x_i} is homogeneous of degree $\alpha - 1$.

Chapter 3

General Optimization

1. Positive Definite Matrix

Convexity is related to minimization, whereas concavity is related to maximization. Further, the concavity and convexity of functions are related to negative and positive definiteness, respectively. To see this, for a function $f \colon \mathbb{R}^n \to \mathbb{R}$ and a point x_0, consider a Taylor expansion:

$$f(x) = f(x_0) + f'(x_0) \cdot (x - x_0) + \frac{1}{2}(x - x_0)^T f''(\xi)(x - x_0),$$

where $\xi = \theta x_0 + (1 - \theta)x$ for some $\theta \in (0, 1)$. At optimum, $f'(x_0) = 0$. Hence, the term $(x - x_0)^T f''(\xi)(x - x_0)$ determines whether or not x_0 is a minimum or maximum point. In particular, x_0 is a maximum point if $y^T f''(\xi)y \leq 0$ for all $y \in \mathbb{R}^n$. The latter condition is the so-called negative definiteness.

An $n \times n$ square symmetric matrix A is said to be

Positive semi-definite $(A \geq 0)$	if $x'Ax \geq 0, \quad \forall\, x$;
Positive definite $(A > 0)$	if $x'Ax > 0, \quad \forall\, x \neq 0$;
Negative semi-definite $(A \leq 0)$	if $x'Ax \leq 0, \quad \forall\, x$;
Negative definite $(A < 0)$	if $x'Ax < 0, \quad \forall\, x \neq 0$.

We deal with symmetric matrices only when we talk about definiteness. From the definition, we obviously have

$$A \geq 0 \Leftrightarrow -A \leq 0; \quad A > 0 \Leftrightarrow -A < 0.$$

Example 3.1. For example, for $A = \begin{pmatrix} 1 & -1 \\ -1 & 1 \end{pmatrix}$, we have

$$(x, y) \begin{pmatrix} 1 & -1 \\ -1 & 1 \end{pmatrix} \begin{pmatrix} x \\ y \end{pmatrix} = x^2 - 2xy + y^2 = (x - y)^2 \geq 0.$$

Thus, by definition, $A \geq 0$. ∎

Example 3.2. Consider $A = \begin{pmatrix} a & b \\ b & c \end{pmatrix}$. We have

$$(x, y)A \begin{pmatrix} x \\ y \end{pmatrix} = ax^2 + 2bxy + cy^2.$$

First, to have $A \geq 0$, if $a = 0$, we need $c \geq 0$ and $b = 0$, otherwise we can easily find a contradiction. Second, if $a \neq 0$, we have

$$(x, y)A \begin{pmatrix} x \\ y \end{pmatrix} = a\left[\left(x + \frac{b}{a}y\right)^2 - \left(\frac{b}{a}y\right)^2\right] + cy^2$$

$$= a\left(x + \frac{b}{a}y\right)^2 + \left(c - \frac{b^2}{a}\right)y^2.$$

Hence, to have $A \geq 0$, we obviously need $a \geq 0$, otherwise $y = 0$ would imply a contradiction. We also obviously need $ac \geq b^2$, otherwise $x = -\frac{b}{a}y$ would imply a contradiction. Therefore, we must have $a \geq 0$ and $ac \geq b^2$ In this case, since $a > 0$, $ac \geq b^2$ implies $c \geq 0$. In summary, by combining the two cases, we find that $A \geq 0$ iff $a \geq 0$, $c \geq 0$ and $ac \geq b^2$. ∎

Given a matrix $A = (a_{ij})_{n \times n}$, for $i_1, \ldots, i_k \in \{1, 2, \ldots, n\}$ with $i_1 < i_2 < \cdots < i_k$ define a k-dimensional minor as

$$d_{(i_1, \ldots, i_k)} \equiv \begin{vmatrix} a_{i_1 i_1} & a_{i_1 i_2} & \cdots & a_{i_1 i_k} \\ a_{i_2 i_1} & a_{i_2 i_2} & & a_{i_2 i_k} \\ \vdots & \vdots & & \vdots \\ a_{i_k i_1} & a_{i_k i_2} & \cdots & a_{i_k i_k} \end{vmatrix}.$$

The k-dimensional minor is the determinant of a $k \times k$ submatrix. In particular, define the principal minors as $d_1 \equiv d_{(1)}, d_2 \equiv d_{(1,2)}, \ldots, d_n \equiv d_{(1,2,\ldots,n)}$. That is,

$$d_1 \equiv a_{11}, d_2 \equiv \begin{vmatrix} a_{11} & a_{12} \\ a_{21} & a_{22} \end{vmatrix}, \quad d_3 \equiv \begin{vmatrix} a_{11} & a_{12} & a_{13} \\ a_{21} & a_{22} & a_{23} \\ a_{31} & a_{32} & a_{33} \end{vmatrix}, \ldots, \quad d_n \equiv |A|.$$

We can use these minors to verify definiteness, as stated in the following theorem.

Theorem 3.1. *For a symmetric matrix A,*

(a) $A > 0 \Leftrightarrow d_k > 0$, *for all k.*
(b) $A < 0 \Leftrightarrow (-1)^k d_k > 0$, *for all k.*
(c) $A \geq 0 \Leftrightarrow d_{(i_1,\ldots,i_k)} \geq 0$, *for all permutations $\{i_1, \ldots, i_k\}$ and all $k = 1, \ldots, n$.*
(d) $A \leq 0 \Leftrightarrow (-1)^k d_{(i_1,\ldots,i_k)} \geq 0$, *for all permutations $\{i_1, \ldots, i_k\}$ and all $k = 1, \ldots, n$.*

Example 3.3. For a symmetric matrix $A \in \mathbb{R}^{n \times n}$, if $A \geq 0$, since $d_{(i)} \geq 0$ for any i, all the diagonal entries of A are non-negative. Let us illustrate this for the case of $n = 2$. By $A \geq 0$, for any $x_1, x_2 \in \mathbb{R}$, we have

$$a_{11} x_1^2 = (x_1, 0) A \begin{pmatrix} x_1 \\ 0 \end{pmatrix} \geq 0, \quad a_{22} x_2^2 = (0, x_2) A \begin{pmatrix} 0 \\ x_2 \end{pmatrix} \geq 0,$$

implying $a_{11} \geq 0$ and $a_{22} \geq 0$. ∎

Note that conditions in Theorem 3.1(c) cannot be reduced to "$d_k \geq 0$ for all k". For example, the following matrix satisfies the conditions $d_1 \geq 0$ and $d_2 \geq 0$, but it is not positive semi-definite.

$$A = \begin{pmatrix} 0 & 0 \\ 0 & -1 \end{pmatrix}.$$

Note also that, for a matrix such as

$$A = \begin{pmatrix} a_{11} & a_{12} \\ a_{21} & a_{22} \end{pmatrix},$$

$A < 0$ is equivalent to

$$B \equiv \begin{pmatrix} -a_{11} & -a_{12} \\ -a_{21} & -a_{22} \end{pmatrix} > 0.$$

By Theorem 3.1(a), this requires the principal minors b_1 and b_2 of B to satisfy

$$b_1 \equiv -a_{11} > 0, \quad b_2 \equiv \begin{vmatrix} -a_{11} & -a_{12} \\ -a_{21} & -a_{22} \end{vmatrix} > 0,$$

which are equivalent to $(-1)^1 d_1 > 0$ and $(-1)^2 d_2 > 0$, where d_1 and d_2 are the principal minors of A. This example shows that Theorems 3.1(b) and 3.1(d) are directly implied by Theorems 3.1(a) and 3.1(c), respectively.

Example 3.4. By Theorem 3.1, we can easily verify $\begin{pmatrix} 1 & -1 \\ -1 & 1 \end{pmatrix} \geq 0$, and we can also easily find conditions for $\begin{pmatrix} a & b \\ b & c \end{pmatrix}$ to be positive semi-definite. These conditions are $a \geq 0, c \geq 0$ and $ac \geq b^2$. ∎

Example 3.5. Verify the following symmetric matrix is negative semi-definite and also negative definite:

$$\begin{pmatrix} -1 & 1 & 0 \\ 1 & -2 & 1 \\ 0 & 1 & -3 \end{pmatrix}. \quad ∎$$

The following proposition lists a few useful properties of a definite matrix.

Proposition 3.1. *For a symmetric matrix $A \in \mathbb{R}^{m \times n}$,*

(a) *$A \geq 0$ iff all its eigenvalues are positive.*
(b) *$A > 0$ iff all its eigenvalues are strictly positive.*
(c) *If $A > 0$, then $A^{-1} > 0$.*
(d) *If A is a tall full-rank matrix, then $A'A > 0$ and $AA' \geq 0$.*
(e) *If $A > 0$ and $|B| \neq 0$, then $B'AB > 0$.* ∎

2. Concavity

Given points $x^1, \ldots, x^k \in \mathbb{R}^n$, a convex combination of the points is

$$y \equiv \lambda_1 x^1 + \cdots + \lambda_m x^m, \quad \lambda_k \geq 0, \quad \sum_{k=1}^{m} \lambda_k = 1.$$

Given any two points $x, y \in \mathbb{R}^n$, consider their convex combination:

$$\lambda x + (1 - \lambda)y = y + \lambda(x - y), \quad \text{for } \lambda \in [0, 1].$$

In a figure, we can see that, for $\lambda \in [0, 1]$, this expression represents the points on the line connecting x and y. Hence, the set of all convex combinations of x and y is the interval $[x, y] \subset \mathbb{R}^n$ connecting the two points, defined by

$$[x, y] \equiv \{z | z = \lambda x + (1 - \lambda)y, \ \lambda \in [0, 1]\}.$$

Similarly, we can define $(x, y]$, $[x, y)$ and (x, y). A set $S \subset \mathbb{R}^n$ is called a convex set if the interval of any two points in S is contained in S:

$$\forall x, y \in S, \quad [x, y] \subset S.$$

The following proposition can be easily proven.

Proposition 3.2 (Properties of Convex Sets).

1. *An intersection of convex sets is also convex.*
2. *A Cartesian product of convex sets is also convex.* ∎

Given a convex set $X \subset \mathbb{R}^n$, a function $f \colon X \to \mathbb{R}$ is concave if

$$f[\lambda x + (1 - \lambda)y] \geq \lambda f(x) + (1 - \lambda)f(y), \quad \forall \lambda \in (0, 1), \quad x, y \in X.$$

If the inequality holds strictly, we say that f is strictly concave. Symmetrically, f is convex if

$$f[\lambda x + (1 - \lambda)y] \leq \lambda f(x) + (1 - \lambda)f(y), \quad \forall \lambda \in (0, 1), \quad x, y \in X.$$

If the inequality holds strictly, we say that f is strictly convex. Figure 3.1 graphically shows a typical concave function. The straight

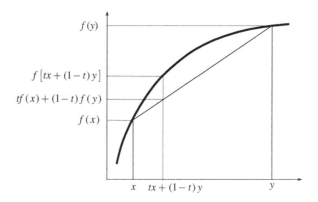

Figure 3.1. A Concave Function

line connecting $(x, f(x))$ and $(y, f(y))$ is described by

$$t(x, f(x)) + (1 - t)(y, f(y)) = (tx + (1 - t)y, \ tf(x) + (1 - t)f(y)),$$
$$t \in [0, 1].$$

Hence, as shown in Figure 3.1, the corresponding value of $tx + (1-t)y$ on the connecting line is $tf(x) + (1 - t)f(y)$.

Proposition 3.3 (Properties of Concave Functions). *Given a convex domain $X \subset \mathbb{R}^n$,*

1. *A function $f\colon X \to \mathbb{R}$ is concave iff $I_l(f) \equiv \{(x, t) \in (X, \mathbb{R}) \mid f(x) \geq t\}$ is convex.*
2. *A function $f\colon X \to \mathbb{R}$ is convex iff $I_u(f) \equiv \{(x, t) \in (X, \mathbb{R}) \mid f(x) \leq t\}$ is convex.*
3. *Concave functions are continuous in the interior of their domains.*
4. *A function $f\colon X \to \mathbb{R}$ is concave iff*

$$f(\lambda_1 x^1 + \cdots + \lambda_k x^k) \geq \lambda_1 f(x^1) + \cdots + \lambda_k f(x^k),$$

for all $k \geq 1$ and all convex combinations $\lambda_1 x^1 + \cdots + \lambda_k x^k$. ∎

The fourth property immediately implies Jensen's inequality:

$$\int_{-\infty}^{\infty} u(x)dF(x) \leq u\left[\int_{-\infty}^{\infty} xdF(x)\right], \quad \text{if } u(x) \text{ is concave,}$$

where $F(x)$ is a distribution function.

The following result is from Varian (1992, p. 313), Chiang (1984, p. 394) and Takayama (1993, p. 58). It is used to verify the concavity or convexity of a function.

Theorem 3.2. *Given a convex set $X \subset \mathbb{R}^n$, and a twice differentiable function $f: X \to \mathbb{R}$,*

1. f *is convex* $\Leftrightarrow f''(x) \geq 0, \forall\, x \in X$.
2. $f''(x) > 0, \forall\, x \in X \Rightarrow f$ *is strictly convex*.
3. f *is concave* $\Leftrightarrow f''(x) \leq 0, \forall\, x \in X$.
4. $f''(x) < 0, \forall\, x \in X \Rightarrow f$ *is strictly concave*. ■

The condition $f''(x) \leq 0$ can be shown using a Taylor expansion and by the fact that when f is convex it achieves the global maximum at any point after a proper transformation of the axes, as shown in Figure 3.2.

The following proposition is a corollary of Theorems 3.1 and 3.2. It appears in Takayama (1993, p. 59). Note that the converses of Statements 3 and 4 in the following proposition are not true.

Proposition 3.4. *Given a convex set $X \subset \mathbb{R}^n$ and a twice differentiable function $f: X \to \mathbb{R}$, let $d_{(i_1,\ldots,i_k)}(x)$ be a k dimensional minor of $f''(x)$. Then,*

1. f *is convex* $\Leftrightarrow d_{(i_1,\ldots,i_k)}(x) \geq 0, \forall\, x \in X, \forall\, k, \forall\, \{i_1,\ldots,i_k\}$.
2. f *is concave* $\Leftrightarrow (-1)^k d_{(i_1,\ldots,i_k)}(x) \geq 0, \forall\, x \in X, \forall\, k, \forall\, \{i_1,\ldots,i_k\}$.

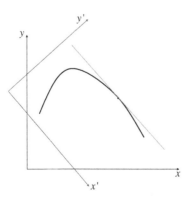

Figure 3.2. Condition $f''(x) \leq 0$ for Concavity

3. $d_k(x) > 0, \forall\, x \in X, \forall\, k \Rightarrow f$ *is strictly convex.*

4. $(-1)^k d_k(x) > 0, \forall\, x \in X, \forall\, k \Rightarrow f$ *is strictly concave.* ∎

Example 3.6. "f is strictly convex" does not imply "$f''(x) > 0$, $\forall\, x \in \mathbb{R}^n$". Consider $f(x) = x^4$ with domain $\mathbb{R}$. Since $h(x) = x^2$ is strictly convex, $f = h \circ h$ is also strictly convex. But, $f''(0) = 0$. ∎

Example 3.7. Consider function $f: \mathbb{R}^2_{++} \to \mathbb{R}$, defined by

$$f(x, y) = x^\alpha + y^\beta, \quad \alpha, \beta \in \mathbb{R}.$$

We have

$$f_x = \alpha x^{\alpha-1}, \quad f_y = \beta y^{\beta-1},$$
$$f_{xx} = \alpha(\alpha - 1)x^{\alpha-2}, \quad f_{yy} = \beta(\beta - 1)y^{\beta-2}, \quad f_{xy} = 0.$$

Then,

$$(-1)^1 d_1 = \alpha(1 - \alpha)x^{\alpha-2},$$
$$(-1)^2 d_2 = \begin{vmatrix} \alpha(\alpha - 1)x^{\alpha-2} & 0 \\ 0 & \beta(\beta - 1)y^{\beta-2} \end{vmatrix}$$
$$= \alpha\beta(1 - \alpha)(1 - \beta)x^{\alpha-2}y^{\beta-2}.$$

Therefore, by Theorem 3.2 and Proposition 3.4, we conclude that

$$f \text{ is } \begin{cases} \text{concave,} & \text{if } 0 \le \alpha, \ \beta \le 1; \\ \text{strictly concave,} & \text{if } 0 < \alpha, \ \beta < 1. \end{cases} \quad ∎$$

Example 3.8. Consider the Cobb–Douglas function $f: \mathbb{R}^2_{++} \to \mathbb{R}$, defined by

$$f(x, y) = x^\alpha y^\beta, \quad \alpha, \beta \ge 0.$$

We have

$$f_x = \alpha x^{\alpha-1}y^\beta, \quad f_y = \beta x^\alpha y^{\beta-1},$$
$$f_{xx} = \alpha(\alpha - 1)x^{\alpha-2}y^\beta, \quad f_{yy} = \beta(\beta - 1)x^\alpha y^{\beta-2},$$
$$f_{xy} = \alpha\beta x^{\alpha-1}y^{\beta-1}.$$

Then,

$$(-1)^1 d_1 = \alpha(1 - \alpha)x^{\alpha-2}y^\beta,$$

$$(-1)^2 d_2 = \begin{vmatrix} \alpha(\alpha - 1)x^{\alpha-2}y^\beta & \alpha\beta x^{\alpha-1}y^{\beta-1} \\ \alpha\beta x^{\alpha-1}y^{\beta-1} & \beta(\beta - 1)x^\alpha y^{\beta-2} \end{vmatrix}$$

$$= \alpha\beta(1 - \alpha - \beta)x^{2(\alpha-1)}y^{2(\beta-1)}.$$

Therefore, by Theorem 3.2 and Proposition 3.4, we conclude that

$$f \text{ is } \begin{cases} \text{concave,} & \text{if } \alpha, \beta \geq 0, \ \alpha + \beta \leq 1; \\ \text{strictly concave,} & \text{if } \alpha, \beta > 0, \ \alpha + \beta < 1. \end{cases} \quad \blacksquare$$

Proposition 3.5. *Let* $f: X \to \mathbb{R}$ *be differentiable. Then,*

- f *is concave* $\Leftrightarrow f'(x) \cdot (y - x) \geq f(y) - f(x)$, *for all* $x, y \in X$.
- f *is strictly concave* $\Leftrightarrow f'(x) \cdot (y-x) > f(y) - f(x)$, *for all* $x, y \in X$, $x \neq y$. $\blacksquare$

Proposition 3.5 is graphically illustrated in Figure 3.3. The tangent line at point x is described by $f(x) + f'(x)(y - x)$. We can see that, if the tangent line is always above the function curve at any point, then the function curve must be concave, and vice versa. This is what Proposition 3.5 states.

Proposition 3.5 can be easily proven using Theorem 3.2. Alternatively, we can use Proposition 3.5 and a Taylor expansion to prove Theorem 3.2, and then prove Proposition 3.5 directly.

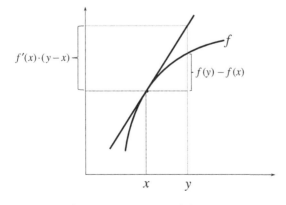

Figure 3.3. A Characterization of Concave Functions

3. Quasi-Concavity

There are three reasons to discuss quasi-concavity and quasi-convexity instead of concavity and convexity.

(a) Some popular functions, such as the Cobb–Douglas function $f(x,y) = Ax^\alpha y^\beta$ with $\alpha + \beta > 1$, are quasi-concave or quasi-convex, but not concave or convex.

(b) Many maximum or minimum value functions, such as the indirect utility function $v(p, I)$, are quasi-concave or quasi-convex.

(c) We generally deal with constrained optimization problems in business. Quasi-concavity is sufficient to ensure maximization from FOCs; and quasi-convexity is adequate to ensure minimization from FOCs. Concavity and convexity are too strong requirements for the purpose.

Given a convex set $X \subset \mathbb{R}^n$, we say that $f: X \to \mathbb{R}$ is quasi-concave if, for any $x, y \in X$,

$$f(y) \geq f(x) \Rightarrow f(z) \geq f(x), \quad \forall z \in (x, y).$$

f is strictly quasi-concave if, for any $x, y \in X$,

$$f(y) \geq f(x) \Rightarrow f(z) > f(x), \quad \forall z \in (x, y).$$

Symmetrically, f is quasi-convex if, for any $x, y \in X$,

$$f(y) \leq f(x) \Rightarrow f(z) \leq f(x), \quad \forall z \in (x, y).$$

f is strictly quasi-convex if, for any $x, y \in X$,

$$f(y) \leq f(x) \Rightarrow f(z) < f(x), \quad \forall z \in (x, y).$$

Hence, f is (strictly) quasi-convex if $-f$ is (strictly) quasi-concave. Figure 3.4 shows two quasi-concave functions when they are monotonic. Figure 3.5 shows that, if an iso-value curve defined by $f(x) = \lambda$ has a straight segment, the function is not strictly quasi-concave.

Note that quasi-concavity may be dependent on the domain of the function. For example, $f(x,y) = xy$ is quasi-concave on $\mathbb{R}^2_+$ but not on $\mathbb{R}^2$.

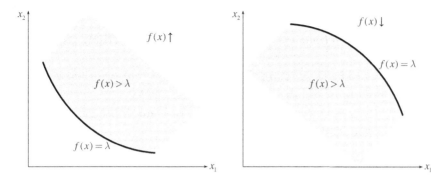

Figure 3.4. Quasi-Concavity

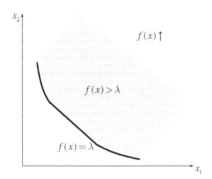

Figure 3.5. Non-Strict Quasi-Concavity

Proposition 3.6. *Given a convex set $X \subset \mathbb{R}^n$,*

- $f: X \to \mathbb{R}$ *is quasi-concave iff the upper level set of the higher-value set $\{x \in X | f(x) \geq t\}$ is convex for all $t \in \mathbb{R}$.*
- $f: X \to \mathbb{R}$ *is quasi-convex iff the lower level set of the lower-value set $\{x \in X | f(x) \leq t\}$ is convex for all $t \in \mathbb{R}$.* ∎

Set $f^{-1}(t) = \{x \in X | f(x) = t\}$ is called a level set or an iso-value set or iso-value curve. In economics, when f is a utility function, an iso-value curve is called an indifference curve; when f is a production function, it is called an isoquant; and when f is a cost function, it is called an isocost curve.

The following proposition states some properties of a quasi-concave function.

Proposition 3.7.

(a) *Concave functions are quasi-concave; convex functions are quasi-convex.*

(b) *Strictly concave functions are strictly quasi-concave. Strictly convex functions are strictly quasi-convex.*

(c) *If $X \subset \mathbb{R}$, monotonic functions $f\colon X \to \mathbb{R}$ are both quasi-concave and quasi-convex.* ■

Quasi-concavity, however, does not necessarily imply concavity. For example, in Figure 3.6, the curve is quasi-concave, but it is not concave.

Note that Proposition 3.7(c) fails when X is multi-dimensional. Consider an increasing function $f\colon \mathbb{R}^2 \to \mathbb{R}$ with iso-value curves shown in Figure 3.7. Monotonicity means that, for any $t \in \mathbb{R}$ and any $x_0 \in \{x | f(x) \geq t\}$, we have $x_0 + \mathbb{R}_+^2 \subset \{x | f(x) \geq t\}$. Figure 3.7 shows that the higher-value sets satisfy this condition. Hence, the implicitly defined function f must be increasing. However, the higher-value set $\{x | f(x) \geq t\}$ is not convex and hence the function is not quasi-concave.

In summary,

$$\text{strict concavity} \quad \Rightarrow \quad \text{concavity}$$
$$\Downarrow \qquad\qquad\qquad \Downarrow$$
$$\text{strict quasi-concavity} \Rightarrow \text{quasi-concavity}$$

The following proposition states that quasi-concavity and quasi-convexity remain under a monotonic transformation.

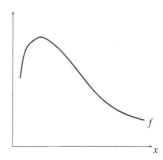

Figure 3.6. A Quasi-Concave Curve

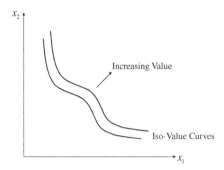

Figure 3.7. An Increasing but Non-Quasi-Concave Function

Proposition 3.8.[1] *Given convex set $X \subset \mathbb{R}^n$ and functions $f: X \rightarrow \mathbb{R}$ and $\phi: \mathbb{R} \rightarrow \mathbb{R}$,*

(a) *If f is quasi-concave (quasi-convex) and ϕ is increasing, then $\phi \circ f$ is quasi-concave (quasi-convex).*

(b) *If f is quasi-concave (quasi-convex) and ϕ is decreasing, then $\phi \circ f$ is quasi-convex (quasi-concave).* ■

The following proposition states that a homogeneous quasi-concave function is often a concave function.

Proposition 3.9.[2] *Given convex cone $X \subset \mathbb{R}^n$ and functions $f: X \rightarrow \mathbb{R}$, suppose that f is quasi-concave and homogeneous of degree α, with $\alpha \in (0, 1]$ and $f(x) > 0$ for all $x \in X, \{0\}$. Then, f is concave.* ■

Given a function $f: X \rightarrow \mathbb{R}$, $X \subset \mathbb{R}^n$, how do we determine whether or not it is quasi-concave? For this purpose, we define the so-called bordered Hessian matrix of f at point x as

$$B_f(x) \equiv \begin{pmatrix} 0 & f_{x_1}(x) & \cdots & f_{x_n}(x) \\ f_{x_1}(x) & f_{x_1 x_1}(x) & \cdots & f_{x_1 x_n}(x) \\ \vdots & \vdots & & \vdots \\ f_{x_n}(x) & f_{x_n x_1}(x) & \cdots & f_{x_n x_n}(x) \end{pmatrix}.$$

---

[1]See Sydsæter *et al.* (2005, p. 70).
[2]See Sydsæter *et al.* (2005, p. 71).

The bordered Hessian matrix is actually the Hessian matrix of the relevant Lagrange function. We will see this later in Section 5. The following theorem provides us a tool to verify quasi-concavity or quasi-convexity.

Theorem 3.3.[3] *Given an open convex set $X \subset \mathbb{R}^n$, a C^2 functions $f: X \to \mathbb{R}$, and principal minors $b_1(x), \ldots, b_{n+1}(x)$ of $B_f(x)$,*

(a) *f is quasi-concave $\Rightarrow (-1)^k b_k(x) \leq 0$, $\forall\, x \in X$, $\forall\, k$.*
(b) *$(-1)^k b_k(x) < 0$, $\forall\, x \in X$, $\forall\, k \geq 2 \Rightarrow f$ is strictly quasi-concave.*
(c) *f is quasi-convex $\Rightarrow b_k(x) \leq 0$, $\forall\, x \in X$, $\forall\, k$.*
(d) *$b_k(x) < 0$, $\forall\, x \in X$, $\forall\, k \geq 2 \Rightarrow f$ is strictly quasi-convex.* ∎

Statements (b) and (d) in Theorem 3.3 immediately imply that any function $f: \mathbb{R} \to \mathbb{R}$ with $f'(x) \neq 0$ for all x must be strictly quasi-concave and quasi-convex.

Chiang (1984, p. 393) and Takayama (1993, p. 65) have the same result as Theorem 3.3 but they require X to be $\mathbb{R}^n_+$. This requirement is unnecessary. Chiang (1984, p. 393) cites $f(x) = x^2$ and $f(x, y) = x, y$ on $\mathbb{R}^2$ as the reason for requiring $\mathbb{R}^n_+$, since they are quasi-concave on $\mathbb{R}^n_+$ but not on $\mathbb{R}^n$. However, our Theorem 3.3 shows that they are not quasi-concave on $\mathbb{R}^2$ since they do not satisfy condition (b) in Theorem 3.3 when $x = 0$.

Example 3.9. Consider function $f: \mathbb{R}^2_{++} \to \mathbb{R}$, defined by

$$f(x, y) = x^\alpha + y^\beta, \quad \alpha, \beta \geq 0.$$

We have

$$f_x = ax^{\alpha-1}, \quad f_y = \beta y^{\beta-1},$$
$$f_{xx} = \alpha(\alpha - 1)x^{\alpha-2}, \quad f_{yy} = \beta(\beta - 1)y^{\beta-2}, \quad f_{xy} = 0.$$

---

[3]See Sydsæter *et al.* (2005, p. 75).

Then, if $\alpha > 0$, we have

$$(-1)^2 b_2 = \begin{vmatrix} 0 & \alpha x^{\alpha-1} \\ \alpha x^{\alpha-1} & \alpha(\alpha-1)x^{\alpha-2} \end{vmatrix}$$

$$= -\alpha^2 x^{2\alpha-2} < 0,$$

and, if $0 < \alpha, \beta \leq 1$ and $\alpha \neq 1$ or $\beta \neq 1$, we have

$$(-1)^3 b_3 = -\begin{vmatrix} 0 & \alpha x^{\alpha-1} & \beta y^{\beta-1} \\ \alpha x^{\alpha-1} & \alpha(\alpha-1)x^{\alpha-2} & 0 \\ \beta y^{\beta-1} & 0 & \beta(\beta-1)y^{\beta-2} \end{vmatrix}$$

$$= \alpha x^{\alpha-1}\begin{vmatrix} \alpha x^{\alpha-1} & \beta y^{\beta-1} \\ 0 & \beta(\beta-1)y^{\beta-2} \end{vmatrix}$$

$$- \beta y^{\beta-1}\begin{vmatrix} \alpha x^{\alpha-1} & \beta y^{\beta-1} \\ \alpha(\alpha-1)x^{\alpha-2} & 0 \end{vmatrix}$$

$$= \alpha^2 x^{2\alpha-2}\beta(\beta-1)y^{\beta-2} + \beta^2 y^{2\beta-2}\alpha(\alpha-1)x^{\alpha-2} < 0.$$

Strict quasi-concavity can then be ensured. Further, for $\alpha = 0$ or $\beta = 0$, quasi-concavity can be verified by looking at the diagram or using monotonicity. Actually, since the function is concave when $\alpha = 0$ or $\beta = 0$ (and $\alpha, \beta \leq 1$), it must be quasi-concave. Therefore, by Theorem 3.3, we conclude that

$$f \text{ is } \begin{cases} \text{quasi-concave,} & \text{if } 0 \leq \alpha, \ \beta \leq 1; \\ \text{strictly quasi-concave,} & \text{if } 0 < \alpha, \ \beta \leq 1 \\ & \text{and } \alpha \neq 1 \text{ or } \beta \neq 1. \end{cases} \blacksquare$$

Example 3.10. Consider the Cobb–Douglas function $f: \mathbb{R}^2_{++} \to \mathbb{R}$, defined by

$$f(x,y) = x^\alpha y^\beta, \quad \alpha, \beta \geq 0.$$

We have

$$f_x = \alpha x^{\alpha-1}y^\beta, \quad f_y = \beta x^\alpha y^{\beta-1},$$

$$f_{xx} = \alpha(\alpha-1)x^{\alpha-2}y^\beta, \quad f_{yy} = \beta(\beta-1)x^\alpha y^{\beta-2},$$

$$f_{xy} = \alpha\beta x^{\alpha-1}y^{\beta-1}.$$

Then, if $\alpha > 0$, we have

$$(-1)^2 b_2 = \begin{vmatrix} 0 & \alpha x^{\alpha-1} y^\beta \\ \alpha x^{\alpha-1} y^\beta & \alpha(\alpha-1) x^{\alpha-2} y^\beta \end{vmatrix}$$

$$= -\alpha^2 x^{2\alpha-2} y^{2\beta} < 0,$$

and, if $\alpha, \beta > 0$, we have

$$(-1)^3 b_3 = - \begin{vmatrix} 0 & \alpha x^{\alpha-1} y^{\beta-1} & \beta x^\alpha y^\beta \\ \alpha x^{\alpha-1} y^{\beta-1} & \alpha(\alpha-1) x^{\alpha-2} y^\beta & \alpha\beta x^{\alpha-1} y^{\beta-1} \\ \beta x^\alpha y^{\beta-1} & \alpha\beta x^{\alpha-1} y^{\beta-1} & \beta(\beta-1) x^\alpha y^{\beta-2} \end{vmatrix}$$

$$= \alpha x^{\alpha-1} y^\beta \begin{vmatrix} \alpha x^{\alpha-1} y^\beta & \beta x^\alpha y^{\beta-1} \\ \alpha\beta x^{\alpha-1} y^{\beta-1} & \beta(\beta-1) x^\alpha y^{\beta-2} \end{vmatrix} - \beta x^\alpha y^{\beta-1}$$

$$\times \begin{vmatrix} \alpha x^{\alpha-1} y^\beta & \beta x^\alpha y^{\beta-1} \\ \alpha(\alpha-1) x^{\alpha-2} y^\beta & \alpha\beta x^{\alpha-1} y^{\beta-1} \end{vmatrix}$$

$$= \alpha x^{\alpha-1} y^\beta [\alpha\beta(\beta-1) - \alpha\beta^2] x^{2\alpha-1} y^{2\beta-2}$$

$$- \beta x^\alpha y^{\beta-1} [\alpha^2\beta - \alpha\beta(\alpha-1)] x^{2\alpha-2} y^{2\beta-1}$$

$$= -\alpha\beta(\alpha+\beta) x^{3\alpha-2} y^{3\beta-2} < 0.$$

Strict quasi-concavity can then be ensured. Further, for $\alpha = 0$ or $\beta = 0$, it can be verified by looking at the diagram or using monotonicity. Therefore, by Theorem 3.3, we conclude that

$$f \text{ is } \begin{cases} \text{quasi-concave,} & \text{if } \alpha, \beta \geq 0, \\ \text{strictly quasi-concave,} & \text{if } \alpha, \beta > 1. \end{cases} \quad \blacksquare$$

Note that a strictly convex function can be strictly quasi-concave. For example, a strictly monotonic function is both strictly quasi-concave and strictly convex.

4. Unconstrained Optimization (Interior Solutions)

Optimization is divided into two categories: unconstrained optimization and constrained optimization. Judging from the names alone, unconstrained optimization is optimization without constraints and constrained optimization is optimization with constraints. However, the real difference between the two is that the former deals with interior solutions whereas the latter deals with boundary solutions. We will explain this in more detail later.

Given a function $f\colon X \to \mathbb{R}$, where $X \subset \mathbb{R}^n$, the maximum value (minimum value) is the largest (smallest) possible value that the function f can obtain on the set X. Here, we say that f can obtain a value y_0 on X if there is $x_0 \in X$ such that $f(x_0) = y_0$. A maximum point (minimum point), or simply a maximum (minimum), is a point in X at which the function f obtains the maximum (minimum) value. An optimal value is either a maximum value or a minimum value, and an optimal point or optimum is either a maximum point or a minimum point. Finally, the global maximum (minimum) gives the maximum (minimum) over the whole set X, while a local maximum (minimum) gives the maximum (minimum) over a neighborhood of a point in X.

We first present the fundamental existence theorem in optimization. This theorem is sometimes called the Weierstrass Theorem.

Theorem 3.4 (Optimal-Value Theorem). *Given function $f\colon X \to \mathbb{R}$, where $X \subset \mathbb{R}^n$, if f is continuous and X is compact, then f has at least one minimum and one maximum.* ∎

For the optimal-value theorem, the continuity and compactness are both necessary conditions. See the following example.

Example 3.11. Consider $f\colon [0, 2] \to \mathbb{R}$,

$$f(x) = \begin{cases} x + 1, & \text{if } x < 1, \\ 1, & \text{if } x = 1, \\ x - 1, & \text{if } x < 1. \end{cases}$$

As shown in Figure 3.8, this function has neither a maximum nor a minimum on $[0, 2]$, simply because it is not continuous at a certain point.

Consider also $g\colon (0, 1) \to \mathbb{R}$, $g(x) = x$. It is continuous, but it has neither a maximum nor a minimum, simply because the domain is not compact. ∎

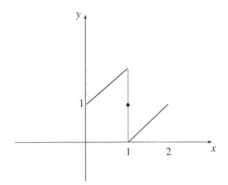

Figure 3.8. A Discontinuous Curve

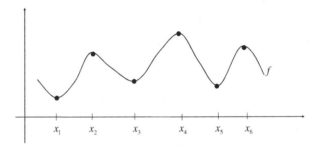

Figure 3.9. Characteristics of the Maximum

Given existence, how do we find an optimal point? Figure 3.9 is suggestive.

We first observe in the figure that the maximum point x_4 implies a zero derivative $f'(x_4) = 0$. However, many other points also satisfy this condition. If we further require $f''(x) < 0$, we can narrow down to three points: x_2, x_4 and x_6. Among these three points, only one is the right solution. However, all three points are maximum points in their neighborhoods; they are the so-called local maxima. We will later show that if a function is strictly quasi-concave, a local maximum is actually a global maximum.

Formally, if there is a neighborhood $N_r(x^*)$ of x^* with radius $r > 0$ such that x^* is the maximum point of f on $N_r(x^*)$, then x^* is a local maximum of f; if $f(x^*) > f(x)$ for any $x \in N_r(x^*)$ and $x \neq x^*$, x^* is a strict local maximum.

We now try to characterize an optimal point. For a function $f: \mathbb{R}^n \to \mathbb{R}$, if $f'(\hat{x}) = 0$, we call $\hat{x}$ or $(\hat{x}, f(\hat{x}))$ a stationary point, and its value $f(\hat{x})$ a stationary value. In a special case when $n = 1$, a stationary point $\hat{x}$ may be a local maximum, a local minimum, or a reflection point:

1. If $f'(x)$ changes sign from positive to negative when x passes $\hat{x}$ from the left, then $\hat{x}$ is a local maximum (or relative maximum).
2. If $f'(x)$ changes sign from negative to positive when x passes $\hat{x}$ from the left, then $\hat{x}$ is a local minimum (or relative minimum).
3. If $f'(x)$ does not change sign when x passes $\hat{x}$ from the left, then $\hat{x}$ or $(\hat{x}, f(\hat{x}))$ is a reflection point.

Example 3.12. Compare $y = x^2$ with $y = x^3$ at $x = 0$. ∎

The Taylor expansion has a more general version. For function $f: \mathbb{R} \to \mathbb{R}$, if $f \in C^m$, for any two points $x_0, x \in X$, there exists $\xi \in (x_0, x)$ such that

$$f(x) = f(x_0) + f'(x_0)(x - x_0) + \frac{1}{2}f''(x_0)(x - x_0)^2 + \cdots$$

$$+ \frac{1}{(m-1)!}f^{(m-1)}(x_0)(x - x_0)^{m-1} + \frac{1}{m!}f^{(m)}(\xi)(x - x_0)^m.$$

Theorem 3.5. *For $m > 1$ and $f: \mathbb{R} \to \mathbb{R}$, suppose*

$$f^{(i)}(x^*) = 0 \quad for \ i = 1, \ldots, m-1, \quad and \quad f^{(m)}(x^*) \neq 0.$$

Then, if m is odd, x^* is a reflection point; if m is even and $f^{(m)}(x^*) > 0$, x^* is a local minimum point; and if m is even and $f^{(m)}(x^*) < 0$, x^* is a local maximum point.

From the above discussion, the first-order condition (FOC): $f'(x^*) = 0$ and the sign of the second-order derivative $f''(x^*)$, called the second-order condition (SOC), seem to be reliable characteristics of an optimal point x^*. When a SOC is necessary for a result, we call it a second-order necessary condition (SONC) for the result; when a SOC is sufficient for a result, we call it a second-order sufficient condition (SOSC) for the result. A prerequisite condition for FOC and SOC to be useful in determining an optimal point is: the optimal point needs to be an interior point of the domain. A point $x_0 \in A$ is an interior point of A if there is a neighborhood $N_r(x_0)$ such that $N_r(x_0) \subset A$. We now present a theorem for an interior optimum.

Theorem 3.6 (Local Maximum).[4] *Given $A \subset \mathbb{R}^n$, consider problem*

$$\max_{x \in A} f(x). \tag{3.1}$$

(a) *If x^* is an interior solution, then*

$$FOC: \quad f'(x^*) = 0,$$
$$SONC: \quad f''(x^*) \leq 0.$$

(b) *For an interior point x^*, if*

$$FOC: \quad f'(x^*) = 0,$$
$$SOSC: \quad f''(x^*) < 0,$$

then x^* is a local maximum point of f. ∎

For $n = 1$, if f is twice differentiable and $f''(\hat{x}) < 0$ at any possible stationary point $\hat{x}$, then the point $\hat{x}$ satisfying $f'(\hat{x}) = 0$ must be the unique global maximum point in the interior A^o of set A. This is intuitive. Consider the function $g(x) = f'(x)$. The graph of function $g(x)$ may cut the horizontal axis a few times. If the graph of $g(x)$ cuts the horizontal axis with negative slopes only, it cannot possibly cut the horizontal axis more than once.

Example 3.13. Let

$$f(x_1, x_2) = x_2 - 4x_1^2 + 3x_1 x_2 - x_2^2.$$

Let us find a maximum of this function on $\mathbb{R}^2$. By the above theorem, we know that a maximum (x_1^*, x_2^*), if it exists, must satisfy the following FOCs:

$$f_{x_1} = -8x_1^* + 3x_2^* = 0, \quad f_{x_2} = 1 + 3x_1^* - 2x_2^* = 0,$$

---

[4]Refer to Chapter 11 of Chiang (1984) for details.

which implies

$$\begin{pmatrix} x_1^* \\ x_2^* \end{pmatrix} = \begin{pmatrix} -8 & 3 \\ 3 & -2 \end{pmatrix}^{-1} \begin{pmatrix} 0 \\ -1 \end{pmatrix} = \frac{1}{7} \begin{pmatrix} -2 & -3 \\ -3 & -8 \end{pmatrix} \begin{pmatrix} 0 \\ -1 \end{pmatrix} = \frac{1}{7} \begin{pmatrix} 3 \\ 8 \end{pmatrix}.$$

This solution is the only stationary point. Let us see if this point satisfies the SOC. We have

$$f''(x) \equiv \begin{pmatrix} f_{x_1 x_1}(x_1, x_2) & f_{x_1 x_2}(x_1, x_2) \\ f_{x_2 x_1}(x_1, x_2) & f_{x_2 x_2}(x_1, x_2) \end{pmatrix} = \begin{pmatrix} -8 & 3 \\ 3 & -2 \end{pmatrix}.$$

We can easily see that the first principal minor of f'' is $(-1)d_1 = 8 > 0$ and the second principal minor of f'' is $(-1)^2 d_2 = |f''| = 7 > 0$. Hence, $f''(x^*) < 0$. Thus, (x_1^*, x_2^*) is a local maximum. ∎

When a maximum x^* is a corner solution, it may not satisfy either the FOC or the SONC. In Figure 3.10, $x^* = b$ is the maximum point, but we do not have either $f(x^*) = 0$ or $f''(x^*) \leq 0$.

The FOC and the SONC are not sufficient for local maximization, even for an interior point. For example, $f(x) = x^3$ satisfies both the FOC and the SONC at $x = 0$, but $x = 0$ is not an optimal point.

Theorem 3.7 (Global Maximum). *For problem* (3.1),

(a) *If f is concave on A, then any point $x^* \in A$ satisfying $f'(x^*) = 0$ is a maximum point.*

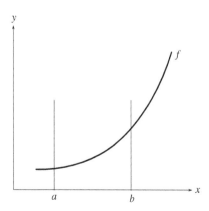

Figure 3.10. Both FOC and SOC Fail

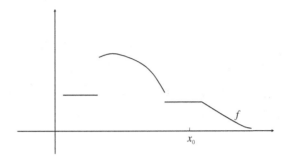

Figure 3.11. A Quasi-Concave Curve

(b) *If f is strictly quasi-concave, a local maximum over a convex set A is the unique global maximum.*[5] ∎

In Theorem 3.7(b), strict quasi-concavity is necessary. Figure 3.11 is illustrative. It indicates that a quasi-concave curve can go up and down, but it can only do so at most once. That is, a quasi-concave function can only have at most one hump. This is the reason why a local maximum of a quasi-concave function is often a global maximum. But, a quasi-concave curve may have a flat area in which $f'(x) = 0$, so that a local maximum may not be a global maximum for a quasi-concave function. In Figure 3.11, x_0 is a local maximum, but not a global maximum. The problem is that the function f is not strictly quasi-concave. A strictly quasi-concave curve does not have a flat area. Hence, a local maximum must be the global maximum for a strictly quasi-concave function.

A FOC and strict quasi-concavity together are also not sufficient to ensure optimality. For example, $f(x) = x^3$ is strictly quasi-concave, but its FOC does not imply a maximum solution.

In Example 3.13, since $f''(x) \leq 0$ for all x, f is concave, implying that (x_1^*, x_2^*) is a global maximum.

---

[5]This result is from Takayama (1993, p. 88). Note that, with strict quasi-concavity only, the FOC cannot guarantee a global maximum, not even a local maximum. For example, $f(x) = x^3$ is strictly quasi-concave, but the FOC does not yield a maximum.

Example 3.14. Let us find a maximum for $f(x_1, x_2) = x_1 + x_2 - \frac{1}{3}x_1^2 + x_1 x_2 - x_2^2$ on $\mathbb{R}^2$. By Theorem 3.6, we know that a maximum (x_1^*, x_2^*), if it exists, must satisfy the following FOCs:

$$f_{x_1} = 1 - \frac{2}{3}x_1^* + x_2^* = 0, \quad f_{x_2} = 1 + x_1^* - 2x_2^* = 0,$$

which imply

$$\begin{pmatrix} x_1^* \\ x_2^* \end{pmatrix} = \begin{pmatrix} -\frac{2}{3} & 1 \\ 1 & -2 \end{pmatrix}^{-1} \begin{pmatrix} -1 \\ -1 \end{pmatrix} = 3 \begin{pmatrix} -2 & -1 \\ -1 & -\frac{2}{3} \end{pmatrix} \begin{pmatrix} -1 \\ -1 \end{pmatrix}$$

$$= 3 \begin{pmatrix} 3 \\ \frac{5}{3} \end{pmatrix} = \begin{pmatrix} 9 \\ 5 \end{pmatrix}.$$

This solution is the only point that satisfies the FOCs. We further have

$$f''(x) \equiv \begin{pmatrix} f_{x_1 x_1}(x_1, x_2) & f_{x_1 x_2}(x_1, x_2) \\ f_{x_2 x_1}(x_1, x_2) & f_{x_2 x_2}(x_1, x_2) \end{pmatrix} = \begin{pmatrix} -\frac{2}{3} & 1 \\ 1 & -2 \end{pmatrix}.$$

We can easily see that the first principal minor of f'' is $(-1)d_1 = 2/3 > 0$ and the second principal minor of f'' is $(-1)^2 d_2 = |f''| = 1/3 > 0$. Hence, $f''(x^*) < 0$, implying that (x_1^*, x_2^*), achieves a local maximum. Actually, since $f''(x) \leq 0$ for all x, f is concave. Thus, f achieves a global maximum at (x_1^*, x_2^*). ∎

Corollary 3.1. *Given $A \subset \mathbb{R}^n$, consider problem*

$$\max_{x \in A} f(x). \tag{3.2}$$

(a) *If x^* is an interior solution, then*

$$\begin{aligned} FOC: \quad & f'(x^*) = 0, \\ SONC: \quad & f''(x^*) \geq 0. \end{aligned}$$

(b) *For an interior point x^*, if*

$$\begin{aligned} FOC: \quad & f'(x^*) = 0, \\ SOSC: \quad & f''(x^*) > 0, \end{aligned}$$

then x^* is a local minimum point of f.

(c) *If f is convex on A, then any point $x^* \in A$ satisfying $f'(x^*) = 0$ is a minimum point.*

(d) *If f is strictly quasi-convex, a local minimum over a convex set A is the unique global minimum.* ■

Example 3.15. Let us find a minimum point for $f(x_1, x_2) = x_1^2 + x_2 - x_1 x_2 - x_3^2$ on $\mathbb{R}^2$. By the above corollary, we know that a minimum point (x_1^*, x_2^*), if it exists, must satisfy the following FOCs:

$$f_{x_1} = 2x_1 - x_2 = 0, \quad f_{x_2} = 1 - x_1 - 3x_2^2 = 0,$$

implying

$$x_2 = 2x_1, (3x_1 + 1)(4x_1 - 1) = 0,$$

which in turn imply two possible solutions: $(-1/3, -2/3)$ and $(1/4, 1/2)$. We have

$$f''(x) \equiv \begin{pmatrix} f_{x_1 x_1}(x_1, x_2) & f_{x_1 x_2}(x_1, x_2) \\ f_{x_2 x_1}(x_1, x_2) & f_{x_2 x_2}(x_1, x_2) \end{pmatrix} = \begin{pmatrix} 2 & -1 \\ -1 & -6x_2 \end{pmatrix}.$$

For the two solutions, we have

$$f'' \left(-\frac{1}{3}, -\frac{2}{3} \right) = \begin{pmatrix} 2 & -1 \\ -1 & 4 \end{pmatrix}, \quad f'' \left(\frac{1}{4}, \frac{1}{2} \right) = \begin{pmatrix} 2 & -1 \\ -1 & -3 \end{pmatrix}.$$

By Theorem 3.1, $f''(-1/3, -2/3) > 0$. Hence, by the SOSC in Corollary 3.1, the first solution is a local minimum. By the SONC in Theorem 3.6 and Corollary 3.1, since the diagonal entries of $f''(1/4, 1/2)$ have changed signs, the function is neither positive semi-definite nor negative semi-definite, and the second solution is neither a local minimum nor a local maximum. ■

5. Constrained Optimization (Boundary Solutions)

We now discuss constrained optimization problems. Consider as an example a basic economic problem. There is a consumer with utility function $u(x_1, x_2)$ and income I. Given market prices p_1 and p_2 for

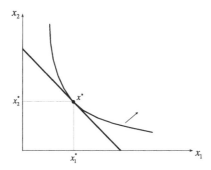

Figure 3.12. A Boundary Solution

the two goods, the consumer's problem is

$$\max_{x \in A} \; u(x_1, x_2), \tag{3.3}$$

where

$$A \equiv \{(x_1, x_2) | x_1 \geq 0, \; x_2 \geq 0, \; p_1 x_1 + p_2 x_2 \leq I\}.$$

This problem can be illustrated by Figure 3.12:

However, from the diagram, we know that the solution to problem (3.3) must be on the boundary of set A. This means that we cannot use Theorem 3.6 to find the solution. We hence face a constrained optimization problem, which should be written as

$$\max_{(x_1, x_2) \in \mathbb{R}^2} \quad u(x_1, x_2)$$
$$\text{s.t.} \qquad p_1 x_1 + p_2 x_2 \leq I,$$
$$x_1 \geq 0,$$
$$x_2 \geq 0.$$

That is, we face a problem with three constraints and the constraints are defined by some functions. Again, from the diagram, if u is strictly increasing, we know that the solution must satisfy $p_1 x_1 + p_2 x_2 = I$. Hence, the problem can be written in a simpler form with one equality constraint only:

$$\max_{(x_1, x_2) \in \mathbb{R}^2} \quad u(x_1, x_2)$$
$$\text{s.t.} \qquad p_1 x_1 + p_2 x_2 = I.$$

This problem can be handled using Theorem 3.8.

From this example, we can see the real difference between unconstrained optimization and constrained optimization: when an optimal point is in the interior, it is an unconstrained problem; when an
optimal point is on the boundary, it is a constrained problem. When
a solution is in the interior, we can ignore the boundary and use
the FOC and SOC in Theorem 3.6 to identify the solution; when a
solution is on the boundary, we need to use the Lagrange approach,
as stated in Theorem 3.8.

We now present the classical theorem on this subject, which
was derived by Takayama (1993, p. 114) and Sydsæter *et al.* (2005,
pp. 118, p. 127). This theorem deals with an optimization problem
when the constraints are defined by a few functions.

Theorem 3.8 (Lagrange). *Given C^2 functions $f: \mathbb{R}^n \to \mathbb{R}$ and
$G: \mathbb{R}^n \to \mathbb{R}^m$, consider problem*

$$
\begin{aligned}
\max_{x \in \mathbb{R}^n} \quad & f(x) \\
\text{s.t.} \quad & G(x) = 0.
\end{aligned}
\tag{3.4}
$$

*Define a Lagrange function $L(x, \lambda) \equiv f(x) + \lambda \cdot G(x)$, where
$\lambda \in \mathbb{R}^m$ is a constant vector.*

(a) *If x^* solves (3.4) and if the row vectors of the derivative $G'(x^*)$
are linearly independent (constraint qualification),[6] then there
exists $\lambda^* \in \mathbb{R}^m$ (a vector of Lagrange multipliers) such that*

  FOC: $L'_x(x^*, \lambda^*) = 0,$
  SONC: $h^T L''_x(x^*, \lambda^*) h \leq 0,$ *for any h satisfying $G'(x^*)h = 0$.*

(b) *If the FOC is satisfied for some pair (x^*, λ^*) satisfying $G(x^*) = 0$
and*

  SOSC: $h^T L''_x(x^*, \lambda^*) h \leq 0,$
     for any $h \neq 0$ satisfying $G'(x^*)h = 0$,   (3.5)

then x^* is a unique local maximum.

---

[6]See Chiang *et al.* (2005, p. 415) and Sydsæter *et al.* (2005, p. 137) for details.

(c) *If the FOC is satisfied for some pair* (x^*, λ^*) *satisfying* $G(x^*) = 0$, $\lambda^* \cdot G(x)$ *is quasi-concave in* x, *and*

$$\text{SOSC: } h^T f''(x^*)h < 0, \quad \text{for any } h \neq 0 \text{ satisfying } G'(x^*)h = 0, \tag{3.6}$$

then x^* *is a unique local maximum.* ■

The Lagrange theorem provides a standard method, called the Lagrange method, for solving problems with equality constraints.

Example 3.16. Given $a > 0$ and $b > 0$, consider

$$F(a, b) \equiv \max_{x_1, x_2} -ax_1^2 - bx_2^2$$
$$\text{s.t.} \quad x_1 + x_2 = 1.$$

We first define the Lagrange function:

$$L(\lambda, x_1, x_2) \equiv -ax_1^2 - bx_2^2 + \lambda(x_1 + x_2 - 1).$$

The FOCs are

$$\frac{\partial L}{\partial x_1} = -2ax_1 + \lambda = 0, \quad \frac{\partial L}{\partial x_2} = -2bx_2 + \lambda = 0,$$

implying

$$x_1 = \frac{\lambda}{2a}, \quad x_2 = \frac{\lambda}{2b}.$$

Substituting these into $x_1 + x_2 = 1$ gives

$$\lambda = \frac{2ab}{a + b}.$$

Hence,

$$x_1^* = \frac{b}{a + b}, \quad x_2^* = \frac{a}{a + b}.$$

This is the only solution from the FOCs. Figure 3.13 illustrates the problem and its solution. ■

Let us try to understand the Lagrange theorem. First, the necessity for quasi-concavity of $\lambda^* \cdot G$ is shown in Appendix A.1.

Second, the full rank requirement on $G'(x^*)$ is not a real constraint. The full rank means that all the constraints defined by

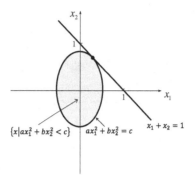

Figure 3.13. Constrained Optimization

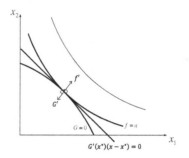

Figure 3.14. The FOC

$G(x) = 0$ are (linearly) independent constraints at x^*; that is, none of them can be implied by others. If one of constraints is redundant, we can drop that constraint without affecting the optimization problem. Hence, we can always be sure that $G'(x^*)$ is of full rank.

Third, let us explain the FOC. By observing Figure 3.14, since the curve $G(x) = 0$ and the indifference curve $f(x) = a$ are tangent at x^*, their gradients must be linearly dependent. In other words, there exists a λ such that $f'(x^*) + \lambda G'(x^*) = 0$, which is the FOC.[7]

Fourth, let us explain the SOC. The tangent line is $G'(x^*)(x - x^*) = 0$. From Figure 3.14, we know that problem (3.4) is

---

[7]In Figure 3.14, G is decreasing and quasi-concave.

equivalent to[8]

$$\max_{x \in \mathbb{R}^n} \quad f(x)$$
$$\text{s.t.} \quad G'(x^*)(x - x^*) = 0,$$

or

$$\max_{h \in V} f(x^* + h),$$

where $V \equiv \{h|G'(x^*)h = 0\}$. In fact, since $V \approx \mathbb{R}^{n-m}$ (equivalence between two Banach spaces or Euclidean spaces), we can treat V as $\mathbb{R}^{n-m}$ and simply write $V = \mathbb{R}^{n-m}$. Let $F(h) \equiv f(x^* + h)$. Since $x = x^*$ is optimal for f, $h^* = 0$ is optimal for F. Since $V = \mathbb{R}^{n-m}$ is a vector space, $h^* = 0$ is an interior solution. Hence, the SOC is that $F(h)$ is concave at $h^* = 0$, which is precisely the SOC in Theorem 3.8. By this explanation, we know that the strict version of this SOC should be locally sufficient. Therefore, the SOC means concavity of f in a subspace and this subspace is defined by $G'(x^*)$.

Finally, how do we verify the SOC? The following theorem is a convenient tool to verify a SOC for a constrained optimization problem. Sydsæter *et al.* (2005, p. 41), Varian (1984, p. 309), Takayama (1993, p. 116, footnote 21) and Chiang (1984, p. 386) similarly refer to this tool. For a more general case, see Varian's Fact A.13 (1984, p. 326). Takayama's Theorem A.10 on p. 603 requires that the first m columns of C in Theorem 3.9 be linearly independent. This is unnecessary since we can move the rows and columns symmetrically so that the first m columns of C are indeed linearly independent. This adjustment amounts to a change of the order of $x_1, x_2, \ldots, x_n$.

Theorem 3.9. *Suppose that $A \in \mathbb{R}^{n \times n}$ is symmetric, $C \in \mathbb{R}^{m \times n}$ has full rank, $m < n$, and let $b_1, \ldots, b_{m+n}$ be the principal minors of $B \equiv \begin{pmatrix} 0 & C \\ C^T & A \end{pmatrix}$.*

Then,

1. $x'Ax > 0$ *for* $x \neq 0$ *satisfying* $Cx = 0 \Leftrightarrow (-1)^m b_k > 0$, $\forall k \geq 2m + 1$.

---

[8]This is true if G is quasi-concave in a neighborhood of x^*.

2. $x'Ax < 0$ *for* $x \neq 0$ *satisfying* $Cx = 0 \Leftrightarrow (-1)^{m+k}b_k > 0, \forall k \geq 2m + 1.$ ∎

With Theorem 3.9, we can easily verify a SOC. For problem (3.4), let

$$B(x) \equiv \begin{pmatrix} 0 & G'(x) \\ [G'(x)]^T & f''(x) \end{pmatrix}.$$

Let $b_i(x), 1, \ldots, n + m$, be the principal minors of $B(x)$. By Theorem 3.9, the SOSC in (3.6) is guaranteed if $(-1)^i b_i(x^*) < 0$ for $i \geq 2m + 1$.

Example 3.17. Verify the SOC for the problem in Example 3.16. Let $g \equiv x_1 + x_2 - 1$. We have

$$B(x) \equiv \begin{pmatrix} 0 & g_{x_1} & g_{x_2} \\ g_{x_1} & f_{x_1 x_1} & f_{x_1 x_2} \\ g_{x_2} & f_{x_2 x_1} & f_{x_2 x_2} \end{pmatrix} = \begin{pmatrix} 0 & 1 & 1 \\ 1 & -2a & 0 \\ 1 & 0 & -2b \end{pmatrix}.$$

Since $(-1)^{1+3} b_3 = 2(a + b) > 0$, by Theorem 3.9, the SOSC defined in the Lagrange theorem is satisfied. Therefore, (x_1^*, x_2^*) is a local maximum. ∎

Example 3.18. Given $a \in (0, 1)$, consider

$$v(p_1, p_2, I) \equiv \max_{x_1, x_2 \geq 0} x_1^a + x_2^a$$
$$\text{s.t.} \quad p_1 x_1 + p_2 x_2 = I.$$

The Lagrange function is

$$L(\lambda, x_1, x_2) \equiv x_1^a + x_2^a + \lambda(I - p_1 x_1 - p_2 x_2).$$

The FOCs are

$$\frac{\partial L}{\partial x_1} = a x_1^{a-1} - \lambda p_1 = 0, \quad \frac{\partial L}{\partial x_2} = a x_2^{a-1} - \lambda p_2 = 0,$$

implying

$$x_1 = \left(\frac{\lambda p_1}{a}\right)^{\frac{1}{a-1}}, \quad x_2 = \left(\frac{\lambda p_2}{a}\right)^{\frac{1}{a-1}}. \tag{3.7}$$

Substituting this solution into the budget constraint yields

$$I = \left(\frac{\lambda}{a}\right)^{\frac{1}{a-1}} \left(p_1^{\frac{a}{a-1}} + p_2^{\frac{a}{a-1}}\right),$$

which determines λ. Substituting this λ into (3.7) determines the solution:

$$x_1^* = \frac{p_1^{\frac{1}{a-1}}}{p_1^{\frac{a}{a-1}} + p_2^{\frac{a}{a-1}}} I, \quad x_2^* = \frac{p_2^{\frac{1}{a-1}}}{p_1^{\frac{a}{a-1}} + p_2^{\frac{a}{a-1}}} I.$$

For the SOC, consider

$$B(x) \equiv \begin{pmatrix} 0 & g_{x_1} & g_{x_2} \\ g_{x_1} & L_{x_1 x_1} & L_{x_1 x_2} \\ g_{x_2} & L_{x_2 x_1} & L_{x_2 x_2} \end{pmatrix}$$

$$= \begin{pmatrix} 0 & p_1 & p_2 \\ p_1 & a(a-1)x_1^{a-2} & 0 \\ p_2 & 0 & a(a-1)x_2^{a-2} \end{pmatrix}.$$

We have

$$(-1)^{1+3} b_3 = -p_1 \begin{vmatrix} p_1 & p_2 \\ 0 & a(a-1)x_2^{a-2} \end{vmatrix} + p_2 \begin{vmatrix} p_1 & p_2 \\ a(a-1)x_2^{a-2} & 0 \end{vmatrix}$$

$$= a(1-a)p_1^2 x_2^{a-2} + a(1-a)p_2^2 x_1^{a-2} > 0.$$

Hence, the SOSC is satisfied. Therefore, (x_1^*, x_2^*) is a local maximum. ∎

Is the SOC related to quasi-concavity? If $m = 1$, by the FOC, we have

$$B(x^*) = \begin{pmatrix} 0 & -\frac{1}{\lambda}f'(x^*) \\ -\frac{1}{\lambda}[f'(x^*)]^T & f''(x^*) \end{pmatrix}.$$

It is easy to see that the signs of the principal minors for $B(x^*)$ are the same as the ones for the following bordered Hessian matrix of f:

$$B_f(x^*) \equiv \begin{pmatrix} 0 & f'(x^*) \\ [f'(x^*)]^T & f''(x^*) \end{pmatrix}.$$

Hence, by Theorems 3.3 and 3.9, the conditions for quasi-concavity of f are basically the same as those for the SOC. This fact is reflected in Figure 3.14, where we can see that the quasi-concavity of f ensures optimality of the tangent point.

In many applications, we have both equality and inequality constraints. The Lagrange theorem allows equality constraints only. We now extend this theorem to allow also inequality constraints. Specifically, given functions $g_i, h_j \colon \mathbb{R}^n \to \mathbb{R}$ for $i = 1, \ldots, m$ and $j = 1, \ldots, k$, we allow constraints of the form:

$$g_1(x) \geq 0, \ldots, g_m(x) \geq 0 \quad \text{and} \quad h_1(x) = 0, \ldots, h_k(x) = 0.$$

An $x \in \mathbb{R}^n$ satisfying the above constraints is said to be admissible. The following Kuhn–Tucker theorem allows us to deal with inequality constraints.

Theorem 3.10 (Kuhn–Tucker).[9] *Given C^1 functions $f, g_i, h_j \colon \mathbb{R}^n \to \mathbb{R}$, $i = 1, \ldots, m$, $j = 1, \ldots, k$, and $k < n$, let $G \equiv (g_1, \ldots, g_m)^T$ and $H \equiv (h_1, \ldots, h_k)^T$. Consider problem*

$$
\begin{aligned}
V = \max_{x \in \mathbb{R}^n} & f(x) \\
\text{s.t.} \quad & G(x) \geq 0, \\
& H(x) = 0.
\end{aligned}
\tag{3.8}
$$

Let $I(x) \equiv \{i | g_i(x) = 0\}$ and $L(x, \lambda, \mu) = f(x) + \lambda \cdot G(x) + \mu \cdot H(x)$, where $\lambda \in \mathbb{R}^m$ and $\mu \in \mathbb{R}^k$ are constant vectors.

(a) *If x^* is a solution and $g_i'(x^*)$ for $i \in I(x^*)$ together with all $h_j'(x^*)$ are linearly independent vectors (constraint qualification or rank condition), then there exist unique $\lambda^* \in \mathbb{R}_+^m$ and $\mu^* \in \mathbb{R}^k$ such that*

$$
\begin{aligned}
\text{FOC:} \quad & L_x'(x^*, \lambda^*, \mu^*) = 0, \\
\text{KTC:} \quad & \lambda^* \cdot G(x^*) = 0.
\end{aligned}
\tag{3.9}
$$

---

[9]Part (a) of this theorem can be found in Sydsæter *et al.* (2005, p. 147), but no proof is provided there. Neither Chiang (1984, 2005) nor Takayama (1993) mentions this result. Sydsæter *et al.* (2005) claim that a proof is available on their website for part (a), but it is actually not. Also, the sufficient conditions in part (b) are my own contribution; they have not been found in the literature.

(b) *Conversely, suppose that a triplet* (x^*, λ^*, μ^*) *satisfies conditions in* (3.9), *where* x^* *is admissible. If* $\lambda_i^* > 0$ *for any* $i \in I(x^*)$ *and* (x^*, λ^*, μ^*) *satisfies the SOSC for the following problem as stated in Theorem* 3.8, *then* x^* *is the unique local maximum for* (3.8).

$$\max_{x \in \mathbb{R}^n} \quad f(x)$$
$$\text{s.t.} \quad g_i(x) = 0, \quad i \in I(x^*) \tag{3.10}$$
$$H(x) = 0. \quad \blacksquare$$

Note that, since $\lambda \geq 0$ and $G \geq 0$, the KTC (Kuhn–Tucker condition) is equivalent to

$$\text{KTC: } \lambda_i g_i(x) = 0, \quad \text{for all } i.$$

Theorem 3.10 is useful. It indicates that, as long as $\lambda_i^* > 0$ for all the binding constraints, we can throw away all the non-binding constraints and use the Lagrange theorem to solve the Kuhn–Tucker problem (3.8). All the FOC, SONC, and SOSC in the Lagrange theorem are valid for the Kuhn–Tucker problem. Specifically, a solution is the unique local maximum if

- $\lambda_i^* > 0$ for all the binding constraints;
- the SOSC in Theorem 3.8 is satisfied when only the binding constraints are included.

Example 3.19. The Kuhn–Tucker theorem is generally difficult to apply since there is no associated mechanical procedure available. We use a simple example to illustrate this point. Consider the standard consumer problem:

$$\max_{(x_1, x_2) \in \mathbb{R}^2} \quad u(x_1, x_2)$$
$$\text{s.t.} \quad p_1 x_1 + p_2 x_2 \leq I,$$
$$x_1 \geq 0,$$
$$x_2 \geq 0.$$

where $p_1 > 0$, $p_2 > 0$, $u_{x_1}(x) > 0$ and $u_{x_2}(x) > 0$ for all $x \in \mathbb{R}^2$. The Lagrange function is

$$L = u(x_1, x_2) + \lambda_1 x_1 + \lambda_2 x_2 + \lambda_3 (I - p_1 x_1 - p_2 x_2).$$

Then, the FOCs and KTCs are

$$u_{x_1} + \lambda_1 = \lambda_3 p_1,$$
$$u_{x_2} + \lambda_2 = \lambda_3 p_2,$$
$$\lambda_1 x_1 = 0, \quad \lambda_2 x_2 = 0,$$
$$\lambda_3(I - p_1 x_1 - p_2 x_2) = 0,$$
$$\lambda_1 \geq 0, \quad \lambda_2 \geq 0, \quad \lambda_3 \geq 0.$$

To find the solution, we first observe that, if $\lambda_3 = 0$, then by the first FOC we have $u_{x_1} + \lambda_1 = 0$, which is impossible since $u_{x_1} > 0$ and $\lambda_1 \geq 0$. Hence, we must have $\lambda_3 > 0$. Thus, $p_1 x_1 + p_2 x_2 = I$. Further, if $x_1 = 0$, we then have $x_2 = I/p_2$, implying $\lambda_2 = 0$, $\lambda_3 = u_{x_2}/p_2$ and $\lambda_1 = \lambda_3 p_1 - u_{x_1}$. That is, one possible solution is

$$x^* = \left(0, \frac{I}{p_2}\right), \quad \lambda_1^* = \frac{p_1 u_{x_2}(x^*)}{p_2} - u_{x_1}(x^*), \quad \lambda_2^* = 0, \quad \lambda_3^* = \frac{u_{x_2}(x^*)}{p_2}.$$

To satisfy the condition $\lambda_i \geq 0$, we need condition

$$\frac{u_{x_2}(x^*)}{p_2} \geq \frac{u_{x_1}(x^*)}{p_1}.$$

Symmetrically, we have another possible solution:

$$x^* = \left(\frac{I}{p_1}, 0\right), \quad \lambda_1^* = 0, \quad \lambda_2^* = \frac{p_2 u_{x_1}(x^*)}{p_1} - u_{x_2}(x^*), \quad \lambda_3^* = \frac{u_{x_1}(x^*)}{p_1},$$

under condition

$$\frac{u_{x_1}(x^*)}{p_1} \geq \frac{u_{x_2}(x^*)}{p_2}.$$

Finally, if $x_1 \neq 0$ and $x_2 \neq 0$, we must have $\lambda_1 = \lambda_2 = 0$, which immediately implies the third possible solution determined by

$$\frac{u_{x_1}(x^*)}{p_1} = \frac{u_{x_2}(x^*)}{p_2}, \quad p_1 x_1^* + p_2 x_2^* = I. \quad \blacksquare$$

So far, we have not mentioned a guarantee for global maximization. The following theorem shows that, with quasi-concavity, the FOC is very much sufficient to guarantee global maximization.

Theorem 3.11 (Global Maximum). *Given differentiable functions* $f, g_i, h_j \colon \mathbb{R}^n \to \mathbb{R}$, *an admissible* $x^* \in \mathbb{R}^n$ *is a global maximum for* *problem* (3.8) *if*

(a) *There are* $\lambda^* \in \mathbb{R}_+^m$ *and* $\mu^* \in \mathbb{R}^k$ *such that* (x^*, λ^*, μ^*) *satisfies the KTC and FOC for* (3.8) *in* (3.9);

(b) $f, \lambda_i^* g_i(\cdot)$ *and* $\mu_j^* h_j(\cdot)$ *are quasi-concave for all* i *and* j; *and*

(c) $f'(x^*) \neq 0$ *or* f *is concave.* ∎

Theorem 3.11 is very useful. Since the quasi-concavity requirement is often satisfied in economics problems, this theorem suggests that we generally do not need to verify the SOCs. That is, a solution from the FOC and KTC is generally the right solution.

This version of the theorem is not found in the literature, even though it is very useful. It is an enhanced version of those in Arrow and Enthoven (1961), Sydsæter *et al.* (2005, p. 146),[10] Chiang (1984, p. 745), Chiang and Wainwright (2005, p. 426) and Takayama (1993, p. 95). *The existing versions do not allow equality constraints.* We extend the existing versions to allow equality constraints. Equality constraints are important since they are involved in most economic problems. By allowing equality constraints, as a special case, Theorem 3.11 provides a global maximization result for the Lagrange problem in Theorem 3.8 for the first time.

Example 3.20. Let us show global maximization in Example 3.16. Since $(-1)^2 b_2 < 0$ and $(-1)^3 b_3 < 0$, the objective function $f = -ax_1^2 - bx_2^2$ is quasi-concave. Alternatively, since $\{x | -ax_1^2 - bx_2^2 \geq c\}$ is convex for any $c \in \mathbb{R}$, the objective function $f = -ax_1^2 - bx_2^2$ is quasi-concave. Further, since $f_{x_1}(x^*) = -ax_1^* \neq 0$, by Theorem 3.11, x^* is the global maximum. ∎

Example 3.21. For $a > 0$ and $b > 0$, consider

$$F(a, b) \equiv \max_{x_1, x_2} x_1 + x_2$$
$$\text{s.t.} \quad ax_1^2 + bx_2^2 \leq 1.$$

The Lagrange function is $L = x_1 + x_2 + \lambda(1 - ax_1^2 - bx_2^2)$. The FOCs are

$$1 = 2a\lambda x_1, \quad 1 = 2b x_2,$$

---

[10]Their proof has a minor error.

implying

$$\hat{x}_1 = \frac{1}{2a\lambda}, \quad \hat{x}_2 = \frac{1}{2b\lambda}.$$

Substituting these into the binding constraint yields $\lambda = \frac{1}{2}\sqrt{a^{-1} + b^{-1}}$. Then,

$$x_1^* = \frac{1}{a\sqrt{a^{-1} + b^{-1}}}, \quad x_2^* = \frac{1}{b\sqrt{a^{-1} + b^{-1}}}.$$

Function $g(x_1, x_2) = 1 - ax_1^2 - bx_2^2$ is quasi-concave since its higher-value sets are convex. To verify condition (b) in Theorem 3.8, consider the matrix:

$$B(x) \equiv \begin{pmatrix} 0 & g_{x_1} & g_{x_2} \\ g_{x_1} & f_{x_1x_1} & f_{x_1x_2} \\ g_{x_2} & f_{x_2x_1} & f_{x_2x_2} \end{pmatrix} = \begin{pmatrix} 0 & -2ax_1 & -2bx_2 \\ -2ax_1 & 0 & 0 \\ -2bx_2 & 0 & 0 \end{pmatrix}.$$

Since $(-1)^{1+3} b_3 = 0$, we cannot use the SOSC. Hence, we have to use Theorem 3.11. The problem is equivalent to

$$F(a, b) \equiv \max_{x_1, x_2} x_1 + x_2$$
$$\text{s.t.} \quad 1 - ax_1^2 - bx_2^2 \geq 0.$$

Then, by Theorem 3.11, since $x_1 + x_2$ and $1 - ax_1^2 - bx_2^2$ are quasi-concave functions, we know that the solution is a global maximum. In fact, from Figure 3.13, we know that it is the unique global maximum. ∎

Example 3.22. Given $\alpha, \beta > 0$, consider

$$v(p_1, p_2, I) \equiv \max_{x_1, x_2 \geq 0} x_1^\alpha x_2^\beta$$
$$\text{s.t.} \quad p_1 x_1 + p_2 x_2 \leq I.$$

The Lagrange function is

$$L = x_1^\alpha x_2^\beta + \lambda(I - p_1 x_1 - p_2 x_2).$$

The FOCs are

$$\lambda p_1 = \alpha x_1^{\alpha-1} x_2^\beta, \quad \lambda p_2 = \beta x_1^\alpha x_2^{\beta-1}.$$

These two conditions imply $\lambda > 0$. Hence, by the KT condition, the constraint is binding. Dividing the first expression above by the second expression yields

$$\frac{\alpha x_2}{\beta x_1} = \frac{p_1}{p_2} \Rightarrow x_2 = \frac{\beta p_1}{\alpha p_2} x_1.$$

Then, by the binding budget constraint, we can determine x_2^* and then x_1^*, which are

$$x_1^*(p_1, p_2, I) = \frac{\alpha I}{(\alpha + \beta) p_1}, \quad x_2^*(p_1, p_2, I) = \frac{\beta I}{(\alpha + \beta) p_2}.$$

Since $u(x_1, x_2)$ is strictly quasi-concave, the solution achieves global maximization. ∎

The following result shows the equivalence between a constrained problem and an unconstrained problem. This result can be found in Sydsæter *et al.* (2005, pp. 140–141). My paper, Wang (1986, Theorem 8), provides a general version in an infinite-dimensional space. This result has limited practical use in business applications due to its strong requirement on the functions. However, it has theoretical value in that it indicates the equivalence, which provides a way to understand constrained optimization. Consequently, many constrained optimization approaches are based on this equivalence.

Proposition 3.10. *Let $f \colon \mathbb{R}^n \to \mathbb{R}$ and $G \colon \mathbb{R}^n \to \mathbb{R}^m$ be concave and $H \colon \mathbb{R}^n \to \mathbb{R}^k$ be linear.*[11] *Also, there exists x_0 such that $G(x_0) \gg 0$. Then, x^* is a solution of*

$$\begin{aligned} \max_{x \in \mathbb{R}^n} \quad & f(x) \\ \text{s.t.} \quad & G(x) \geq 0, \\ & H(x) = 0, \end{aligned}$$

iff $G(x^*) \geq 0, H(x^*) = 0$, and there exist $\lambda \in \mathbb{R}_+^m$ and $\mu \in \mathbb{R}^k$ such that $\lambda \cdot G(x^*) = 0$ and x^* is a solution of

$$\max_{x \in \mathbb{R}^n} L(x, \lambda, \mu) \equiv f(x) + \lambda \cdot G(x) + \mu \cdot H(x). \quad \blacksquare$$

---

[11]A linear H means that there is $A \in \mathbb{R}^{k \times n}$ and $\alpha \in \mathbb{R}^k$ such that $H(x) = \alpha + Ax$.

6. Envelope Theorem

We often deal with maximum and minimum value functions in business applications. In this section, we provide two theorems on the derivatives of such a function. The first theorem requires the optimal point to be in the interior of the domain and the second theorem allows the optimal point to be on the boundary.

Theorem 3.12 (Envelope). *Given differentiable $f: X \times A \to \mathbb{R}$, $X \subset \mathbb{R}^n$ and $A \subset \mathbb{R}^k$, if $x^*(a)$ is an interior optimal point of*

$$F(a) \equiv \max_{x \in X} f(x, a),$$

then

$$\frac{dF(a)}{da} = \left. \frac{\partial f(x, a)}{\partial a} \right|_{x = x^*(a)}. \quad \blacksquare$$

The key advantage of the Envelope Theorem is that we can find the derivative of function $F(a)$ without actually solving $F(a)$. Given the knowledge of $x^*(a)$, we can use function $f(x, a)$ to find $F'(a)$.

Theorem 3.13 (Envelope). *Given set $A \subset \mathbb{R}^l$ and C^1 functions $f, g_i, h_j: \mathbb{R}^n \times A \to \mathbb{R}$, let $G \equiv (g_1, \ldots, g_m)^T$, $H \equiv (h_1, \ldots, h_k)^T$, and*

$$L(x, a, \lambda, \mu) \equiv f(x, a) + \lambda \cdot G(x, a) + \mu \cdot H(x, a).$$

If $x^*(a)$ is a solution of the following problem:

$$F(a) \equiv \max_{x \in \mathbb{R}^n} f(x, a)$$
$$\text{s.t.} \quad G(x, a) \geq 0,$$
$$H(x, a) = 0,$$

and $\lambda^*(a)$ and $\mu^*(a)$ are the corresponding Lagrange multipliers, then

$$\frac{\partial F(a)}{\partial a} = \left. \frac{\partial L(x, a, \lambda, \mu)}{\partial a} \right|_{x = x^*(a), \lambda = \lambda^*(a), \mu = \mu^*(a)} \qquad (3.11)$$

under the conditions[12]:

(a) *There is a neighborhood* $\mathbb{N}_r(a^*) \subset A$ *such that, for every* $a \in \mathbb{N}_r(a^*)$, *the problem has a solution, and at* a^*, *the problem has a unique solution* $x^* = x^*(a^*)$.

(b) *Gradients* $g'_{ix}(x^*, a^*)$, $i = 1, \ldots, m$, *corresponding to binding constraints are linearly independent.* ■

The key in Theorem 3.13 is that, although the Lagrange multipliers are dependent on a, we can assume that they are independent of a when we use the envelope formula (3.11). Hence, taking a derivative of a value function is equivalent to taking the derivative of the corresponding Lagrange function when treating the choice variables and Lagrange multipliers as constants.

Example 3.23. From Example 3.16, we have

$$F(a, b) = -a \left(\frac{b}{a+b} \right)^2 - b \left(\frac{a}{a+b} \right)^2 = -\frac{ab}{a+b},$$

which gives the derivative:

$$\frac{\partial F(a, b)}{\partial a} = -\frac{b(a+b) - ab}{(a+b)^2} = -\left(\frac{b}{a+b} \right)^2.$$

We can also directly find the derivative using the Envelope Theorem:

$$\frac{\partial F(a, b)}{\partial a} = -(x_1^*)^2 = -\left(\frac{b}{a+b} \right)^2. \quad ■$$

---

[12]This result is from Sydsæter *et al.* (2005, p. 149). There is no concavity condition on the functions, otherwise we can simply use Proposition 3.10 to arrive at this result. See also Afriat (1971, pp. 355–357) and Samuelson (1947). Chiang (1984, 2005) does not give this result. Takayama (1993, p. 131), however, gives a similar one. Sydsæter *et al.* (2005) do not mention the domain A. The domain A is added by us. We can also restrict x to a set $X \subset \mathbb{R}^n$.

Example 3.24. Consider the following problem:

$$v(p_1, \ldots, p_n, I) \equiv \max_{x \geq 0} u(x_1, \ldots, x_n)$$
$$\text{s.t.} \quad p_1 x_1 + \cdots + p_n x_n \leq I.$$

We first translate it into an unconstrained problem:

$$v(p_1, \ldots, p_n, I) \equiv \max_{x \geq 0} \ u(x_1, \ldots, x_n) + \lambda(I - p_1 x_1 - \cdots - p_n x_n),$$

where $\lambda \geq 0$ is a Lagrange multiplier. By Theorem 3.13, we have

$$\frac{\partial v}{\partial p_i} = -\lambda x_i^*, \quad \frac{\partial v}{\partial I} = \lambda,$$

implying

$$x_i^* = -\frac{\partial v}{\partial p_i} \bigg/ \frac{\partial v}{\partial I}.$$

This is the well-known Roy's Identity, which means that the demand is the ratio of the marginal utility of price to the marginal utility of income. ∎

Example 3.25. For Example 3.21, find $\frac{\partial F(a,b)}{\partial a}$. By the Envelope Theorem, with the Lagrange function being $L = x_1 + x_2 + \lambda(1 - ax_1^2 - bx_2^2)$, we have

$$\frac{\partial F(a,b)}{\partial a} = \frac{\partial L}{\partial a} = -\lambda x_1^2 = -\frac{1}{2}\sqrt{a^{-1} + b^{-1}} \left(\frac{1}{a\sqrt{a^{-1} + b^{-1}}} \right)^2$$

$$= -\frac{1}{2a^2 \sqrt{a^{-1} + b^{-1}}}.$$

To verify this, we first find that

$$F(a,b) = \left(\frac{1}{a} + \frac{1}{b} \right) \frac{1}{\sqrt{a^{-1} + b^{-1}}} = \sqrt{a^{-1} + b^{-1}}.$$

Then,

$$\frac{\partial F(a,b)}{\partial a} = -\frac{1}{2a^2 \sqrt{a^{-1} + b^{-1}}}. \quad \blacksquare$$

The envelop theorems are often used to give a few needed equations in addition to FOCs when we try to solve an optimization problem, especially in dynamic programming.

Notes

Two good references are Sydsæter *et al.* (2005, Chapters 2 and 3) and Chiang (1984, Chapters 9, 11, 12, and 21). Chiang offers extensive discussions. We provide only a condensed list of useful results, but these results are basically sufficient for business applications.

The best software for dealing with math problems is Mathcad. It has several advantages. What you see on the screen is what you will see on paper; there is no need to learn a programming language. It can solve multiple equations with equality and inequality constraints. It can also solve optimization problems with equality and inequality constraints. Further, the optimization problem can carry a free parameter, by which we can solve for an optimal function.

Appendix

A.1. *A Counterexample*

We now show the necessity of quasi-concavity in Theorem 3.8(c) through an example. We show that the following SOC, together with the FOC, is not sufficient for optimality:

$$h^T f''(x^*)h < 0, \quad \text{for } h \neq 0 \text{ satisfying } G'(x^*)h = 0.$$

Consider

$$\max_{x_1, x_2} x_1^a + x_2^a$$

$$\text{s.t.} \quad \frac{1}{x_1} + \frac{1}{x_2} = 1,$$

where $a \in (0,1)$. Let $L = x_1^a + x_2^a + \lambda(x_1^{-1} + x_2^{-1} - 1)$. The FOCs are

$$ax_1^{a-1} = \lambda x_1^{-2}, \quad ax_2^{a-1} = \lambda x_2^{-2},$$

implying

$$x_1 = x_2 = \left(\frac{\lambda}{a}\right)^{\frac{1}{a+1}}.$$

The constraint in the optimization problem can then determine λ, which implies

$$x_1^* = x_2^* = 2, \quad \lambda^* = a^{a+2}.$$

The bordered Hessian matrix is

$$B(x) \equiv \begin{pmatrix} 0 & g_{x_1} & g_{x_2} \\ g_{x_1} & f_{x_1 x_1} & f_{x_1 x_2} \\ g_{x_2} & f_{x_2 x_1} & f_{x_2 x_2} \end{pmatrix}$$

$$= \begin{pmatrix} 0 & -\dfrac{1}{x_1^2} & -\dfrac{1}{x_2^2} \\ -\dfrac{1}{x_1^2} & a(a-1)x_1^{a-2} & 0 \\ -\dfrac{1}{x_2^2} & 0 & a(a-1)x_2^{a-2} \end{pmatrix}.$$

Since

$$(-1)^{1+3}b_3 = \begin{vmatrix} 0 & -\dfrac{1}{x_1^2} & -\dfrac{1}{x_2^2} \\ -\dfrac{1}{x_1^2} & a(a-1)x_1^{a-2} & 0 \\ -\dfrac{1}{x_2^2} & 0 & a(a-1)x_2^{a-2} \end{vmatrix}$$

$$= \frac{1}{x_1^2}\begin{vmatrix} -\dfrac{1}{x_1^2} & -\dfrac{1}{x_2^2} \\ 0 & a(a-1)x_2^{a-2} \end{vmatrix} - \frac{1}{x_2^2}\begin{vmatrix} -\dfrac{1}{x_1^2} & -\dfrac{1}{x_2^2} \\ a(a-1)x_2^{a-2} & 0 \end{vmatrix}$$

$$= \frac{a(1-a)x_2^{a-2}}{x_1^4} + \frac{a(1-a)x_1^{a-2}}{x_2^4} > 0,$$

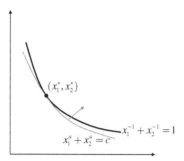

Figure 3.15. A Counterexample

the SOSC as defined in Theorem 3.8(c) is satisfied. However, as shown in Figure 3.15 (for the case when a is close to 1), this (x_1^*, x_2^*) is obviously not a local maximum.

However, the other bordered Hessian matrix, relating to Theorem 3.8(b), is

$$\bar{B}(x) \equiv \begin{pmatrix} 0 & g_{x_1} & g_{x_2} \\ g_{x_1} & L_{x_1 x_1} & L_{x_1 x_2} \\ g_{x_2} & L_{x_2 x_1} & L_{x_2 x_2} \end{pmatrix}$$

$$= \begin{pmatrix} 0 & -\dfrac{1}{x_1^2} & -\dfrac{1}{x_2^2} \\ -\dfrac{1}{x_1^2} & a(a-1)x_1^{a-2} + \dfrac{2\lambda}{x_1^3} & 0 \\ -\dfrac{1}{x_2^2} & 0 & a(a-1)x_2^{a-2} + \dfrac{2\lambda}{x_2^3} \end{pmatrix}.$$

Then,

$$(-1)^{1+3} b_3 = \begin{vmatrix} 0 & -\dfrac{1}{x_1^2} & -\dfrac{1}{x_2^2} \\ -\dfrac{1}{x_1^2} & a(a-1)x_1^{a-2} + \dfrac{2\lambda}{x_1^3} & 0 \\ -\dfrac{1}{x_2^2} & 0 & a(a-1)x_2^{a-2} + \dfrac{2\lambda}{x_2^3} \end{vmatrix}$$

$$= \frac{1}{x_1^2} \begin{vmatrix} -\dfrac{1}{x_1^2} & -\dfrac{1}{x_2^2} \\ 0 & a(a-1)x_2^{a-2} + \dfrac{2\lambda}{x_2^3} \end{vmatrix}$$

$$- \frac{1}{x_2^2} \begin{vmatrix} -\dfrac{1}{x_1^2} & -\dfrac{1}{x_2^2} \\ a(a-1)x_2^{a-2} + \dfrac{2\lambda}{x_1^3} & 0 \end{vmatrix}$$

$$= \frac{1}{x_1^4}\left[a(1-a)x_2^{a-2} - \frac{2\lambda}{x_2^3}\right] + \frac{1}{x_2^4}\left[a(1-a)x_1^{a-2} - \frac{2\lambda}{x_1^3}\right]$$

$$= 2^{-3}[a(1-a)2^{a-2} - 2^{-2}a^{a+2}]$$

$$= 2^{a-5}a^2\left[\frac{1}{a} - 1 - \left(\frac{a}{2}\right)^a\right],$$

which is not positive when a is close to 1. That is, the condition in Theorem 3.8(b) is not satisfied, which is consistent with the situation in Figure 3.15, where (x_1^*, x_2^*) is not a local maximum. The reason for the failure is because $g = x_1^{-1} + x_2^{-1} - 1$ is not quasi-concave. Therefore, the quasi-concavity of $\lambda^* \cdot G$ is necessary.

A.2. *Lemmas*

We present a few lemmas that are useful for the proof of Theorem 3.11.

Lemma 3.1[13] *Given a convex set $X \subset \mathbb{R}^n$ and a differentiable function $f: X \to \mathbb{R}$,*

(a) *f is quasi-concave iff, for all $x, y \in X$,*

$$f(y) \geq f(x) \Rightarrow f'(x) \cdot (y - x) \geq 0. \tag{3.12}$$

---

[13]This result is obtained from Sydsæter *et al.* (2005, p. 74) and Chiang (1984, p. 393).

(b) f *is strictly quasi-concave iff, for all* $x, y \in X, x \neq y$,

$$f(y) \geq f(x) \Rightarrow f'(x) \cdot (y - x) > 0. \qquad (3.13)$$

Proof. We prove the necessity of (3.12) only. Define

$$g(t) \equiv f[x + t(y - x)], \text{for } t \in [0, 1].$$

By the quasi-concavity of f, g achieves the minimum at $t = 0$. Hence, $g'(0) \geq 0$, implying

$$g'(0) = f'(x) \cdot (y - x) \geq 0. \quad \blacksquare$$

Figure 3.16 illustrates (3.12) graphically. The circular area is the higher-value set $\{x | f(x) \geq c\}$ for some constant c. This means that the gradient $f'(x)$ should point inward and is orthogonal to the iso-value curve $\{x | f(x) = c\}$ at point x. In other words, for any point y within the higher-value set, if the higher-value set is convex, the angle between the two vectors $f'(x)$ and $y - x$ cannot be larger than 90°, implying $f'(x) \cdot (y - x) \geq 0$. This explains the conclusion in (3.12).

Corollary 3.2. *Given a convex set* $X \subset \mathbb{R}^n$ *and a differentiable function* $f: X \to \mathbb{R}^n$,

(c) f *is quasi-convex iff, for all* $x, y \in X$,

$$f(y) \geq f(x) \Rightarrow f'(y) \cdot (y - x) \geq 0. \qquad (3.14)$$

(d) f *is strictly quasi-convex iff, for all* $x, y \in X, x \neq y$,

$$f(y) \geq f(x) \Rightarrow f'(y) \cdot (y - x) > 0. \quad \blacksquare \qquad (3.15)$$

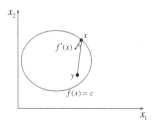

Figure 3.16. Quasi-Concavity

Notice that (3.12) implies

$$f'(x) \cdot (y - x) < 0 \Rightarrow f(y) < f(x).$$

But it may not imply

$$f'(x) \cdot (y - x) = 0 \Rightarrow f(y) \leq f(x).$$

The following lemma ensures this.

Lemma 3.2.[14] *Given a convex set $X \subset \mathbb{R}^n$ and a differentiable quasi-concave function $f \colon X \to \mathbb{R}$, if $f'(x_0) \neq 0$ for $x_0 \in X$, then for any $x \in X$,*

$$f'(x_0) \cdot (x - x_0) = 0 \Rightarrow f(x) \leq f(x_0). \qquad (3.16)$$

Proof. Suppose that (3.16) is false, namely there is $x \in X$ such that

$$f'(x_0) \cdot (x - x_0) = 0 \quad \text{and} \quad f(x) > f(x_0).$$

Since f is continuous, there is $h \in \mathbb{R}^n$ such that $f(x + h) \geq f(x_0)$. Furthermore, since $f'(x_0) \neq 0$, we can choose such an h such that $f'(x_0) \cdot h < 0$. Then,

$$0 = f'(x_0) \cdot (x - x_0) = f'(x_0) \cdot (x + h - x_0) - f'(x_0) \cdot h,$$

implying $f'(x_0) \cdot (x + h - x_0) < 0$. Then, by (3.12), we have $f(x+h) < f(x_0)$, which is a contradiction. Therefore, (3.16) must hold. ∎

Lemma 3.2 is quite intuitive and is illustrated in Figure 3.17.

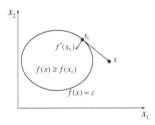

Figure 3.17. A Property from Quasi-Concavity

---

[14]This result is obtained from Takayama (1993, p. 612) — the best source on quasi-concave optimization.

By (3.12) and (3.16), we have the following lemma.

Lemma 3.3. *Given a convex set $X \subset \mathbb{R}^n$ and a differentiable quasi-concave function $f : X \to \mathbb{R}^n$, for all $x, y \in X$, if $f'(x_0) \neq 0$ for $x_0 \in X$, then*

$$f'(x_0) \cdot (x - x_0) \leq 0 \Rightarrow f(x) \leq f(x_0). \quad \blacksquare \qquad (3.17)$$

Lemma 3.4.[15] *If $g : \mathbb{R}^n \to \mathbb{R}$ is quasi-concave and C^2, then for any x^* satisfying $g'(x^*) \neq 0$, we have*

$$h^T g''(x^*) h \leq 0, \quad \text{for } h \in \mathbb{R}^n \text{ satisfying } g'(x^*) \cdot h = 0.$$

Proof. For any $h \in \mathbb{R}^n, \varepsilon > 0$ and $x = x^* + \varepsilon h$, we have

$$g(x) = g(x^*) + g'(x^*) \cdot (x - x^*) + \frac{1}{2}(x - x^*)^T g''(\xi)(x - x^*),$$

where $\xi \in (x, x^*)$. That is,

$$g(x) = g(x^*) + \frac{1}{2}\varepsilon^2 h^T g''(\xi) h \quad \text{for any } h \text{ satisfying } g'(x^*) \cdot h = 0.$$

By Lemma 3.2, since g is quasi-concave and $g'(x^*) \neq 0$, we have $g(x) \leq g(x^*)$, implying

$$h^T g''(\xi) h \leq 0 \quad \text{for any } h \text{ satisfying } g'(x^*) \cdot h = 0 \quad \text{and} \quad \varepsilon > 0.$$

As $\varepsilon \to 0$, we have $\xi \to x^*$. Then, $h^T g''(x^*) h \leq 0$ for any h satisfying $g'(x^*) \cdot h = 0$. $\quad \blacksquare$

A.3. *Proofs of Propositions*

Proof of Proposition 3.1

We prove property (a) only. The rest of the properties are good exercises for students.

---

[15]This lemma is new to the literature.

By Theorem 1.22 in Chapter 1, since A is symmetric, there exists an orthogonal matrix T such that

$$T^{-1}AT = diag\{\lambda_1, \ldots, \lambda_n\}.$$

This implies that λ_i's are the eigenvalues. Then, for any $x \in \mathbb{R}^n$, since $T^{-1} = T'$, we have

$$\begin{aligned}
x'Ax &= (T'x)'T^{-1}AT(T^{-1}x) \\
&= (T'x)'[diag\{\lambda_1, \ldots, \lambda_n\}](T'x) = \lambda_1 y_1^2 + \cdots + \lambda_n y_n^2,
\end{aligned}$$

where $y = T^{-1}x$. Hence, $x'Ax \geq 0$ for all $x \in \mathbb{R}^n$ is equivalent to $\lambda_i \geq 0$ for all λ_i's.

Here is an alternative proof. Given an eigenvalue λ and an eigenvector $\xi \neq 0$ of λ, we have $A\xi = \lambda\xi$. Then, $\xi'A\xi = \lambda\xi'\xi$. Since $\xi'A\xi \geq 0$, we have $\lambda \geq 0$.

Proof of Proposition 3.3

The third property can be illustrated graphically. The fourth property can be easily proven by mathematical induction. Hence, we prove the first property only.

Suppose that f is concave. If

$$(x, t), (y, d) \in I(f) \equiv \{(x, t) \in (X, \mathbb{R}) | f(x) \geq t\},$$

i.e., $f(x) \geq t$ and $f(y) \geq d$, then for any $\lambda \in (0, 1)$, we have

$$f[\lambda x + (1 - \lambda)y] \geq \lambda f(x) + (1 - \lambda)f(y) = \lambda t + (1 - \lambda)d,$$

implying

$$(\lambda x + (1 - \lambda)y, \lambda t + (1 - \lambda)d) \in I(f),$$

i.e.,

$$\lambda(x, t) + (1 - \lambda)(y, d) \in I(f).$$

That is, $I(f)$ is convex.

Conversely, suppose that $I(f)$ is convex. Since

$$(x, f(x)), \quad (y, f(y)) \in I(f),$$

we have

$$(\lambda x + (1 - \lambda)y, \lambda f(x) + (1 - \lambda)f(y)) \in I(f).$$

That is,

$$f[\lambda x + (1 - \lambda)y] \geq \lambda f(x) + (1 - \lambda)f(y).$$

Hence, f is concave.

Proof of Proposition 3.6

We prove the first property only.

$\Rightarrow$: For $f(x) \geq t$ and $f(y) \geq t$, suppose $f(y) \geq f(x)$. Then, $f[\tau x + (1 - \tau)y] \geq f(x)$, implying $f[\tau x + (1 - \tau)y] \geq f(x) \geq t$, for any $\tau \in [0, 1]$. That is, for any $x, y \in \{x \in X | f(x) \geq t\}$, we have $\tau x + (1 - \tau)y \in \{x \in X | f(x) \geq t\}$ for $\tau \in [0, 1]$. Hence, $\{x \in X | f(x) \geq t\}$ is convex.

$\Leftarrow$: If $f(y) \geq f(x)$, we have $x, y \in \{z | f(z) \geq f(x)\}$. Since $\{z | f(z) \geq f(x)\}$ is convex, we have $\tau x + (1 - \tau)y \in \{z | f(z) \geq f(x)\}$, implying $f[\tau x + (1 - \tau)y] \geq f(x)$, for $\tau \in [0, 1]$. Hence, f is quasi-concave.

Proof of Proposition 3.7

(a) Given a concave function f, for any $\lambda \in (0, 1), x, y \in X$, if $f(y) \geq f(x)$, then

$$f[\lambda x + (1 - \lambda)y] \geq \lambda f(x) + (1 - \lambda)f(y) \geq \lambda f(x) + (1 - \lambda)f(x) = f(x).$$

Hence, f is quasi-concave.

(c) If f is monotonic, its higher-value set $f^{-1}[[t, \infty)]$ and lower-value set $f^{-1}[(-\infty, t]]$ are half-lines, which are convex. Hence, f is quasi-concave and quasi-convex.

A.4. Proofs of Theorems

Proof of Theorem 3.2

We prove the third property only. Suppose that f is concave. Then, for any $x, y \in X$ and $\lambda \in [0, 1]$, we have

$$f[\lambda x + (1 - \lambda)y] \geq \lambda f(x) + (1 - \lambda)f(y).$$

Define

$$g(\lambda) \equiv f[\lambda x + (1 - \lambda)y] - \lambda[f(x) - f(y)].$$

We have $g(\lambda) \geq f(y)$ for $\lambda \in [0, 1]$, and $g(0) = f(y)$ and $g(1) = f(y)$. Thus, there must exist a maximum point $\lambda^* \in (0, 1)$ of $g(\lambda)$. Then,

$$g'(\lambda^*) = 0 \quad \text{and} \quad g''(\lambda^*) \leq 0,$$

implying

$$g''(\lambda^*) = (x - y)' f''[\lambda^* x + (1 - \lambda^*)y](x - y) \leq 0.$$

Let $y = x + \varepsilon h$, where $\varepsilon > 0$ and $h \in \mathbb{R}^n$. Then,

$$h' f''[x + (1 - \lambda_\varepsilon^*)\varepsilon h]h \leq 0.$$

As $\varepsilon \to 0$, we have

$$h' f''(x)h \leq 0, \quad \forall h \in \mathbb{R}^n.$$

That is, $f''(x) \leq 0$ for any $x \in X$.

Proof of Theorem 3.3

We prove Part (b) only. For an arbitrary point $x^* \in X$, consider problem

$$\begin{aligned} &\max_{x \in X} \quad f(x) \\ &\text{s.t.} \quad f'(x^*) \cdot (x - x^*) \leq 0. \end{aligned} \qquad (3.18)$$

Let $L(x) = f(x) + \lambda f'(x^*) \cdot (x - x^*)$. The optimization conditions are

FOC: $\quad 0 = f'(x^*) + \lambda f'(x^*),$

SOSC: $\quad x' f''(x^*)x < 0$ for any $x \neq 0$ satisfying $f'(x^*) \cdot x = 0.$

By Theorem 3.9, since $(x, \lambda) = (x^*, -1)$ satisfies the FOC and SOSC, x^* is a strict local maximum. This means that:

For x close to x^*, $x \neq x^*$, we have $f'(x^*)(x - x^*) \leq 0$
$$\Rightarrow f(x) < f(x^*).$$

This is equivalent to:

For x close to x^*, $x \neq x^*$, we have $f(x) \geq f(x^*)$
$$\Rightarrow f'(x^*)(x - x^*) > 0. \qquad (3.19)$$

Now, for any $x, y \in X, x \neq y$, suppose $f(y) \geq f(x)$. Let

$$g(t) \equiv f[ty + (1 - t)x], \quad \text{for } t \in [0, 1].$$

Consider problem

$$\min_{t \in [0,1]} g(t). \qquad (3.20)$$

It must have a solution, which we denote by t^*. Since $f(y) \geq f(x)$, we can assume $t^* \in [0, 1)$. If $t^* > 0$, it must satisfy the FOC:

$$f'[t^*y + (1 - t^*)x] \cdot (y - x) = 0. \qquad (3.21)$$

However, by (3.19), when t is close to t^*, we have

$$f'[t^*y + (1 - t^*)x] \cdot (t - t^*)(y - x) > 0,$$

which contradicts (3.21). Hence, we must have $t^* = 0$. Hence,

$$f[ty + (1 - t)x] \geq f(x), \quad \text{for } t \in [0, 1].$$

Further, the equality cannot hold for any interior $t_0 \in (0, 1)$. Such a t_0 would be an interior solution of (3.20), which we have shown to be impossible. Hence,

$$f[ty + (1 - t)x] > f(x), \quad \text{for } t \in [0, 1].$$

In other words, f is strictly quasi-concave.

Proof of Theorem 3.6

We prove (d) only. Suppose that x^* is a local maximum. If it is not the unique global maximum, there is an $\bar{x}$ such that $f(\bar{x}) \geq f(x^*)$. Then, by strictly quasi-concavity, we have

$$f[\lambda \bar{x} + (1 - \lambda)x^*] > f(x^*), \quad \text{for } \lambda \in (0, 1).$$

When λ is close to zero, we have a contradiction of the fact that x^* is a local maximum. Hence, x^* must be the unique global maximum.

Proof of Theorem 3.8

We prove Part (a) first. Denote $\hat{x} \equiv (x_{m+1}, \ldots, x_n)$. Since $G'(x^*)$ has full rank, for simplicity, assume the first m columns of $G'(x^*)$ are linearly independent (corresponding to variables $x_1, \ldots, x_m$). Then, by the implicit function theorem, there exist C^1 functions $h_j(\hat{x})$ in a neighborhood $N_r(x^*)$ of x^* such that

$$x_j = h_j(x_{m+1}, \ldots, x_n), \quad \text{for } j = 1, \ldots, m.$$

Then

$$f(x) = f[h_1(\hat{x}), \ldots, h_m(\hat{x}), \hat{x}].$$

and problem (3.4) becomes the following unconstrained maximization problem:

$$\max_{\hat{x} \in \mathbb{R}^{n-m}} f[h_1(\hat{x}), \ldots, h_m(\hat{x}), \hat{x}].$$

The FOC for $\hat{x}^*$ implies that, at x^*, we have

$$f_{x_1} h_{1x_k} + \cdots + f_{x_m} h_{mx_k} + f_{x_k} = 0, \quad \text{for } k = m+1, \ldots, n,$$

which can be written as

$$\begin{pmatrix} h_{1x_{m+1}} & \cdots & h_{mx_{m+1}} \\ \vdots & & \vdots \\ h_{1x_n} & \cdots & h_{mx_n} \end{pmatrix} \begin{pmatrix} f_{x_1} \\ \vdots \\ f_{x_m} \end{pmatrix} = \begin{pmatrix} f_{x_{m+1}} \\ \vdots \\ f_{x_n} \end{pmatrix}. \tag{3.22}$$

The constraints in (3.4) also imply

$$g_j[h_1(\hat{x}), \ldots, h_m(\hat{x}), \hat{x}] = 0, \quad \text{for } j = 1, \ldots, m. \tag{3.23}$$

Taking derivative of these equations w.r.t. $\hat{x}$ yields

$$g_{jx_1} h_{1x_k} + \cdots + g_{jx_m} h_{mx_k} + g_{jx_k} = 0, \quad \text{for } k = m+1, \ldots, n,$$
$$j = 1, \ldots, m,$$

which can be written as

$$\begin{pmatrix} h_{1x_{m+1}} & \cdots & h_{mx_{m+1}} \\ \vdots & & \vdots \\ h_{1x_n} & \cdots & h_{mx_n} \end{pmatrix} \begin{pmatrix} g_{jx_1} \\ \vdots \\ g_{jx_m} \end{pmatrix} = \begin{pmatrix} g_{jx_{m+1}} \\ \vdots \\ g_{jx_n} \end{pmatrix}, \quad \text{for } j = 1, \ldots, m.$$
$$\tag{3.24}$$

Since the first m columns of $G'(x^*)$ are linearly independent, there must exist constants $\lambda_1, \ldots, \lambda_m$ such that

$$\begin{pmatrix} f_{x_1} \\ \vdots \\ f_{x_m} \end{pmatrix}_{x=x^*} = \lambda_1 \begin{pmatrix} g_{1x_1} \\ \vdots \\ g_{1x_m} \end{pmatrix}_{x=x^*} + \cdots + \lambda_m \begin{pmatrix} g_{mx_1} \\ \vdots \\ g_{mx_m} \end{pmatrix}_{x=x^*}. \quad (3.25)$$

By (3.22) and (3.24), this implies

$$\begin{pmatrix} f_{x_{m+1}} \\ \vdots \\ f_{x_n} \end{pmatrix}_{x=x^*} = \lambda_1 \begin{pmatrix} g_{1x_{m+1}} \\ \vdots \\ g_{1x_n} \end{pmatrix}_{x=x^*} + \cdots + \lambda_m \begin{pmatrix} g_{mx_{m+1}} \\ \vdots \\ g_{mx_n} \end{pmatrix}_{x=x^*}. $$
$$(3.26)$$

Hence, by (3.25) and (3.26), we have

$$\begin{pmatrix} f_{x_1} \\ \vdots \\ f_{x_n} \end{pmatrix}_{x=x^*} = \lambda_1 \begin{pmatrix} g_{1x_1} \\ \vdots \\ g_{1x_n} \end{pmatrix}_{x=x^*} + \cdots + \lambda_m \begin{pmatrix} g_{mx_1} \\ \vdots \\ g_{mx_n} \end{pmatrix}_{x=x^*}. $$

That is,

$$f'(x^*) - \sum_{j=1}^{m} \lambda_j g_j'(x^*) = 0,$$

which is the FOC in Theorem 3.8.

We now prove the necessity of the SONC.[16] Let $L(x) \equiv L(x, \lambda^*)$. By Taylor expansion, we have

$$L(x) = L(x^*) + L'(x^*) \cdot (x - x^*) + \frac{1}{2}(x - x^*)^T L''(\xi)(x - x^*),$$
$$G(x) = G(x^*) + G'(\eta) \cdot (x - x^*),$$

---

[16] This proof is new and cannot be found in existing books.

where $\xi, \eta \in (x, x^*)$. For $x = [h_1(\hat{x}), \ldots, h_m(\hat{x}), \hat{x}]$, by the FOC and $G(x) = G(x^*) = 0$, the above two equations imply

$$f(x) = f(x^*) + \frac{1}{2}(x - x^*)^T L''(\xi)(x - x^*),$$
$$G'(\eta) \cdot (x - x^*) = 0.$$

Since $f(x) \leq f(x^*)$, we have

$$(x - x^*)^T L''(\xi)(x - x^*) \leq 0 \quad \text{and} \quad G'(\eta) \cdot (x - x^*) = 0. \quad (3.27)$$

Here, $\hat{x}$ is completely free. Let $\hat{x} = \hat{x}^* + \varepsilon \hat{z}$, where $\hat{z} \in \mathbb{R}^{n-m}$ is an arbitrary vector and $\varepsilon > 0$. Denote the corresponding ξ and η by ξ_ε and η_ε, respectively, and denote

$$x_\varepsilon = [h_1(\hat{x}^* + \varepsilon \hat{z}), \ldots, h_m(\hat{x}^* + \varepsilon \hat{z}), \hat{x}^* + \varepsilon \hat{z}].$$

By the uniqueness of the solution of $G(x) = 0$, when $\varepsilon = 0$, we have $x_0 = x^*$. Then, (3.27) becomes

$$(x_\varepsilon - x^*)^T L''(\xi_\varepsilon)(x_\varepsilon - x^*) \leq 0, \quad (3.28)$$
$$G'(\eta_\varepsilon) \cdot (x_\varepsilon - x^*) = 0. \quad (3.29)$$

Equation (3.29) can be expanded

$$G'(\eta_\varepsilon) \cdot \begin{pmatrix} \dfrac{h_1(\hat{x}^* + \varepsilon \hat{z}) - h_1(\hat{x}^*)}{\varepsilon} \\ \vdots \\ \dfrac{h_m(\hat{x}^* + \varepsilon \hat{z}) - h_m(\hat{x}^*)}{\varepsilon} \\ \hat{z} \end{pmatrix} = 0.$$

As $\varepsilon \to 0$, the above becomes

$$G'(x^*) \cdot \begin{pmatrix} h_1'(\hat{x}^*) \cdot \hat{z} \\ \vdots \\ h_m'(\hat{x}^*) \cdot \hat{z} \\ \hat{z} \end{pmatrix} = 0. \quad (3.30)$$

Let $H(\hat{x}) \equiv (h_1(\hat{x}), \ldots, h_m(\hat{x}))$. Then, (3.30) becomes

$$G'(x^*)_{m \times n} \begin{pmatrix} H'(\hat{x}^*) \\ I_{n-m} \end{pmatrix}_{n \times m} \hat{z} = 0. \tag{3.31}$$

Similarly, (3.28) becomes

$$\left[\begin{pmatrix} H'(\hat{x}^*) \\ I_{n-m} \end{pmatrix} \hat{z} \right]^T L''(x^*) \begin{pmatrix} H'(\hat{x}^*) \\ I_{n-m} \end{pmatrix} \hat{z} \leq 0. \tag{3.32}$$

For any vector $z \in \mathbb{R}^n$ satisfying $G'(x^*)z = 0$ or

$$\left(\frac{\partial G(x^*)}{\partial(x_1, \ldots, x_m)}, \frac{\partial G(x^*)}{\partial(x_{m+1}, \ldots, x_n)} \right) \begin{pmatrix} z_1 \\ \vdots \\ z_m \\ \hat{z} \end{pmatrix} = 0,$$

since the first m columns of $G'(x^*)$ are linearly independent, the above equation becomes

$$\begin{pmatrix} z_1 \\ \vdots \\ z_m \end{pmatrix} = -\left[\frac{\partial G(x^*)}{\partial(x_1, \ldots, x_m)} \right]^{-1} \frac{\partial G(x^*)}{\partial(x_{m+1}, \ldots, x_n)} \hat{z}. \tag{3.33}$$

By definition of $H(x)$, we have

$$G[h_1(\hat{x}), \ldots, h_m(\hat{x}), \hat{x}] = 0 \quad \text{or} \quad G[H(\hat{x}), \hat{x}] = 0,$$
$$\text{for any } \hat{x} \in \mathbb{R}^{n-m}.$$

Then, taking a derivative w.r.t. $\hat{x}$ implies

$$\frac{\partial G(x)}{\partial(x_1, \ldots, x_m)} H'(\hat{x}) + \frac{\partial G(x)}{\partial \hat{x}} = 0.$$

Hence, expression (3.33) becomes

$$\begin{pmatrix} z_1 \\ \vdots \\ z_m \end{pmatrix} = H'(\hat{x}^*)\hat{z}.$$

That is, for any vector $z \in \mathbb{R}^n$ satisfying $G'(x^*)z = 0$, we must have

$$z = \begin{pmatrix} H'(\hat{x}^*) \\ I_{n-m} \end{pmatrix} \hat{z},$$

where $\hat{z} = (z_{m+1}, \dots, z_n)$ can be arbitrary. Therefore, (3.31) and (3.32) mean that, for any $z \in \mathbb{R}^n$ satisfying $G'(x^*)z = 0$, we have $z^T L''(x^*)z \le 0$, which is the SONC.

We now prove part (b). Let $G(x) \equiv (g_1(x), \dots, g_m(x))$. Suppose that (x^*, λ^*) satisfy

$$G(x^*) = 0, \tag{3.34}$$

$$f'(x^*) + \lambda^* \cdot G'(x^*) = 0, \tag{3.35}$$

$$h^T L_x''(x^*, \lambda)h < 0, \quad \text{for } h \ne 0 \text{ satisfying } G'(x^*)h = 0. \tag{3.36}$$

Let $L(x) \equiv f(x) + \lambda^* \cdot G(x)$. By Taylor expansion, for any $h \in \mathbb{R}^n$, there exists $\theta \in (0,1)$ such that

$$L(x^* + h) = L(x^*) + L'(x^*) \cdot h + \frac{1}{2}h'L''(x^* + \theta h)h,$$

which can be written as

$$f(x^* + h) - f(x^*) = \lambda^* \cdot G(x^* + h) + \frac{1}{2}h'L''(x^* + \theta h)h. \tag{3.37}$$

By (3.37), to show that $f(x^*+h) - f(x^*) < 0$ for $h \in N_\varepsilon(0)$ satisfying $G(x^* + h) = 0$, we only need to show that $h'L''(x^* + \theta h)h < 0$ for such a h. To utilize condition (3.5), we use the mean-value theorem to yield

$$g_i(x^* + h) = g_i(x^* + h) - g_i(x^*) = g_i'(x^* + \theta_i h)h, \tag{3.38}$$

for some $\theta_i \in (0,1), i = 1, \ldots, m$. Define the bordered Hessian matrix:

$$B(x^0, x^1, \ldots, x^m)$$

$$\equiv \begin{pmatrix} & & g_{1x_1}(x^1) & \cdots & g_{1x_n}(x^1) \\ & 0 & \vdots & & \vdots \\ & & g_{mx_1}(x^m) & \cdots & g_{mx_n}(x^m) \\ g_{1x_1}(x^1) & \cdots & g_{mx_1}(x^m) & L_{x_1x_1}(x^0) & \cdots & L_{x_1x_n}(x^0) \\ \vdots & & \vdots & \vdots & & \vdots \\ g_{1x_n}(x^1) & \cdots & g_{mx_n}(x^m) & L_{x_nx_1}(x^0) & \cdots & L_{x_nx_n}(x^0) \end{pmatrix},$$

$$(n+m) \times (n+m)$$

and denote its kth principal minor by $b_k(x^0, x^1, \ldots, x^m)$. By Theorem 3.9, condition (3.5) implies

$$(-1)^{m+k} b_k(x^*, x^*, \ldots, x^m) > 0, \quad \forall\, k \geq 2m+1.$$

By the continuity of $b_k(x^0, x^1, \ldots, x^m)$, there exists $\varepsilon > 0$ such that, when $h^i \in N_\varepsilon(0)$ for $i = 0, 1, \ldots, m$, we have

$$(-1)^{m+k} b_k(x^* + h^0, x^* + h^1, \ldots, x^* + h^m) > 0, \quad \forall\, k \geq 2m+1.$$

Hence, for any $h \in N_\varepsilon(0)$, we have

$$(-1)^{m+k} b_k(x^* + \theta h, x^* + \theta_1 h, \ldots, x^* + \theta_m h) > 0, \quad \forall\, k \geq 2m+1.$$

By Theorem 3.9, this implies

$$x^T L_x''(x^* + \theta h) x < 0, \quad \text{for } x \neq 0 \text{ satisfying } g_i'(x^* + \theta_i h) \cdot x = 0, \quad \forall\, i.$$

In particular, for $h \in N_\varepsilon(0)$, we have

$$h^T L_x''(x^* + \theta h) h < 0, \quad \text{for } h \neq 0 \text{ satisfying } g_i'(x^* + \theta_i h) \cdot h = 0, \quad \forall\, i. \tag{3.39}$$

Therefore, for $h \in N_\varepsilon(0)$ satisfying $G(x^* + h) = 0$, by (3.38) and (3.39), we have

$$h^T L_x''(x^* + \theta h) h < 0,$$

implying

$$f(x^* + h) - f(x^*) < 0.$$

That is, x^* is a local maximum.

We now prove part (c). Since $\lambda^* \cdot G(x)$ is quasi-concave, for any $h \in \mathbb{R}^n$ satisfying $\sum_i \lambda_i g_i'(x^*) \, h = 0$, by Lemma 3.4, we have $h^T [\sum_i \lambda_i^* g_i''(x^*)] h \leq 0$. If so, by (3.6), for any h satisfying $G'(x^*)h = 0$, we have $\sum_i \lambda_i g_i'(x^*)h = 0$ and hence

$$h^T L_x''(x^*, \lambda^*)h = h^T f''(x^*)h + h^T \left[\sum_i \lambda_i^* g_i''(x^*) \right] h \leq h^T f''(x^*)h < 0.$$

Then, by Theorem 3.8 (b), x^* is a local maximum.

Proof of Theorem 3.10

Part (a): For simplicity, assume $I(x^*) = \{1, 2, \ldots, \bar{m}\}$ for some $\bar{m} \leq m$. Consider the following problem:

$$\begin{aligned} \max_{x \in \mathbb{R}^n, \, y \in \mathbb{R}^m} \quad & f(x) \\ \text{s.t.} \quad & g_i(x) = y_i^2, \quad i = 1, \ldots, m, \qquad (3.40) \\ & H(x) = 0. \end{aligned}$$

Then, for $y^* \equiv (0, \sqrt{g_{\bar{m}+1}(x^*)}, \ldots, \sqrt{g_m(x^*)}) \in \mathbb{R}^m, (x^*, y^*) \in \mathbb{R}^{n+m}$ is a strict local maximum of (3.40). By Theorem 3.8(a), there exist $\lambda \in \mathbb{R}^m, \mu \in \mathbb{R}^k$, and

$$L(x, y, \lambda, \mu) \equiv f(x) + \sum_{i=1}^m \lambda_i [g_i(x) - y_i^2] + \sum_{j=1}^k \mu_j h_j(x)$$

such that

$$\frac{\partial L}{\partial x} = f'(x^*) + \sum_{i=1}^m \lambda_i, g_i'(x^*) + \sum_{j=1}^k \mu_j, h_j'(x^*) = 0,$$

$$\frac{\partial L}{\partial y_i} = -2\lambda_i \sqrt{g_i(x^*)} = 0, \quad \text{for } i = \bar{m} + 1, \ldots, n.$$

We have the FOC and $\lambda_i = 0$ for $i = \bar{m} + 1, \ldots, n$. Hence, the KT condition is satisfied. Further, we have

$$\frac{\partial}{\partial(x,y)} \begin{pmatrix} g_1(x) - y_1^2 \\ \vdots \\ g_m(x) - y_m^2 \\ H(x) \end{pmatrix}_{(x^*,y^*)}$$

$$= \begin{pmatrix} g_{1x_1} & \cdots & g_{1x_n} & -2y_1 & \cdots & 0 \\ \vdots & & \vdots & \vdots & & \vdots \\ g_{mx_1} & \cdots & g_{mx_n} & 0 & \cdots & -2y_m \\ h_{1x_1} & \cdots & h_{1x_n} & 0 & \cdots & 0 \\ \vdots & & \vdots & \vdots & & \vdots \\ h_{kx_1} & \cdots & h_{kx_n} & 0 & \cdots & 0 \end{pmatrix}_{(x^*,y^*)}.$$

Since $y_1^* = \cdots = y_m^* = 0$, a vector of the form $z_{n+i} = (0, \ldots, 0, 1, 0, \ldots, 0) \in \mathbb{R}^{n+m}$ satisfies the condition:

$$\frac{\partial}{\partial(x,y)} \begin{pmatrix} g_1(x) - y_1^2 \\ \vdots \\ g_m(x) - y_m^2 \\ H(x) \end{pmatrix}_{(x^*,y^*)} z_i = 0,$$

where 1 is in the $(n + i)$th column of z_{n+i} and $i = 1, \ldots, \bar{m}$. By the SONC in Theorem 3.8(a), we have

$$z_i^T L''_{(x,y)}(x^*, y^*) z_i = -2\lambda_i \leq 0,$$

implying $\lambda_i \geq 0$ for $i = 1, \ldots, \bar{m}$.

Part (b): The idea is to construct a problem with equality constraints and use the sufficiency conditions in Theorem 3.8 to show that x^* is a solution or part of a solution of this problem and a solution of this problem must mean a solution of (3.10). Consider the following problem:

$$\begin{aligned} \max_{x \in \mathbb{R}^n, y \in \mathbb{R}^{\bar{m}}} \quad & f(x) \\ \text{s.t.} \quad & g_i(x) = y_i^2, \quad i = 1, \ldots, \bar{m}, \\ & H(x) = 0. \end{aligned} \qquad (3.41)$$

Let us show that $(x^*, 0) \in \mathbb{R}^{n+\bar{m}}$ is a unique local maximum of (3.41). Define a Lagrange function:

$$L(x, y) \equiv f(x) + \sum_{i=1}^{\bar{m}} \lambda_i^*[g_i(x) - y_i^2] + \sum_{j=1}^{k} \mu_j^* h_j(x).$$

By (3.9), the FOC and the constraints are satisfied by $(x^*, 0)$. The bordered Hession matrix for the SOSC is

$$B(x, y) \equiv \begin{pmatrix}
& & & 0 & & & \\
g_{1x_1}(x) & \cdots & g_{\bar{m}x_1}(x) & h_{1x_1}(x) & \cdots & h_{kx_1}(x) \\
\vdots & & \vdots & \vdots & & \vdots \\
g_{1x_n}(x) & \cdots & g_{\bar{m}x_n}(x) & h_{1x_n}(x) & \cdots & h_{kx_n}(x) \\
-2y_1 & \cdots & 0 & 0 & \cdots & 0 \\
\vdots & & \vdots & \vdots & & \vdots \\
0 & \cdots & -2y_{\bar{m}} & 0 & \cdots & 0 \\
\end{pmatrix}$$

$$\begin{pmatrix}
g_{1x_1}(x) & \cdots & g_{1x_n}(x) & -2y_1 & \cdots & 0 \\
\vdots & & \vdots & \vdots & & \vdots \\
g_{\bar{m}x_1}(x) & \cdots & g_{\bar{m}x_n}(x) & 0 & \cdots & -2y_{\bar{m}} \\
h_{1x_1}(x) & \cdots & h_{1x_n}(x) & 0 & \cdots & 0 \\
\vdots & & \vdots & \vdots & & \vdots \\
h_{kx_1}(x) & \cdots & h_{kx_n}(x) & 0 & \cdots & 0 \\
L_{x_1x_1}(x, y) & \cdots & L_{x_1x_n}(x, y) & 0 & \cdots & 0 \\
\vdots & & \vdots & \vdots & & \vdots \\
L_{x_nx_1}(x, y) & \cdots & L_{x_nx_n}(x, y) & 0 & \cdots & 0 \\
0 & \cdots & 0 & -2\lambda_1^* & \cdots & 0 \\
\vdots & & \vdots & \vdots & & \vdots \\
0 & \cdots & 0 & 0 & \cdots & -2\lambda_{\bar{m}}^* \\
\end{pmatrix}$$

If we take out the last $\bar{m}$ columns and the last $\bar{m}$ rows, $B(x^*, 0)$ is the same as the bordered Hession matrix $\bar{B}(x^*)$ for problem (3.10). Let b_k be the kth principal minor of $B(x^*, 0)$ and $\bar{b}_k$ be the kth principal minor of $\bar{B}(x^*)$. We have

$$(-1)^{\bar{m}+i} b_i = (-1)^{\bar{m}+i} \bar{b}_i > 0,$$
$$\text{for } i = 2(\bar{m} + k) + 1, \dots, \bar{m} + n + k,$$
$$(-1)^{2\bar{m}+n+k+1} b_{\bar{m}+n+k+1} = 2(-1)^{2\bar{m}+n+k} \bar{b}_{\bar{m}+n+k} \lambda_1^* > 0,$$
$$(-1)^{2\bar{m}+n+k+2} b_{\bar{m}+n+k+2} = 2^2 (-1)^{2\bar{m}+n+k} \bar{b}_{\bar{m}+n+k} \lambda_1^* \lambda_2^* > 0,$$
$$\vdots$$
$$(-1)^{2\bar{m}+n+k+\bar{m}} b_{\bar{m}+n+k+\bar{m}} = 2^{\bar{m}} (-1)^{2\bar{m}+n+k} \bar{b}_{\bar{m}+n+k} \lambda_1^* \lambda_2^* \cdots \lambda_{\bar{m}}^* > 0.$$
$$\tag{3.42}$$

Then, by Theorem 3.9, the SOSC for $(x^*, 0)$ is satisfied. Hence, by Theorem 3.8(b), $(x^*, 0)$ is a unique local maximum of (3.41). Then, by the continuity[17] of $g_i(\cdot)$ for $i = 1, \dots, \bar{m}$, x^* is a local maximum of the following problem:

$$\begin{aligned} \max_{x \in \mathbb{R}^n} \quad & f(x) \\ \text{s.t.} \quad & g_i(x) \geq 0, \quad i = 1, \dots, \bar{m}; \\ & H(x) = 0. \end{aligned}$$

This implies that x^* must be a local maximum of the following more restrictive problem:

$$\begin{aligned} \max_{x \in \mathbb{R}^n} \quad & f(x) \\ \text{s.t.} \quad & g_i(x) \geq 0, \quad i = 1, \dots, m; \\ & H(x) = 0. \end{aligned}$$

This completes the proof.

---

[17]In a neighborhood of x^*, a vector y satisfying $g_i(x) = y_i^2$ must be in a neighborhood of 0.

Proof of Theorem 3.11

Let $x \in \mathbb{R}^n$ satisfy $G(x) \geq 0$ and $H(x) = 0$. By the KT condition, we have

$$\lambda_i^* g_i(x) \geq \lambda_i^* g_i(x^*), \quad \text{for all } i = 1, \ldots, m;$$
$$\mu_j^* h_j(x) = \mu_j^* h_j(x^*), \quad \text{for all } j = 1, \ldots, k.$$

Since $\lambda_i^* g_i(\cdot)$ and $\mu_j^* h_j(\cdot)$ are quasi-concave, by (3.12),

$$\lambda_i^* g_i'(x^*) \cdot (x - x^*) \geq 0,$$
$$\mu_j^* h_j'(x^*) \cdot (x - x^*) \geq 0.$$

Then by the FOC,

$$f'(x^*) \cdot (x - x^*) = -\sum_{i=1}^{m} \lambda_i^* g_i'(x^*) \cdot (x - x^*) - \sum_{j=1}^{k} \mu_j^* h_j'(x^*) \leq 0.$$

Since $f'(x^*) \neq 0$, by (3.17), we have

$$f(x) \leq f(x^*), \quad \text{for all } x.$$

That is, x^* is a global maximum.

Proof of Theorem 3.12

We have $F(a) = f[x(a), a]$. Taking a derivative of $F(a)$ w.r.t. a gives

$$F'(a) = f_x[x(a), a] x'(a) + f_a[x(a), a].$$

By the FOC, $f_x[x(a), a] = 0$, we have $F'(a) = f_a[x(a), a]$.

Proof of Theorem 3.13[18]

Since $F(a) = f[x^*(a), a]$, we have

$$\frac{\partial F(a)}{\partial a} = \frac{\partial f[x^*(a), a]}{\partial x} \frac{\partial x^*(a)}{\partial a} + \frac{\partial f[x^*(a), a]}{\partial a}. \qquad (3.43)$$

---

[18]Sydsæter *et al.* (2005) do not provide a proof.

By the FOC, $L'_x[x^*(a), \lambda^*(a), \mu^*(a), a] = 0$, we have

$$f'_x[x^*(a), a] = -\lambda^*(a)G'_x[x^*(a), a] - \mu^*(a)H'_x[x^*(a), a].$$

Also,

$$L'_a(x, \lambda, \mu, a) = f'_a(x, a) + \lambda G'_a(x, a) + \mu H'_a(x, a).$$

Substituting these two into (3.43) yields

$$\frac{\partial F(a)}{\partial a} = \{-\lambda^*(a)G'_x[x^*(a), a] - \mu^*(a)H'_x[x^*(a), a]\}x^{*'}(a)$$

$$+ L'_a[x^*(a), \lambda^*(a), \mu^*(a), a] - \lambda^*(a)G'_a[x^*(a), a]$$

$$- \mu^*(a)H'_a[x^*(a), a]$$

$$= L'_a[x^*(a), \lambda^*(a), \mu^*(a), a] - \lambda^*(a)\{G'_x[x^*(a), a]x^{*'}(a)$$

$$+ G'_a[x^*(a), a]\} - \mu^*(a)\{H'_x[x^*(a), a]x^{*'}(a) + H'_a[x^*(a), a]\}.$$

Since $H[x^*(a), a] = 0$ for all a, we have

$$H'_x[x^*(a), a]x^{*'}(a) + H'_a[x^*(a), a] = 0. \tag{3.44}$$

Since $\lambda^*(a) \cdot G[x^*(a), a] = 0$ for all a, we have

$$\lambda^{*'}(a)G[x^*(a), a] + \lambda^*(a)\{G'_x[x^*(a), a]x^{*'}(a) + G'_a[x^*(a), a]\} = 0. \tag{3.45}$$

We either have $g_i[x^*(a), a] = 0$ or $g_i[x^*(a), a] > 0$ for any i. If $g_i[x^*(a), a] > 0$, $\lambda^*(a)$ is zero in a neighborhood of this a, implying $\lambda^{*'}(a) = 0$. Hence, we always have

$$\lambda^{*'}(a)G[x^*(a), a] = 0.$$

Hence, by (3.44) and (3.45), we have

$$\frac{\partial F(a)}{\partial a} = L'_a[x^*(a), \lambda^*(a), \mu^*(a), a].$$

This completes the proof.

Chapter 4

Dynamic Optimization

Dynamic optimization is a special case of general optimization in the last chapter. However, since the emphasis of dynamic optimization is on some special features of a dynamic problem, dynamic optimization is treated as a separate problem and some special techniques are used to solve a dynamic problem.

There are two important features in a dynamic model: presence of uncertainty and continuity of time. They lead to four types of models, as shown in Table 4.1:

Table 4.1. Four Types of Dynamic Models

	Discrete time	Continuous time
Deterministic	Type 1 $\sqrt{}$	Type 3 $\sqrt{}$
Stochastic	Type 2 $\sqrt{}$	Type 4 $\times$

We cover the first three types. Type 1 is actually included as a special case of Type 2. We will not discuss Type 4, since it is technically difficult and is in fact not very useful for non-finance majors.

Each dynamic problem can have two alternative setups: with or without state variables.

There are also two forms of solutions to the same dynamic problem: the open-loop solution and the closed-loop solution. The latter is also called a feedback solution. Typically, for a problem without state variables, we solve for its open-loop solution; for a problem with state variables, we solve for its closed-loop solution.

There are several well-known approaches to solving dynamic problems: backward induction, the Bellman equation, the Lagrangian method, and the Hamiltonian method. All these methods must satisfy the principle of dynamic optimization. We can also use phase diagrams to illustrate the short-run dynamics of a solution.

1. Discrete-Time Stochastic Models

1.1. *An Example*

We start with an example to motivate the standard approaches in dynamic optimization.

Dynamic Optimization under Certainty

Consider a two-period consumption problem with a single good and a fixed lifetime income I. The consumer's problem is

$$\max_{c_0, c_1} u(c_0) + \beta u(c_1)$$
$$\text{s.t. } c_0 + \frac{1}{R} c_1 \leq I, \tag{4.1}$$

where $R = 1 + r$ is the gross interest rate and c_i is consumption at time i. Using the Lagrange method (the Kuhn–Tucker theorem), the Lagrange function is

$$L = u(c_0) + \beta u(c_1) + \lambda \left(I - c_0 - \frac{1}{R} c_1 \right).$$

The FOCs are

$$u'(c_0) = \lambda, \quad \beta u'(c_1) = \frac{\lambda}{R},$$

which imply the so-called Euler equation:

$$u'(c_0) = \beta R u'(c_1). \tag{4.2}$$

The optimal solution $(c_0^* c_1^*)$ of (4.1) is determined by this Euler equation and the binding constraint in (4.1).

We can also solve it by backward induction. Given c_0, the optimization problem at time $t = 1$ is

$$V(c_0) = \max_{c_1} u(c_1)$$
$$\text{s.t. } c_1 \leq R(I - c_0), \qquad (4.3)$$
$$\text{given } c_0.$$

We obviously have $V(c_0) = u[R(I - c_0)]$. Then, at time $t = 0$, the optimization problem is

$$V_0 = \max_{c_0 \geq 0} u(c_0) + \beta V(c_0).$$

The FOC is

$$u'(c_0) + \beta V'(c_0) = 0,$$

which is the same as the Euler equation (4.2). We also have the binding constraint in (4.3), which is the same as the binding constraint in (4.1). Hence, backward induction implies the same two conditions for the optimal solution as those from the Lagrange method.

In a special case when $u(c) = \frac{1}{1-\gamma}c^{1-\gamma}$, we find

$$c_0^* = \frac{I}{1 + \beta^{\frac{1}{\gamma}} R^{\frac{1}{\gamma}-1}}, \quad c_1^* = \frac{\beta^{\frac{1}{\gamma}} R^{\frac{1}{\gamma}}}{1 + \beta^{\frac{1}{\gamma}} R^{\frac{1}{\gamma}-1}} I.$$

Dynamic Optimization under Uncertainty

If the interest rate $\tilde{r}$ is random at $t = 0$, then the consumer's problem is

$$\max_{c_0, \tilde{c}_1} \quad u(c_0) + \beta E[u(\tilde{c}_1)]$$
$$\text{s.t.} \quad c_0 + \frac{1}{\tilde{R}}\tilde{c}_1 \leq I, \qquad (4.4)$$

where $\tilde{R} \equiv 1 + \tilde{r}$ is random and E is the expectation operator. Using the Lagrange method, the Lagrange function is

$$L = u(c_0) + \beta E[u(\tilde{c}_1)] + E\left[\tilde{\lambda}\left(I - c_0 - \frac{1}{\tilde{R}}\tilde{c}_1\right)\right], \qquad (4.5)$$

where $\tilde{\lambda}$ is the Lagrange multiplier and is random. We will explain why the Lagrange function is defined this way later. The FOCs are

$$u'(c_0) = E(\tilde{\lambda}), \quad \beta u'(\tilde{c}_1) = \frac{\tilde{\lambda}}{\tilde{R}}.$$

We have used the Hamilton method for the second FOC, which is obtained by maximizing the term inside the expectation operator for each possible event. The Hamilton method will also be explained later. These two conditions imply the Euler equation:

$$u'(c_0) = \beta E[\tilde{R}u'(\tilde{c}_1)]. \tag{4.6}$$

The optimal solution (c_0^*, c_1^*) of (4.4) is determined by this Euler equation and the binding constraint in (4.4).

We can also solve it by backward induction. Given c_0 the optimization problem at time $t = 1$ is

$$\begin{aligned} V(c_0) &= \max_{c_1} u(c_1) \\ \text{s.t. } c_1 &\leq \tilde{R}(I - c_0), \\ &\text{given } c_0. \end{aligned} \tag{4.7}$$

We obviously have $V(c_0) = u[\tilde{R}(I - c_0)]$. Then, at time $t = 0$, the optimization problem is

$$V_0 = \max_{c_0 \geq 0} u(c_0) + \beta E[V(c_0)].$$

The FOC is

$$u'(c_0) + \beta E[V'(c_0)] = 0,$$

implying

$$u'(c_0) = \beta E[\tilde{R}u'(\tilde{c}_1)],$$

which is the same as the Euler equation (4.6). We also have the binding constraint in (4.7), which is the same as the binding constraint in (4.4). Hence, the two methods imply the same two conditions that determine the optimal solution.

In a special case when $u(c) = \frac{1}{1-\gamma}c^{1-\gamma}$, we find

$$c_0^* = \frac{I}{1 + [\beta E(\tilde{R}^{1-\gamma})]^{\frac{1}{\gamma}}}, \quad c_1^* = \frac{[\beta E(\tilde{R}^{1-\gamma})]^{\frac{1}{\gamma}}}{1 + [\beta E(\tilde{R}^{1-\gamma})]^{\frac{1}{\gamma}}} I\tilde{R}.$$

The Lagrange Function under Uncertainty

We will now explain the Lagrange function in (4.5). A random variable is a function of random outcomes. Hence, we can write $\tilde{R}$ as a function $R(\omega)$ of random outcome ω. Then, problem (4.4) can be written as

$$\max_{c_0, c_1} u(c_0) + \beta E u(\tilde{c}_1)$$
$$\text{s.t. } c_0 + \frac{1}{R(\omega)}c_1(\omega) \leq I, \quad \text{for all } \omega.$$

That is, it is a problem with infinite constraints. For each constraint, there is a corresponding Lagrange multiplier $\mu(\omega)$. Then, the Lagrange function should be

$$L = u(c_0) + \beta E[u(\tilde{c}_1)] + \sum_{\omega} \left[\mu(\omega) \left(I - c_0 - \frac{1}{R(\omega)}c_1(\omega) \right) \right].$$

More appropriately, we should write the above summation over ω as an integral, i.e.,

$$L = u(c_0) + \beta E[u(\tilde{c}_1)] + \int \mu(\omega) \left(I - c_0 - \frac{1}{R(\omega)}c_1(\omega) \right) d\omega.$$

For convenience, we further write the integral as an expected term. Let $f(\omega)$ be the density function of ω and denote $\tilde{f} \equiv f(\omega)$ and $\tilde{\mu} \equiv \mu(\omega)$. Then,

$$L = u(c_0) + \beta E[u(\tilde{c}_1)] + \int \frac{\mu(\omega)}{f(\omega)} \left(I - c_0 - \frac{1}{R(\omega)}c_1(\omega) \right) f(\omega) d\omega$$
$$= u(c_0) + \beta E[u(\tilde{c}_1)] + E\left[\tilde{\lambda} \left(I - c_0 - \frac{1}{R(\omega)}\tilde{c}_1 \right) \right],$$

where $\tilde{\lambda} \equiv \tilde{\mu}/\tilde{f}$. That is, we have the expression in (4.5).

Figure 4.1. A Random Process

1.2. *Markov Process*

What is a Markov process? Given a set of possible outcomes Ω, called the sample space, a set $\mathbb{E}$ of subsets in Ω is the event space. A measurable real-valued function $\xi \colon \Omega \to \mathbb{R}$ is called a random variable, where the measurability means $\{\omega | \xi(\omega) \le t\} \in \mathbb{E}$ for all $t \in \mathbb{R}$.

Suppose that we have a sequence of random variables $\{x_t\}$ depending on time t as shown in Figure 4.1. At time, we know x_0 but we do not know x_1. Suppose that we know the distribution function of x_1 conditional on our knowledge of x_0, i.e.,

$$x_1 \sim F_0(\cdot | x_0),$$

where F_0 is the distribution function of x_1 at time $t = 0$. In general, at t, we know $x_0, \ldots, x_t$ and we also know the distribution function of x_{t+1}, i.e.,

$$x_{t+1} \sim F_t(\cdot | x_t, x_{t-1}, \ldots, x_0).$$

In general, the distribution function is time-dependent. In this case, we say that $\{x_t\}_{t=0}^{\infty}$ is a random process. If the distribution function is time-independent, i.e.,

$$x_{t+1} \sim F(\cdot | x_t, x_{t-1}, \ldots, x_0), \quad \text{for all } t,$$

we say that $\{x_t\}_{t=0}^{\infty}$ is a stationary process. In addition, if the distribution function's dependence on past history has a fixed time length, i.e., there exists an integer n such that[1]

$$x_{t+1} \sim F(\cdot | x_t, \ldots, x_{t-n+1}), \quad \text{for all } t,$$

---

[1]In this case, for $t < n$, we assume $x_1 \sim F(\cdot | x_0)$, $x_2 \sim F(\cdot | x_0, x_1), \ldots, x_n \sim F(\cdot | x_0, \ldots, x_{n-1})$.

we say that $\{x_t\}_{t=0}^{\infty}$ is an nth-order Markov process. For example, a first-order Markov process $\{x_t\}_{t=0}^{\infty}$ is defined by

$$x_{t+1} \sim F(\cdot|x_t), \quad \text{for all } t.$$

First-order Markov processes are the most popular processes in business applications.

1.3. Backward Induction

A popular method of solving a finite-period model is the so-called backward induction. This method is based on the so-called principle of dynamic optimization. This principle is an axiom that applies to all dynamic problems.

Let $x_t \in \mathbb{R}^n, u_t \in \mathbb{R}^k$, $f_t \colon \mathbb{R}^n \times \mathbb{R}^k \to \mathbb{R}$, $g_t \colon \mathbb{R}^n \times \mathbb{R}^k \to \mathbb{R}^n$, and $\varphi_{T+1} \colon \mathbb{R}^n \to \mathbb{R}$. Consider a recursive dynamic problem[2]:

$$
\begin{aligned}
J(x_0) &\equiv \max_{(u_0,\ldots,u_T)} E_0 \left[\sum_{t=0}^{T} f_t(x_t, u_t) + \varphi_{T+1}(x_{T+1}) \right] \\
&\text{s.t. } x_{t+1} = g_t(x_t, u_t, \varepsilon_{t+1}), \quad t = 0, 1, \ldots, T \\
&\text{given } x_0,
\end{aligned}
\tag{4.8}
$$

where $\varepsilon_t \in \mathbb{R}^m$ is a random vector unknown until period t, $\{\varepsilon_t\}$ is a random process, E_t is the mathematical expectation operator conditional on the information set Φ_t containing information available at t. Here, u_t is called the control and x_t is called the state. The following is a general theorem on backward induction.

Theorem 4.1 (Backward Induction). *Let*

$$
\begin{aligned}
\varphi_T(x_T) &\equiv \max_{u_T} E_T[f_T(x_T, u_T) + \varphi_{T+1}(x_{T+1})] \\
&\text{s.t. } x_{T+1} = g_T(x_T, u_T, \varepsilon_{T+1}), \\
&\text{given } x_T,
\end{aligned}
\tag{4.9}
$$

---

[2]The key here is that this recursive system ensures that its solution under the dynamic programming principle can be dependent only on the current state and not on the past history.

$$\varphi_{T-1}(x_{T-1}) \equiv \max_{u_{T-1}} E_{T-1}[f_{T-1}(x_{T-1}, u_{T-1}) + \varphi_T(x_T)]$$

$$\text{s.t. } x_T = g_{T-1}(x_{T-1}, u_{T-1}, \varepsilon_T),$$

$$\text{given } x_{T-1}, \tag{4.10}$$

$$\vdots$$

$$\varphi_0(x_0) \equiv \max_{u_0} E_0[f_0(x_0, u_0) + \varphi_1(x_1)]$$

$$\text{s.t. } x_1 = g_0(x_0, u_0, \varepsilon_1),$$

$$\text{given } x_0. \tag{4.11}$$

Then, a solution of (4.9)–(4.11) *must be a solution of* (4.8) *and* $J(x_0) = \varphi_0(x_0)$. ∎

Example 4.1. Consider a three-period consumer's problem:

$$V \equiv \max_{c_0, \tilde{c}_1, \tilde{c}_2} E_0\{u(c_0) + \beta u(\tilde{c}_1) + \beta^2 u(\tilde{c}_2)\}$$

$$\text{s.t. } c_0 + \frac{1}{\tilde{R}_1}\tilde{c}_1 + \frac{1}{\tilde{R}_2\tilde{R}_1}\tilde{c}_2 \leq I, \tag{4.12}$$

where $\tilde{R}_t \equiv 1 + \tilde{r}_t$ is random at $t-1$ but becomes known at t, and E_t is the expectation operator conditional on information at t. Assume $u'(0) = +\infty$. We now use Backward Induction to solve the problem. There are two approaches to solve this problem by backward induction, depending on whether or not a state variable is introduced.

Approach I: Backward Induction without a State Variable

First, given c_0 and c_1, the problem at $t = 2$ is

$$V_2(c_0, c_1) \equiv \max_{c_2} u(c_2)$$

$$\text{s.t. } c_2 \leq R_2[R_1(I - c_0) - c_1].$$

The solution is

$$c_2 = R_2[R_1(I - c_0) - c_1],$$
$$V_1(c_0, c_1) = u\{R_2[R_1(I - c_0) - c_1]\}.$$

Second, given c_0, the problem at $t = 1$ is

$$V_1(c_0) \equiv \max_{c_1} u(c_1) + \beta E_1[V_2(c_0, c_1)]$$

$$\text{s.t. } c_1 \leq R_1(I - c_0).$$

The Lagrange function is

$$L = u(c_1) + \beta E_1[V_2(c_0, c_1)] + \lambda_1[R_1(I - c_0) - c_1]$$
$$= u(c_1) + \beta E_1[u\{\tilde{R}_2[R_1(I - c_0) - c_1]\}] + \lambda_1[R_1(I - c_0) - c_1].$$
$$(4.13)$$

The FOC is

$$u'(c_1) - \beta E_1[\tilde{R}_2 u'\{\tilde{R}_2[R_1(I - c_0) - c_1]\}] - \lambda_1 = 0. \qquad (4.14)$$

The KT condition is

$$\lambda_1[R_1(I - c_0) - c_1] = 0.$$

If $\lambda_1 \neq 0$, by the KT condition, (4.14) implies $u'(c_1) = \beta E_1[\tilde{R}_2 u'(0)] + \lambda_1$. Since $u'(0) = +\infty$, this implies $c_1 = 0$, which cannot possibly be optimal. Hence, we must have $\lambda_1 = 0$. Then, (4.14) implies

$$u'(c_1) = \beta E_1[\tilde{R}_2 u'(\tilde{c}_2)]. \qquad (4.15)$$

Third, the problem at $t = 0$ is

$$V \equiv \max_{c_0 \in [0,I]} u(c_0) + \beta E_0[V_1(c_0)].$$

The FOC is

$$u'(c_0) + \beta E_0[V_1'(c_0)] = 0. \qquad (4.16)$$

By the Envelope Theorem, from (4.13), we have

$$V_1'(c_0) \equiv -\beta E_1[\tilde{R}_2 R_1 u'\{\tilde{R}_2[R_1(I - c_0) - c_1]\}] = -\beta R_1 E_1[\tilde{R}_2 u'(c_2)].$$

Then, (4.15) and (4.16) imply

$$u'(c_0) = \beta^2 E_0\{\tilde{R}_1 E_1[\tilde{R}_2 u'(c_2)]\} = \beta E_0[\tilde{R}_1 u'(\tilde{c}_1)],$$

where we have used the filtering property of conditional expectations: $E_0 E_1(\tilde{x}) = E_0(\tilde{x})$ for any random variable x.[3] In summary,

---

[3]Formally, let $\tilde{x}$ be a random variable defined in a probability space (P, Ω, F). Then, for any σ-algebras $\mathcal{F}_1$ and $\mathcal{F}_2$, $\mathcal{F}_1 \mathcal{F}_2 \subset \mathcal{F}$, we have $E[E(\tilde{x}|\mathcal{F}_1)|\mathcal{F}_2] = E(\tilde{x}|\mathcal{F}_1 \cap \mathcal{F}_2)$. See Miermont (2006, p. 10).

the optimal solution (c_0^*, c_1^*, c_2^*) is determined by

$$u'(c_t^*) = \beta E_t[\tilde{R}_{t+1} u'(c_{t+1}^*)], \quad \text{for } t = 0, 1;$$
$$c_2^* = \tilde{R}_2[\tilde{R}_1(I - c_0^*) - c_1^*]. \quad (4.17)$$

Approach II: Backward Induction with a State Variable

In problem (4.12), we have a lifetime/overall budget constraint. There is no state variable in the problem. We now introduce a state variable A_t, which is the wealth available at the beginning of period t. The initial wealth is $A_0 = I$. We have $A_{t+1} = R_{t+1}(A_t - c_t)$ for $t = 1, 2$. Then, the problem becomes

$$V \equiv \max_{c_0, \tilde{c}_1, \tilde{c}_2, A_1, A_2, A_3} E_0\{u(c_0) + \beta u(\tilde{c}_1) + \beta^2 u(\tilde{c}_2)\}$$
$$\text{s.t. } A_{t+1} = R_{t+1}(A_t - c_t), \quad \text{for } t = 0, 1, 2,$$
$$\text{given } A_0. \quad (4.18)$$

In problem (4.18), instead of a lifetime/overall budget constraint, it has a per-period constraint. Let us now solve the problem by backward induction. First, given A_2 the problem at $t = 2$ is

$$V_2(A_2) \equiv \max_{c_2, A_3 \geq 0} u(c_2)$$
$$\text{s.t. } A_3 = \tilde{R}_3(A_2 - c_2).$$

Since A_3 does not contribute to welfare, the consumer will choose $A_3 = 0,$[4] which implies

$$c_2^* = A_2, \quad V_2(A_2) = u(A_2). \quad (4.19)$$

Second, given A_1, the problem at $t = 1$ is

$$V_1(A_1) \equiv \max_{c_1, A_2} u(c_1) + \beta E_1[V_2(A_2)]$$
$$\text{s.t. } A_2 = \tilde{R}_2(A_1 - c_1).$$

This problem can be written as

$$V_1(A_1) = \max_{c_1} u(c_1) + \beta E_1\{V_2[\tilde{R}_2(A_1 - c_1)]\}.$$

---

[4]This is a transversality condition. The condition $A_3 \geq 0$ is called the non-Ponzi condition.

The FOC is

$$u'(c_1^*) = \beta E_1\{\tilde{R}_2 V_2'[\tilde{R}_2(A_1 - c_1^*)]\}.$$

By (4.19), we have

$$u'(c_1^*) = \beta E_1\{\tilde{R}_2 u'(A_2)\} = \beta E_1\{\tilde{R}_2 u'(c_2^*)\}.$$

Also, by the Envelope Theorem,

$$V_1'(A_1) = \beta E_1\{\tilde{R}_2 V_2'[\tilde{R}_2(A_1 - c_1)]\} = u'(c_1^*). \qquad (4.20)$$

Third, given A_0, the problem at $t = 0$ is

$$V_0(A_0) \equiv \max_{c_0, A_1} u(c_0) + \beta E_1[V_1(A_1)]$$

$$\text{s.t. } A_1 = \tilde{R}_1(A_0 - c_0).$$

The problem becomes

$$\max_{c_0} u(c_0) + \beta E_0\{V_1[\tilde{R}_1(A_0 - c_0)]\}.$$

The FOC is

$$u'(c_0^*) = \beta E_0\{\tilde{R}_1 V_1'[\tilde{R}_1(A_0 - c_0^*)]\}.$$

By (4.20), we have

$$u'(c_0^*) = \beta E_0[\tilde{R}_1 u'(c_1^*)].$$

Hence, we have the same equations for the optimal solution as in (4.17).

1.4. *Bellman Equation*

When there are infinite periods, backward induction is done using the Bellman equation. To use this method, the dynamic problem is required to be recursive.

Let $x_t \in \mathbb{R}^n, u_t \in \mathbb{U} \subset \mathbb{R}^k, f_t: \mathbb{R}^n \times \mathbb{R}^k \to \mathbb{R}$, and $g_t: \mathbb{R}^n \times \mathbb{R}^k \times \mathbb{R}^m \to \mathbb{R}^n$.[5] Consider a recursive dynamic problem with infinite

---

[5]The choice set $\mathbb{U}$ can also be dependent on the state, such as $\mathbb{U}(x_t)$. Most of the results still hold.

periods:

$$V_0(x_0) \equiv \max_{u_0, u_1, \ldots, \in \mathbb{U}} E_0 \sum_{t=0}^{\infty} \beta^t f_t(x_t, u_t)$$

$$\text{s.t. } x_{t+1} = g_t(x_t, u_t, \varepsilon_{t+1}), \quad t = 0, 1, \ldots$$

$$x_0 \text{ is given and known}, \tag{4.21}$$

where $\beta \in (0, 1)$ is a discount factor, $\varepsilon_t \in \mathbb{R}^m$ is a random vector unknown until period t, and E_t is the mathematical expectation operator conditional on the information set Φ_t at t. In this problem, uncertainty is injected by the random process $\{\varepsilon_t\}$ through the motion equation. Here, u_t is the control and x_t is the state.

Example 4.2. Consider a consumer who, at each time t, consumes c_t units of goods and has wealth A_t. The consumer has an initial endowment of A_0. The gross return is $R_t = 1 + r_t$ at time t. The consumer's problem is then

$$V_0(A_0) \equiv \max_{c_0, c_1, \ldots} E_0 \sum_{t=0}^{\infty} \beta^t u(u_t)$$

$$\text{s.t. } A_{t+1} = R_{t+1}(A_t - c_t),$$

$$\text{given } A_0.$$

Example 4.3. Consider a firm that, at each time t, employs l_t units of labor, utilizes an existing capital stock k_t, invests s_t units into the capital stock at time t, and produces y_t, units of output. The firm's problem is then[6]:

$$\max_{\{l_t, s_t\}} E_0 \sum_{t=0}^{\infty} \beta^t (y_t - w_t l_t - s_t)$$

$$\text{s.t. } y_{t+1} = f(k_t, l_t, \varepsilon_{t+1}),$$

$$k_{t+1} = (1 - \delta)k_t + s_t,$$

---

[6]Here, s_t, y_t, and w_t are in the same unit of measure and the price of the good has been normalized to 1. This treatment implicitly assumes that we are in the Arrow–Debreu world.

where $\beta \equiv (1+r)^{-1}$, r is the interest rate, δ is the depreciation rate, and w_t is the wage rate. ∎

In a dynamic problem, the control at time t is the set of choice variables at t The state can be the set of remaining variables or the set of remaining endogenous variables. The latter definition for the state is more convenient. For example, in the above example, the control at t is $u_t \equiv (l_t, s_t)$ and the state is either $x_t \equiv (y_t, k_t, w_t, \varepsilon_t)$ or simply $x_t \equiv (y_t, k_t)$.

Denote a solution of (4.21) by $\{u_t^*\}_{t=0}^{\infty}$. This solution is dependent on time and is called an open-loop solution. Alternatively, consider the following seemingly more general problem (actually an equivalent problem). At each time t, the problem is:

$$V_t(x_t) \equiv \max_{u_t, u_{t+1}, \ldots} E_t \left\{ \sum_{s=t}^{\infty} \beta^{s-t} f_s(x_s, u_s) \right\}$$

$$\text{s.t. } x_{s+1} = g_s(x_s, u_s, \varepsilon_{s+1}), \quad s \geq t,$$

$$\text{given } x_t. \tag{4.22}$$

The first control u_t^* of this problem should generally be dependent on the initial state x_t (and the past shocks). That is, $u_t^* = \varphi_t(x_t)$. By this, for each $t \geq 0$, we can find an optimal control $\varphi_t(x_t)$. Then, $\{\varphi_t(x_t)\}_{t=0}^{\infty}$ is a solution of (4.21). The key feature of this solution is that each optimal control $\varphi_t(x_t)$ at time t depends on the state at time t. We call this solution a closed-loop solution, feedback solution, or simply policy. We now develop an approach that leads to a closed-loop solution.

We have[7]

$$V_t(x_t) = \max_{u_t \in \mathbb{U}} \left\{ f_t(x_t, u_t) + \beta \max_{u_{t+1}, u_{t+2}, \ldots} E_t \sum_{s=t+1}^{\infty} \beta^{s-t-1} f_s(x_s, u_s) \right\}$$

---

[7]Two comments are in order here. First, we can interchange the operator E_t and the max operation; in discrete time, it means $\max_{x_1, \ldots, x_n} \sum_{t=1}^{n} f(x_t, t) = \sum_{t=1}^{n} \max_{x_t} f(x_t, t)$ which is obvious. Second, $V_t(x_t)$ actually depends on the past shocks, i.e., $V_t(x_t) = V_t(x_t, \varepsilon_t, \ldots, \varepsilon_{t-n+1})$ if $\{\varepsilon_s\}$ is an nth-order Markov process.

$$= \max_{u_t \in \mathbb{U}} \left\{ f_t(x_t, u_t) + \beta E_t \max_{u_{t+1}, u_{t+2}, \dots} E_{t+1} \sum_{s=t+1}^{\infty} \beta^{s-t-1} f_s(x_s, u_s) \right\}$$

$$= \max_{u_t \in \mathbb{U}} \{ f_t(x_t, u_t) + \beta E_t V_{t+1}(x_{t+1}) \}.$$

Thus, a solution of (4.21) must be a solution of the following so-called Bellman equation:

$$V_t(x_t) \equiv \max_{u_t \in \mathbb{U}} f_t(x_t, u_t) + \beta E_t[V_{t+1}(x_{t+1})]$$

$$\text{s.t. } x_{t+1} = g_t(x_t, u_t, \varepsilon_{t+1}). \tag{4.23}$$

Conversely, a solution $\{x_t^*\}$ of the Bellman equation (4.23) is generally a solution of (4.21) if the following so-called transversality condition is satisfied:

$$\lim_{t \to \infty} \beta^t E_t[V_{t+1}(x_{t+1}^*)] = 0. \tag{4.24}$$

Transversality conditions ensure optimality of initial and terminal values. A dynamic problem that is equivalent to the Bellman equation is called a recursive problem.

As before, a typical way of solving problem (4.23) is to use the FOC and the Envelope Theorem. The FOC is

$$f_{t,u}(x_t, u_t) + \beta E_t[V'_{t+1}(x_{t+1}) g_{t,u}(x_t, u_t, \varepsilon_{t+1})] = 0. \tag{4.25}$$

When V_t is known, this will give us a feedback solution: $u_t^* = h_t(x_t)$. To determine V_t, we may use the Envelope Theorem to take the derivative of (4.23) w.r.t. x:

$$V'_t(x_t) = f_{t,x}(x_t, u_t) + \beta E_t[V'_{t+1}(x_{t+1}) g_{t,x}(x_t, u_t, \varepsilon_{t+1})]. \tag{4.26}$$

(4.25) and (4.26) together determine the solution of two functions h_t and V_t.

When functions $f_t(x, u)$ and $g_t(x, u, \varepsilon)$ are independent of time t and the error sequence ε_t is a Markov process, we call problem (4.21) autonomous. In this case, Equations (4.25) and (4.26) lead to a solution pair $(V(x_t), u^*(x_t))$ with both $V(x)$ and $u^*(x)$ being independent of t.

Theorem 4.2. *If $f_t = f, g_t = g$ and $\{\varepsilon_t\}$ is a first-order Markov process, then V_t defined in (4.22) is time invariant.*[8] ∎

By Theorem 4.2, a solution $(h_t V_t)$ from (4.25) and (4.26) will be time invariant: $u_t^* = h(x_t)$ and $V_t(x_t) = V(x_t)$. We show how to use the Bellman equation in the following two examples.

Example 4.4. Let us solve the consumer's problem in Example 4.2:

$$V_0(A_0) \equiv \max_{c_0, c_1, \dots} E_0 \sum_{t=0}^{\infty} \beta^t u(c_t)$$

$$\text{s.t. } A_{t+1} = R_{t+1}(A_t - c_t).$$

Here, A_t is the state and c_t is the control. Assume that R_t, c_t, and A_t are known at the beginning of period t. To have a recursive structure, assume that $\{R_t\}$ follows a first-order Markov process, with $F(R|R_t) \equiv \Pr\{R_{t+1} \le R|R_t\}$. The key here is that the conditional distribution F is time-invariant. By Theorem 4.2, V_t is time-invariant. Then, the Bellman equation is

$$V(A_t) \equiv \max_{c_t} u(c_t) + \beta E_t V[R_{t+1}(A_t - c_t)], \quad \text{given } A_t.$$

The two conditions are

$$\text{FOC: } u'(c_t) = \beta E_t[V'(A_{t+1})R_{t+1}],$$
$$\text{Envelope: } V'(A_t) = \beta E_t[V'(A_{t+1})R_{t+1}],$$

which imply $u'(c_t) = V'(A_t)$. Substituting this back into the FOC gives

$$u'(c_t) = \beta E_t[u'(c_{t+1})R_{t+1}]. \tag{4.27}$$

This is the Euler equation, which determines the optimal consumption sequence.

To find out more about the solution, assume $u(c) = \ln c$. One can then show that the optimal consumption c_t must be proportional

---

[8] If $\mathbb{U}$ is compact, using the contraction mapping theorem, Sydsæter *et al.* (2005, p. 436) show the uniqueness of the solution of the Bellman equation.

to A_t. Hence, let $c_t = \gamma A_t$, where γ is a constant. Substituting this into (4.27) gives

$$\frac{1}{\gamma A_t} = \beta E_t \frac{R_{t+1}}{\gamma R_{t+1}(A_t - \gamma A_t)}.$$

Since A_t is known at time t and therefore can be taken out of the expectation operator, this equation implies $\gamma = 1 - \beta$. The optimal consumption is thus

$$c_t = (1 - \beta)A_t.$$

This is a feedback solution and is consistent with the Permanent Income Hypothesis. ∎

Example 4.5. Let us solve the firm's problem Example 4.3:

$$\max_{\{l_t, s_t, k_t, y_t\}} E_0 \sum_{t=0}^{\infty} \beta^t (y_t - w_t l_t - s_t)$$
$$\text{s.t. } y_{t+1} = f(k_t, l_t, \varepsilon_{t+1}),$$
$$k_{t+1} = (1 - \delta)k_t + s_t.$$

Here, the state is $x_t = (k_t, y_t)$ and the control is $u_t = (l_t, s_t)$. The Bellman equation is

$$V(k_t, y_t) = \max_{l_t, s_t} y_t - w_t l_t - s_t + \beta E_t V[(1 - \delta)k_t + s_t, f(k_t, l_t, \varepsilon_{t+1})].$$

The conditions are

$$\text{FOC on } l_t: \ -w_t + \beta E_t[V_y(x_{t+1})f_l(k_t, l_t, \varepsilon_{t+1})] = 0,$$
$$\text{FOC on } s_t: \ -1 + \beta E_t[V_k(x_{t+1})] = 0,$$
$$\text{Envelope on } k_t: \ V_k(x_t) = \beta E_t[(1 - \delta)V_k(x_{t+1})$$
$$+ V_y(x_{t+1})f_k(k_t, l_t, \varepsilon_{t+1})],$$
$$\text{Envelope on } y_t: \ V_y(x_t) = 1.$$

Then,

$$w_t = \beta E_t[f_l(k_t, l_t, \varepsilon_{t+1})],$$
$$1 = \beta E_t[V_k(x_{t+1})],$$

$$V_k(x_t) = \beta \left[(1-\delta)\frac{1}{\beta} + E_t f_k(k_t, l_t, \varepsilon_t) \right]$$
$$= 1 - \delta + \beta E_t[f_k(k_t, l_t, \varepsilon_{t+1})].$$

Then,

$$w_t = \beta E_t[f_l(k_t, l_t, \varepsilon_{t+1})],$$
$$1 = \beta E_t\{1 - \delta + \beta E_{t+1}[f_k(k_{t+1}, l_{t+1}, \varepsilon_{t+2})]\}.$$

We thus have two equations:

$$w_t = \beta E_t[f_l(k_t, l_t, \varepsilon_{t+1})],$$
$$r + \delta = \beta E_t[f_k(k_{t+1}, l_{t+1}, \varepsilon_{t+2})],$$

where $\beta \equiv \frac{1}{1+r}$. Given r and $\{w_t\}$, these two equations together with the two constraints in the problem determine the solution $\{(l_t^*, s_t^*, k_t^*, y_t^*)\}$.

Here, we have only solved the demand for labor. The supply of labor can be derived from the consumer's problem. We can add a term in the consumer's problem to generate the supply of labor for a more interesting problem. We have also assumed away a financial market. Here, the firm finances its own capital stock. We can alternatively allow the consumer to provide funds for the capital stock in the financial market through savings. ∎

1.5. *Lagrange Method*

We restate the Kuhn–Tucker theorem in Chapter 3.

Theorem 4.3 (Kuhn–Tucker). *For differentiable $f: \mathbb{R}^n \to \mathbb{R}$ and $G: \mathbb{R}^n \to \mathbb{R}^m$, let $L(\lambda, x) \equiv f(x) + \lambda \cdot G(x)$. If x^* is a solution of*

$$\max_{x \in \mathbb{R}^n} f(x)$$
$$\text{s.t. } G(x) \geq 0,$$

then there exists $\lambda \in \mathbb{R}_+^m$ such that

$$FOC: \quad L_x'(\lambda, x^*) = 0,$$
$$KTC: \quad \lambda \cdot G(x^*) = 0. \quad \blacksquare$$

We explain how to use the Lagrange method in a dynamic problem with an example first.

Example 4.6. Consider Example 4.1 again. The consumer's problem is

$$V \equiv \max_{c_0, \tilde{c}_1, \tilde{c}_2} E_0\{u(c_0) + \beta u(\tilde{c}_1) + \beta^2 u(\tilde{c}_2)\}$$

$$\text{s.t. } c_0 + \frac{1}{\tilde{R}_1}\tilde{c}_1 + \frac{1}{\tilde{R}_2\tilde{R}_1}\tilde{c}_2 \leq I, \tag{4.28}$$

where $\tilde{R}_t \equiv 1 + \tilde{r}_t$ is random at $t - 1$ but becomes known at t and E_t is the expectation operator conditional on information at t. Assume $u'(0) = +\infty$. We use the Lagrange method to solve the problem. There are two approaches, one without a state variable and the other with a state variable.

The original Lagrange approach disregards the dynamic nature of a problem. In our approaches, we will define Lagrange functions in such a way as to take into account the dynamic nature.

Approach I: The Lagrange Method without a State Variable

We can use the Lagrange method to solve (4.28). The Lagrange function for c_t at time t is

$$L_t = E_t\{u(c_0) + \beta u(\tilde{c}_1) + \beta^2 u(\tilde{c}_2)\}$$

$$+ E_t\left[\tilde{\lambda}\left(I - c_0 - \frac{1}{R_1}\tilde{c}_1 - \frac{1}{R_2R_1}\tilde{c}_2\right)\right], \tag{4.29}$$

where $t = 0, 1$ or 2. Here, c_t^* should be based on information at time t. Hence, the FOCs for c_0^*, c_1^* and c_2^* are respectively

$$u'(c_0) = E_0(\tilde{\lambda}), \quad \beta u'(c_1) = E_1\left(\frac{\tilde{\lambda}}{\tilde{R}_1}\right), \quad \beta^2 u'(c_2) = E_2\left(\frac{\tilde{\lambda}}{\tilde{R}_1\tilde{R}_2}\right).$$

Since R_t is known at t and $E_t E_{t+1}(\tilde{x}) = E_t(\tilde{x})$ for any random variable $\tilde{x}$, the above implies

$$\beta E_0[\tilde{R}_1 u'(\tilde{c}_1^*)] = E_0(\tilde{\lambda}) = u'(c_0^*),$$
$$\beta^2 R_1 E_1[\tilde{R}_2 u'(\tilde{c}_2^*)] = E_1(\tilde{\lambda}) = \beta R_1 u'(c_1^*),$$

implying

$$u'(c_0^*) = \beta E_0[\tilde{R}_1 u'(\tilde{c}_1^*)], \quad u'(c_1^*) = \beta E_1[\tilde{R}_2 u'(\tilde{c}_2^*)].$$

Hence, we have the same Euler equations as in (4.17).

Approach II: The Lagrange Method with a State Variable

We can also use the Lagrange method to solve (4.18), which is a reformulated version of (4.28) using the state variable A_t. The Lagrange function for $(c_t A_t)$ is

$$L_t = E_t\{u(c_0) + \beta u(c_1) + \beta^2 u(c_2)\}$$

$$+ E_t\left\{\sum_{t=0}^{2} \lambda_{t+1}[R_{t+1}(A_t - c_t) - \Lambda_{t+1}]\right\}.$$

The key here is information. The control variable c_t is decided at t and hence its Lagrange function is conditional on information Φ_t at time t. The state variable A_{t+1} is also decided at t, but the information set would be different when it is time to decide A_{t+1}. When we choose A_{t+1}, it becomes a known variable, which means that we have information set Φ_{t+1}. Hence, we use L_{t+1} to decide A_{t+1}. We can think of it this way: as shown in Figure 4.2, c_t is decided in period t conditional on Φ_t and A_{t+1} is decided at the end of period t or the beginning of period $t + 1$ conditional on Φ_{t+1}.

With the above properly defined Lagrange functions, we can now use FOCs to solve the problem. The FOCs for c_0, c_1 and c_2 are

$$u'(c_0) = E_0(\lambda_1 R_1), \quad \beta u'(c_1) = E_1(\lambda_2 R_2), \quad \beta^2 u'(c_2) = E_2(\lambda_3 R_3).$$

The FOCs for A_1, A_2, and A_3 are

$$E_1(\lambda_2 R_2) = \lambda_1, \quad E_2(\lambda_3 R_3) = \lambda_2, \quad \frac{\partial \hat{L}_2}{\partial A_3} < 0.$$

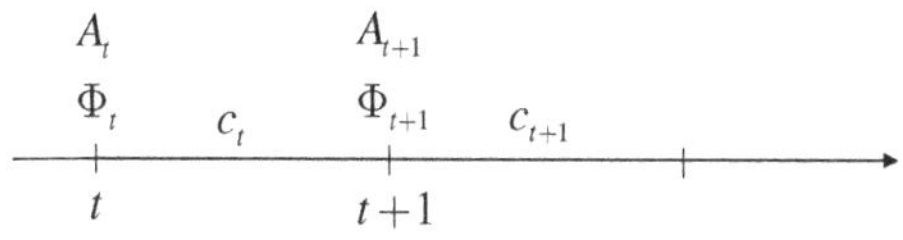

Figure 4.2. Choice Variables and Their Relevant Information Sets

There are six equations plus three motion equations in (4.18) and they determine three consumption variables c_0, c_1 and c_2, three state variables A_1, A_2 and A_3, and three Lagrange multipliers. From the last inequality, we have $A_3^* = 0$. Hence,

$$u'(c_0) = E_0(\lambda_1 R_1) = E_0[E_1(\lambda_2 R_2) R_1] = \beta E_0[u'(c_1) R_1],$$
$$\beta u'(c_1) = E_1(\lambda_2 R_2) = E_1[E_2(\lambda_3 R_3) R_2] = \beta^2 E_1[u'(c_2) R_2],$$

which also imply the two Euler equations in (4.17). Further, by the Envelope Theorem, we find

$$V_0(A_0) \equiv \max_{c_0, c_1, c_2} L_0 \Rightarrow V_0'(A_0) \equiv E_0(\lambda_1 R_1) = u'(c_0),$$
$$V_1(A_1) \equiv \max_{c_1, c_2} L_1 \Rightarrow V_1'(A_1) = E_1(\lambda_2 R_2) = \beta u'(c_1),$$
$$V_2(A_2) \equiv \max_{c_2} L_2 \Rightarrow V_2'(A_2) = E_2(\lambda_3 R_3) = \beta^2 u'(c_2). \quad \blacksquare$$

To illustrate the Lagrange method in general, as in the case of the Bellman equation, let us consider (4.21) again. The Lagrange function for (u_t, x_t) is

$$L_t = E_t \sum_{s=t}^{\infty} \beta^{s-t} \{ f_x(x_s, u_s) + \lambda_{s+1} \cdot [g_s(x_s, u_s, \varepsilon_{s+1}) - x_{s+1}] \}.$$

$$(4.30)$$

The problem becomes[9]

$$V_t(x_t)$$

$$= \max_{\substack{u_t, u_{t+1}, \ldots \\ x_t, x_{t+1}, \ldots}} E_t \sum_{s=t}^{\infty} \beta^{s-t} \{ f_s(x_s, u_s) + \lambda_{s+1} \cdot [g_s(x_s, u_s, \varepsilon_{s+1}) - x_{s+1}] \}.$$

---

[9]Problem (4.21) is equivalent to

$$V_t(x_t) \equiv \max_{\substack{u_t, u_{t+1}, \ldots \\ x_{t+1}, x_{t+2}, \ldots}} E_t \sum_{s=t}^{\infty} \beta^{s-t} f_s(x_s, u_s)$$
$$\text{s.t. } x_{s+1} = g_s(x_s, u_s, \varepsilon_{s+1}), \quad s \geq t$$
$$\text{given } x_t.$$

This problem is equivalent to (4.21) since $x_t, x_{t+1}, \ldots$ have already been determined by the constraints. For example, we have $x_{t+2} = g_{t+1}[g_t(x_t, u_t, \varepsilon_{t+1}), u_{t+1}, \varepsilon_{t+2}]$. Given x_t, x_{t+2} is determined by $u_t, u_{t+1}, \varepsilon_{t+1}$ and ε_{t+2}. Hence, although we are allowed to choose x_{t+2}, it is already determined by the motion equations. However, in the Lagrange problem, the constraints are incorporated into the Lagrange function by introducing Lagrange multipliers. We need the FOCs from the optimal choice of $\{x_s\}$ in order to determine the Lagrange multipliers.

In a Lagrange problem, there are no state variables and both $\{u_t\}$ and $\{x_{t+1}\}$ are choice variables. The FOCs for the choice variables u_t and x_{t+1} are

$$0 = \frac{\partial L_t}{\partial u_t} = f_{t,u}(x_t, u_t) + E_t[\lambda_{t+1} \cdot g_{t,u}(x_t, u_t, \varepsilon_{t+1})], \quad (4.31)$$

$$0 = \frac{\partial L_{t+1}}{\partial x_{t+1}} = -\lambda_{t+1} + \beta E_{t+1}[f_{t+1,x}(x_{t+1}, u_{t+1})$$

$$+ \lambda_{t+2} \cdot g_{t+1,x}(x_{t+1}, u_{t+1}, \varepsilon_{t+2})]. \quad (4.32)$$

By the Envelope Theorem, we also have

$$V_t'(x_t) = E_t[f_{t,x}(x_t, u_t) + \lambda_{t+1} \cdot g_{t,x}(x_t, u_t, \varepsilon_{t+1})]. \quad (4.33)$$

By (4.32) and (4.33), we have

$$\lambda_t = \beta V_t'(x_t).$$

Substituting this into (4.31) and (4.33) yields

$$f_{t,u}(x_t, u_t) + \beta E_t[V_{t+1}'(x_{t+1}) \cdot g_{t,u}(x_t, u_t, \varepsilon_{t+1})] = 0,$$
$$V_t'(x_t) = f_{t,x}(x_t, u_t) + \beta E_t[V_{t+1}'(x_{t+1}) \cdot g_{t,x}(x_t, u_t, \varepsilon_{t+1})].$$

These two equations are the same as (4.25) and (4.26) from the Bellman equation.

The above derivation for (4.21) is illustrative. It shows that the Bellman equation and the Lagrange method are equivalent in solving problems of the type in (4.21). However, the Lagrange method can solve more general problems. For a problem to which the Bellman equation is not applicable, the Lagrange method should be employed.

In summary, there are two types of model setups: A model with an overall lifetime constraint and a model with a motion equation at each time that determines the evolution of the state. We have covered three methods in this section: backward induction, the Bellman equation, and the Lagrange method. Generally speaking, backward induction works for models of finite periods; the Bellman equation is convenient for recursive models of the type in (4.21); and the Lagrange method can work for any type of model.

2. Continuous-Time Deterministic Models

In this section, we present the standard approach in solving a dynamic model with continuous time under certainty. We first present an example to motivate the approach.

Example 4.7.[10] What is the shortest path from one point (x_0, y_0) to another (x_1, y_1) on $\mathbb{R}^2$? The answer is obvious: the straight line from (x_0, y_0) to (x_1, y_1). Let us show this rigorously. To do so, let the set of admissible paths be[11]

$$\mathcal{Y} = \{y : [x_0, x_1] \to \mathbb{R} | y(x) \text{ is piecewise smooth}\}.$$

Given a path $y(x) \in \mathcal{Y}$ connecting the two points, and assuming $x_0 < x_1$, the distance is

$$\int_{(x_0,y_0)}^{(x_1,y_1)} \sqrt{dx^2 + dy^2} = \int_{x_0}^{x_1} \sqrt{1 + \left(\frac{dy}{dx}\right)^2} dx.$$

Denoting by $\dot{y}(x)$ the first derivative of $y(x)$, our problem is

$$\min_{y \in \mathcal{Y}} \int_{x_0}^{x_1} \sqrt{1 + [\dot{y}(x)]^2} dx$$
$$\text{s.t. } y(x_0) = y_0, y(x_1) = y_1.$$

As we will show later, a necessary condition for the optimal path is

$$\frac{d}{dx}\left(\frac{d}{d\dot{y}}\sqrt{1 + \dot{y}^2}\right) = 0.$$

Denoting by $\ddot{y}(x)$ the second derivative of $y(x)$, the above equation becomes

$$0 = \frac{d}{dx}\frac{\dot{y}}{\sqrt{1 + \dot{y}^2}} = \frac{\ddot{y}\sqrt{1 + \dot{y}^2} - \dot{y}\frac{\dot{y}\ddot{y}}{\sqrt{1+\dot{y}^2}}}{1 + \dot{y}^2} = \frac{\ddot{y}}{(1 + \dot{y}^2)^{3/2}},$$

---

[10]This example is from Leitmann (1981, p. 3).
[11]A function is piecewise smooth if it is differentiable and its derivative is continuous except at finite points.

implying $\ddot{y}(x) = 0$, i.e., $y(x)$ must be a linear function. Therefore, the optimal path is linear, i.e., a straight line connecting the two points. ∎

2.1. *Dynamic Programming: The General Case*

There are two approaches in dynamic optimization: (1) the calculus of variations and (2) optimal control. In appearance, an optimal control problem involves state variables, while the calculus of variations does not. This section covers the so-called calculus of variations. The following theorem is from Kamien and Schwartz (1981, p. 16).

Theorem 4.4 (Hamilton). *Suppose that* $H: \mathbb{R} \times \mathbb{R}^k \times \mathbb{R}^k \to \mathbb{R}$ *is continuous w.r.t. its first argument, and continuously differentiable w.r.t. its second and third arguments. Let the set of admissible controls be:*

$$\mathbb{U} \equiv \{ \text{continuously differentiable functions } u: [0, T] \to \mathbb{R}^k \}.$$

Then, the optimal solution u^* *of*

$$\max_{u \in \mathbb{U}} \int_0^T H[t, u(t), \dot{u}(t)] dt$$
$$\text{s.t. } u(0) = u_0, \quad u(T) = u_T \tag{4.34}$$

must satisfy the Euler equation:

$$\frac{d}{dt} H_{\dot{u}}[t, u^*(t), \dot{u}^*(t)] = H_u[t, u^*(t), \dot{u}^*(t)], \quad t \in (0, T). \tag{4.35}$$

Here, T *can be either finite or infinite, and the initial and terminal values* $u(0)$ *and* $u(T)$ *can be either fixed or free. If the initial value* $u(0)$ *is free, the following so-called transversality condition must be satisfied:*

$$H_{\dot{u}}[0, u^*(0), \dot{u}^*(0)] = 0. \tag{4.36}$$

If the terminal value $u(T)$ *is free, the transversality condition is*

$$H_{\dot{u}}[T, u^*(T), \dot{u}^*(T)] = 0. \tag{4.37}$$

If the terminal condition is $u(T) \geq 0$, the transversality conditions are

$$u^*(T)H_{\dot{u}}[T, u^*(T), \dot{u}^*(T)] = 0, \quad H_{\dot{u}}[T, u^*(T), \dot{u}^*(T)] \leq 0. \quad (4.38)$$

Conversely, if $H(t, u, \dot{u})$ is concave in $(u, \dot{u})$, then any $u^* \in \mathbb{U}$ satisfying the Euler equation (4.35) and the initial and terminal conditions is a solution of (4.34). ∎

The concavity condition of $H(t, u, \dot{u})$ in $(u, \dot{u})$ is too strong. This condition often fails for a business application. A weaker second-order condition is needed. In the proof of the above theorem in the Appendix, the SOC $g''(0) \leq 0$ implies

$$H_{\dot{u}\dot{u}}[t, u^*(t), \dot{u}^*(t)] \leq 0.$$

This is the so-called Legendre condition, which is a second-order necessary condition. However, this condition turns out to be too weak. A strict inequality of this condition is not sufficient even for a locally optimal solution. Generally speaking, we do not have a proper SOC for a continuous-time dynamic problem.

Since the Euler equation is a second-order ordinary differential equation for u, two boundary conditions are needed to pin down the two arbitrary (vectors of) constants in the general solution. Transversality conditions are for optimality of boundary values. When a boundary condition is missing, a transversality condition replaces it. For example, for problem (4.34), the two boundary conditions for the Euler equation are $u(0) = u_0$, and $u(T) = u_T$; but for problem (4.82), the two boundary conditions are $u(0) = u_0$ and (4.37). Condition (4.37) says that diverting from the optimal path $u^*(t)$ at the last minute will not affect the maximum value, which is intuitive. Similarly, when T is free but $u(T) = u_T$ is fixed, we have the following necessary condition:

$$[H - \dot{u}H_{\dot{u}}]_{t=T} = 0. \quad (4.39)$$

Example 4.8. A well-known contract problem is

$$\max_{a,s(\cdot)} \int v[y - s(y)]f(y,a)dy$$

$$\text{s.t.} \int u[s(y)]f(y,a)dy \geq c(a) + \bar{u}. \tag{4.40}$$

The Lagrangian for (4.40) is

$$L \equiv \int v[y - s(y)]f(y,a)dy + \lambda \left[\int u[s(y)]f(y,a)dy - c(a) - \bar{u} \right],$$

where $\lambda \geq 0$. Then, (4.40) is equivalent to

$$\max_{a,s(\cdot),\lambda} \int v[y - s(y)]f(y,a)dy + \lambda \left[\int u[s(y)]f(y,a)dy - c(a) - \bar{u} \right]. \tag{4.41}$$

The Hamiltonian for (4.41) (or simply for the Lagrangian L) is

$$H \equiv [v(y - s) + \lambda u(s) - \lambda c(a) - \lambda \bar{u}]f(y,a).$$

The Euler equation is $H_s = 0$, implying

$$v'(y - s^*) = \lambda u'(s^*),$$

which determines the optimal contract $s^*(y)$. ∎

Problem (4.41) is a mixed problem with variables (a, λ) and a function $s(\cdot)$. For a complete solution, we also need the FOCs for a and λ from (4.41), with $\lambda > 0$.

Example 4.9. Consider

$$\max_{x(\cdot)} \int_{\underline{\theta}}^{\bar{\theta}} \{u[x(\theta), \theta] + v[x(\theta), \theta]\}dF(\theta)$$

$$\text{s.t.} \ \dot{x}(\theta) \geq 0, \tag{4.42}$$

where $F(\theta)$ is the distribution function of random variable θ. The Lagrange function is

$$L = \int_{\underline{\theta}}^{\bar{\theta}} \{u[x(\theta), \theta] + v[x(\theta), \theta] + \lambda(\theta)\dot{x}(\theta)\}dF(\theta), \tag{4.43}$$

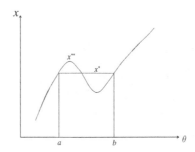

Figure 4.3. The Solutions With and Without the Motion Equation

where $\lambda(\theta) \geq 0$ is the Lagrange multiplier. Then, the Hamilton function is

$$H(x, \dot{x}, \lambda, \theta) = u(x, \theta) + v(x, \theta) + \lambda(\theta)\dot{x}.$$

The conditions are:

Euler equation:	$\dot{\lambda} = u_x(x^*, \theta) + v_x(x^*, \theta),$
Motion equation:	$\dot{x}^*(\theta) \geq 0,$
Transversality conditions:	$\lambda(\underline{\theta}) = \lambda(\bar{\theta}) = 0,$
KT conditions:	$\lambda(\theta)\dot{x}^*(\theta) = 0.$

Let $x^{**}(\theta)$ be the solution when the motion equation $\dot{x}(\theta) \geq 0$ is missing. By the KT condition, we know that, in an open interval, if x^* is strictly increasing, then $\lambda = 0$ and $x^* = x^{**}$ in that interval. Thus, x^* is either constant or coincides with x^{**}, as shown in Figure 4.3. ∎

2.2. *Dynamic Programming with State Variables*

Problem (4.34) is an unconstrained problem. However, economic problems often have constraints, such as consumer budget constraints, government budget constraints, and resource constraints. For a dynamic problem, one special constraint is the so-called motion equation, which describes the movement of state variables over time. Problem (4.44) contains such a constraint and is a so-called optimal control problem. It turns out that this problem can be treated as a special case of problem (4.34).

Theorem 4.5. *Let* $x \in \mathbb{R}^n, u \in \mathbb{R}^k, g \colon \mathbb{R}^n \times \mathbb{R}^k \times \mathbb{R} \to \mathbb{R}^n$, *and* $f \colon \mathbb{R}^n \times \mathbb{R}^k \times \mathbb{R} \to \mathbb{R}$, *where f and g are continuously differentiable w.r.t. their first and second arguments and continuous w.r.t. their third argument. For problem*

$$J(x_0) \equiv \max_u \int_0^T f[x(t), u(t), t] dt$$
$$\text{s.t. } \dot{x}(t) = g[x(t), u(t), t],$$
$$x(t_0) = x_0, \quad x(T) \geq 0, \tag{4.44}$$

define the Hamiltonian as

$$H = f(x, u, t) + \lambda(t) \cdot g(x, u, t).$$

If u^* is a solution, then there exists a function $\lambda \colon [0, T] \to \mathbb{R}^n$ such that u^* is a solution of

$$H_u = 0, \tag{4.45}$$
$$\dot{\lambda} = -H_x, \tag{4.46}$$

with transversality conditions:

$$\lim_{t \to T} \lambda(t) x(t) = 0, \quad \lambda(T) \geq 0. \tag{4.47}$$

If the terminal value $x(T)$ is free, the transversality condition is

$$\lambda(T) = 0. \quad \blacksquare$$

By Arrow's Theorem (Sydsæter *et al.*, 2005, p. 363; Chiang, 1992, p. 218), conditions (4.45) and (4.46) are sufficient if the following function is concave in x for all t:

$$\hat{H}(t, x) \equiv f[x, u^*(t), t] + \lambda(t) \cdot g[x, u^*(t), t].$$

Theorem 4.6. *Let* $g \colon \mathbb{R}^n \times \mathbb{R}^k \times \mathbb{R} \to \mathbb{R}^n$, $f \colon \mathbb{R}^n \times \mathbb{R}^k \to \mathbb{R}$, $x \in \mathbb{R}^n$, $u \in \mathbb{R}^k$, *where f and g are continuously differentiable w.r.t. their first and second arguments and g is continuous w.r.t. its third argument.*

For problem

$$J(x_0) \equiv \max_u \int_0^T f[x(t), u(t)]e^{-\rho t} dt$$
$$\text{s.t. } \dot{x}(t) = g[x(t), u(t), t],$$
$$x(0) = x_0, \quad x(T) \geq 0,$$

define the Hamiltonian as

$$H = f(x, u) + \lambda(t) \cdot g(x, u, t).$$

If u^* is a solution, there exists a function $\lambda\colon [0, T] \to \mathbb{R}^n$ such that u^* is a solution of

$$H_u = 0, \tag{4.48}$$
$$\dot{\lambda} = \rho\lambda - H_x, \tag{4.49}$$

with transversality conditions

$$\lim_{t \to T} \lambda(t)x(t)e^{-\rho t} = 0, \quad \lambda(T) \geq 0. \quad \blacksquare \tag{4.50}$$

Example 4.10. The corresponding continuous-time version of the consumer's problem in Example 4.2 is

$$J(A_0) \equiv \max_{c(\cdot)} \int_0^\infty u[c(t)]e^{-\rho t} dt$$
$$\text{s.t. } \dot{A} = rA - c,$$
$$A(0) = A_0, \quad A(\infty) \geq 0.$$

The Hamiltonian is

$$H \equiv u(c) + \lambda(t)(rA - c).$$

By Theorem 4.6, the conditions are

$$\begin{aligned}
&H_c = 0: && u'(c) = \lambda, \\
&\dot{\lambda} = \rho\lambda - H_A: && \dot{\lambda} = \rho\lambda - \lambda r, \\
&\text{transversality:} && \lim_{t \to \infty} \lambda(t)A(t)e^{-\rho t} = 0,
\end{aligned}$$

where $\lambda(\infty) \geq 0$ is obviously satisfied. They imply

$$u''(c)\dot{c} = (\rho - r)u'(c),$$

which in turn implies the continuous-time version of the Euler equation in (4.27):

$$\dot{c} = (\rho - r)\frac{u'(c)}{u''(c)}.$$

Denote $\alpha(c) \equiv -\frac{cu''(c)}{u'(c)}$, which is the relative risk aversion. Then,

$$\frac{\dot{c}}{c} = \frac{r - \rho}{\alpha(c)}.$$

That is, consumption growth is determined by risk aversion, the interest rate and the discount rate in a simple way. If $u(c) = \ln(c)$, then $\dot{c} = (r - \rho)c$, implying $c^*(t) = c_0 e^{(r-\rho)t}$, where c_0 is the starting point $c(0) = c_0$. ∎

Example 4.11. Many other types of constraints can be handled as in Theorem 4.6. For example, consider the following problem:

$$J(x_0, x_T) \equiv \max_u \int_0^T f[x(t), u(t), t]dt$$
$$\text{s.t. } \dot{x}(t) = g[x(t), u(t), t],$$
$$\int_0^T h[x(t), u(t), t]dt = c,$$
$$x(0) = x_0, \quad x(T) = x_T.$$

By the Lagrange theorem, there exists a constant μ such that the problem is equivalent to

$$J(x_0, x_T) \equiv \max_{u,x} \int_0^T f(x, u, t)dt + \mu \left[\int_0^T h[x(t), u(t), t]dt - c \right]$$
$$\text{s.t. } \dot{x}(t) = g[x(t), u(t), t],$$
$$x(0) = x_0, \quad x(T) = x_T,$$

which can be handled using Theorem 4.5 with Hamiltonian:

$$H(x, u, t) \equiv f(x, u, t) + \lambda(t) \cdot g(x, u, t) + \mu \cdot h(x, u, t). \quad ∎$$

Example 4.12. Condider the following problem:

$$V = \max_{x(\cdot)} \int_0^1 \{\theta v[x(\theta)] - c[x(\theta)]\}dF(\theta)$$

$$\text{s.t.} \int_0^1 c[x(\theta)]dF(\theta) \leq I, \qquad (4.51)$$

where $v(x)$ is concave and $c(x)$ is convex. Let us show that V is increasing and concave in income:

$$\frac{\partial V}{\partial I} \geq 0, \quad \frac{\partial^2 V}{\partial I^2} \leq 0.$$

The Lagrange function is

$$L = \int_0^1 \{\theta v[x(\theta)] - c[x(\theta)]\}dF(\theta) + \lambda \left[I - \int_0^1 c[x(\theta)]dF(\theta)\right],$$

where $\lambda \geq 0$ is the Lagrange multiplier and is generally a function of I. By the Envelope theorem,

$$\frac{\partial V}{\partial I} = \lambda \geq 0.$$

The Hamilton function implied by L is

$$H = \theta v(x) - (1 + \lambda)c(x).$$

Then, the Euler equation is

$$\theta v'(x) = (1 + \lambda)c'(x).$$

Taking a derivative of the above equation w.r.t. I yields

$$\theta v''(x)\frac{\partial x}{\partial I} = (1 + \lambda)c''(x)\frac{\partial x}{\partial I} + \frac{\partial \lambda}{\partial I}c'(x). \qquad (4.52)$$

If the constraint in (4.52) is non-binding, then $\lambda = 0$. If the constraint is binding, taking its derivative w.r.t. I yields

$$\int_0^1 c'[x(\theta)]\frac{\partial x}{\partial I}dF(\theta) = 1. \qquad (4.53)$$

Solving for $\frac{\partial x}{\partial I}$ from (4.52) and substituting it into (4.53) yields

$$1 = \frac{\partial \lambda}{\partial I} \int_0^1 \frac{[c'(x)]^2}{\theta v''(x) - (1 + \lambda)c''(x)} dF(\theta),$$

which implies $\frac{\partial \lambda}{\partial I} \leq 0$. Hence, we always have

$$\frac{\partial^2 V}{\partial I^2} = \frac{\partial \lambda}{\partial I} \leq 0. \quad \blacksquare$$

Sometimes, we face a mixed problem in which we are required to solve for some optimal variables and some optimal functions. The trick here is to define an expanded state vector that includes both the original state vector and the variables. After this, we can then apply Theorem 4.5 to find the optimal solution. The following result is from Leitmann (1981, Section 13.14).

Theorem 4.7 (Mixed Problem). *Let $x \in \mathbb{R}^n, u \in \mathbb{R}^k, g: \mathbb{R}^n \times \mathbb{R}^k \times \mathbb{R}^m \times \mathbb{R} \to \mathbb{R}^n$, and $f: \mathbb{R}^n \times \mathbb{R}^k \times \mathbb{R}^m \times \mathbb{R} \to \mathbb{R}$, where f and g are continuously differentiable w.r.t. their first three arguments and continuous w.r.t. their fourth argument. For problem*

$$J(x_0, x_T) \equiv \max_{a \in \mathbb{A}, u \in \mathcal{A}} \int_0^T f[x(t), u(t), a, t]dt$$
$$\text{s.t. } \dot{x}(t) = g[x(t), u(t), a, t],$$
$$x(0) = x_0, \quad x(T) = x_T,$$

define the Hamiltonian as

$$H = f(x, u, a, t) + \lambda(t) \cdot g(x, u, a, t).$$

If $(u^*(\cdot), a^*)$ is a solution, there exists a function $\lambda : [0, T] \to \mathbb{R}^n$ such that $(u^*(\cdot), a^*)$ is a solution of

$$H_u = 0, \tag{4.54}$$

$$\dot{\lambda} = -H_x, \tag{4.55}$$

$$\frac{\partial}{\partial a} \int_0^T H[x(t), u(t), a, t]dt = 0. \quad \blacksquare \tag{4.56}$$

Theorem 4.7 is very much like Theorem 4.5 except that it also specifies the m FOCs in (4.56) for the m variables $a_1, \ldots, a_m$. A crucial part of this result is that $\lambda(t)$ does not depend on a.

Another extension is that the value space of u is a subspace $\mathbb{U}$ of $\mathbb{R}^k$, rather than $\mathbb{R}^k$. In this case, condition (4.45) in Theorem 4.5 is replaced by the following condition:

$$\max_{u \in \mathbb{U}} H(x, u, t). \tag{4.57}$$

Condition (4.45) is the FOC if the optimal u^* is an interior solution in $\mathbb{U}$ otherwise condition (4.57) may imply a boundary solution. This is the Pontryagin maximum principle. We restate Theorem 4.5 with the Pontryagin maximum principle in the following.

Theorem 4.8 (Pontryagin). *Let* $x \in \mathbb{R}^n, u \in \mathbb{U} \subset \mathbb{R}^k$, $g \colon \mathbb{R}^n \times \mathbb{R}^k \times \mathbb{R} \to \mathbb{R}^n$, *and* $f \colon \mathbb{R}^n \times \mathbb{R}^k \times \mathbb{R} \to \mathbb{R}$, *where* f *and* g *are continuously differentiable w.r.t. their first two arguments and continuous w.r.t. their third argument. For problem*

$$J(x_0) \equiv \max_{u \in \mathbb{U}} \int_0^T f[x(t), u(t), t]dt$$
$$\text{s.t. } \dot{x}(t) = g[x(t), u(t), t],$$
$$x(0) = x_0, \quad x(T) \geq 0,$$

define the Hamiltonian as

$$H = f(x, u, t) + \lambda(t) \cdot g(x, u, t).$$

If u^* *is a solution, there exists a function* $\lambda \colon [0, T] \to \mathbb{R}^n$ *such that* u^* *is a solution of*

$$H(x, u, t), \tag{4.58}$$
$$\dot{\lambda} = -H_x. \quad \blacksquare \tag{4.59}$$

This Pontryagin result can be extended to the following form.

Theorem 4.9 (Pontryagin). *Suppose that* $H \colon \mathbb{R} \times \mathbb{R}^k \times \mathbb{R}^n \times \mathbb{R}^n \to \mathbb{R}$, *is continuous w.r.t. its first argument, and continuously differentiable w.r.t. its second and third arguments. Let the set of admissible* *controls be:*

$\mathcal{X} \equiv \{continuously\ differentiable\ functions\ x\colon [0,T] \to \mathbb{R}^n\},$

$\mathcal{U} \equiv \{piecewise\ continuous\ functions\ u\colon [0,T] \to \mathbb{U}\}.$

Then, the optimal solution (u^*, x^*) of

$$\max_{u \in \mathcal{U}, x \in \mathcal{X}} \int_0^T H[t, u(t), x(t), \dot{x}(t)]dt$$
$$\text{s.t. } x(0) = x_0, \quad x(T) = x_T \tag{4.60}$$

must satisfy the following conditions:

$$H[t, u, x, \dot{x}], \tag{4.61}$$

$$\frac{d}{dt} H_{\dot{x}}[t, u^*(t), x^*(t), \dot{x}^*(t)] = H_x[t, u^*(t), x^*(t), \dot{x}^*(t)], \quad t \in (0, T). \tag{4.62}$$

In (4.61), x and $\dot{x}$ are treated as constants. ∎

2.3. Transversality Conditions

Boundary conditions can take various forms. In this section, we list a few of the boundary conditions and their corresponding transversality conditions from Kamien and Schwartz (1991, p. 155).

Consider problem

$$\max_u \int_0^T f(t, x, u)dt + \varphi[T, x(T)]$$
$$\text{s.t. } \dot{x}_i = g_i(t, x, u), \quad \forall\, i$$
$$x_i(0) = x_{i0}, \quad x_i(T) = x_{iT}, \text{ and other conditions,}$$

where $x(t) \in \mathbb{R}^n$ and $u(t) \in \mathbb{R}^m$. Let the Hamiltonian be

$$H(t, x, u, \lambda) = f(t, x, u) + \lambda(t) \cdot g(t, x, u),$$

where $g = (g_1, \ldots, g_k)$. We have

1. The multiplier equation is

$$\dot{\lambda} = -H_x.$$

2. The optimality condition is

$$H[t, x^*(t), u, \lambda(t)] \text{ is maximized by } u = u^*(t).$$

3. Transversality conditions are

   (a) If condition $x_i(T)$ is free for some i, then

   $$\lambda_i(T) = \frac{\partial \varphi[T, x(T)]}{\partial x_i}. \qquad (4.63)$$

   (b) If condition $x_i(T) \geq 0$ for some i, then

   $$\lambda_i(T) \geq \frac{\partial \varphi[T, x(T)]}{\partial x_i}, \quad x_i(T)\left\{\lambda_i(T) - \frac{\partial \varphi[T, x(T)]}{\partial x_i}\right\} = 0.$$

   (c) If $\psi[x_k(T), \ldots, x_l(T)] \geq 0$ for a continuously differentiable $\psi \colon \mathbb{R}^{k-l+1} \to \mathbb{R}$, there exists $\mu \geq 0$ such that

   $$\lambda_i(T) = \frac{\partial \varphi[T, x(T)]}{\partial x_i} + \mu \frac{\partial \psi[x_k(T), \ldots, x_l(T)]}{\partial x_i},$$
   $$\mu \psi[x_k(T), \ldots, x_l(T)] = 0, \quad i = k, \ldots, l.$$

   (d) If $\psi[x_k(T), \ldots, x_l(T)] = 0$ for a continuously differentiable $\psi \colon \mathbb{R}^{k-l+1} \to \mathbb{R}$, there exists $\mu \in \mathbb{R}$ such that

   $$\lambda_i(T) = \frac{\partial \varphi[T, x(T)]}{\partial x_i} + \mu \frac{\partial \psi[x_k(T), \ldots, x_l(T)]}{\partial x_i}, \quad i = k, \ldots, l.$$

   (e) If T is free, then

   $$H[Tx(T), u(T), \lambda(T)] + \frac{\partial \varphi[T, x(T)]}{\partial t} = 0.$$

   (f) If T is partially free with condition $T \leq \bar{T}$ for some constant $\bar{T} > 0$, then

   $$H[Tx(T), u(T), \lambda(T)] + \frac{\partial \varphi[T, x(T)]}{\partial t} \geq 0,$$

   with equality if the optimal T satisfies $T < \bar{T}$.

(g) If $\psi[x_k(T), \ldots, x_l(T), T] \geq 0$ for a continuously differentiable $\psi \colon \mathbb{R}^{k-l} \to \mathbb{R}$, there exists a constant $\mu \geq 0$ such that

$$\lambda_i(T) = \frac{\partial \varphi[T, x(T)]}{\partial x_i} + \mu \frac{\partial \psi[x_k(T), \ldots, x_l(T), T]}{\partial x_i},$$

$$H[T, x(T), u(T), \lambda(T)] + \frac{\partial \varphi[T, x(T)]}{\partial t}$$

$$+ \mu \frac{\partial \psi[x_k(T), \ldots, x_l(T), T]}{\partial x_i} = 0,$$

$$\mu \psi[x_k(T), \ldots, x_l(T)] = 0, \quad i = k, \ldots, l.$$

2.4. Equivalence between Continuous-Time and Discrete-Time Models

Continuous-time and discrete-time models are equivalent. We use an example to illustrate this equivalence in this section.

Suppose that a representative consumer faces the following problem:

$$V(A_0) \equiv \max_{\{c_t\}} \sum_{t=0}^{\infty} \beta^t u(c_t)$$

$$\text{s.t. } A_{t+1} = R_{t+1}(A_t + y_t - c_t),$$

$$\text{given } A_0, \tag{4.64}$$

where A_t is the total wealth, y_t is the exogenous random wage income, R_{t+1} is the exogenous random gross interest rate, and c_t is consumption. The Bellman equation is

$$V(A_t) = \max_{c_t} u(c_t) + \beta V[R_{t+1}(A_t + y_t - c_t)].$$

It implies

FOC: $\qquad u'(c_t) = \beta V'(A_{t+1})R_{t+1},$
Envelope Theorem: $\quad V'(A_t) = \beta V'(A_{t+1})R_{t+1}.$

Then,

$$u'(c_t) = V'(A_t), \tag{4.65}$$

implying

$$u'(c_t) = \beta u'(c_{t+1})R_{t+1}.$$

This in turn implies the discrete-time version of the well-known Euler equation:

$$1 = \beta \frac{u'(c_{t+1})}{u'(c_t)} R_{t+1}. \tag{4.66}$$

With c_0^* being determined by (4.65), the Euler equation determines the optimal consumption path $\{c_t^*\}$.

Let us now convert the discrete-time version of the consumer's problem (4.64) to its continuous-time version. If r_t is the net interest rate, then $R_t = 1 + r_t$. Since

$$(1 + r_t)(1 - r_t) = 1 - r_t^2 \approx 1,$$

we have

$$R_t \approx \frac{1}{1 - r_t}. \tag{4.67}$$

Then, the budget constraint $A_{t+1} = R_{t+1}(A_t + y_t - c_t)$ implies

$$A_{t+1}(1 - r_{t+1}) \approx A_t + y_t - c_t \Rightarrow A_{t+1} - A_t \approx r_{t+1}A_{t+1} + y_t - c_t.$$

Hence, the continuous-time version of the budget constraint is

$$\dot{A} = rA + y - c,$$

where $A(t), r(t), y(t)$, and $c(t)$ are functions of t. Then, the corresponding continuous-time version of the consumer's problem is[12]

$$J(A_0) \equiv \max_{c(\cdot)} \int_0^\infty u[c(t)]e^{-\rho t}dt$$

$$\text{s.t. } \dot{A} = rA + y - c,$$

$$\text{given } A(0) = A_0,$$

---

[12]The Euler equation will be the same if we use a time-dependent $\rho(t)$ instead of a constant ρ. If so, we should replace ρt by $\int_0^t \rho(\tau)d\tau$.

where $\beta \equiv e^{-\rho}$ in (4.64). The Hamiltonian is

$$H \equiv u(c) + \lambda(t)(rA + y - c).$$

The conditions are

$$
\begin{aligned}
H_c = 0: && u'(c) = \lambda, \\
\dot{\lambda} = \rho\lambda - H_A: && \dot{\lambda} = \rho\lambda - \lambda r, \\
\text{transversality}: && \lim_{t\to\infty} \lambda A e^{-\rho t} = 0.
\end{aligned}
$$

They imply

$$u''(c)\dot{c} = (\rho - r)u'(c),$$

in turn implying the continuous-time version of the well-known Euler equation:

$$\dot{c} = (\rho - r)\frac{u'(c)}{u''(c)}.$$

We say that continuous-time and discrete-time models are equivalent if they imply the same results as the time interval $\Delta t \to 0$. Let us now show that the continuous-time and discrete-time versions of the consumer's problem imply the same Euler equation when $\Delta t \to 0$. We have

$$\beta = e^{-\rho} \approx 1 - \rho \approx \frac{1}{1+\rho}.$$

Together with (4.67), (4.66) becomes

$$u'(c_t)(1 + \rho)(1 - r_{t+1}) \approx u'(c_{t+1}). \tag{4.68}$$

Let the length of a period be Δt. Then, (4.68) becomes

$$u'(c_t)(1 + \rho\Delta t)(1 - r_{t+\Delta t}\Delta t) \approx u'(c_{t+\Delta t}),$$

i.e.,

$$u'(c_t)(\rho - r_{t+\Delta t} - \rho r_{t+\Delta t}\Delta t) \approx \frac{u'(c_{t+\Delta t}) - u'(c_t)}{\Delta t}.$$

Letting $\Delta t \to 0$ implies (the above approximation becomes precise when $\Delta t \to 0$):

$$u'(c_t)(\rho - r_t) = u''(c_t)\frac{dc_t}{dt},$$

which is the continuous-time version of the Euler equation.

3. Phase Diagram

A phase diagram is often used to analyze a dynamic solution, particularly when the solution cannot be explicitly solved.

A dynamic system may be derived from optimization or from some equilibrium conditions. In the case of an optimization problem, the Euler equation and the motion equation of a continuous-time dynamic problem often lead to two equations of the form:

$$\begin{cases} \dot{x} = f(x, y, t), \\ \dot{y} = g(x, y, t), \end{cases} \qquad (4.69)$$

where $x(t)$ and $y(t)$ are real-valued functions of t, $\dot{x}(t) \equiv x'(t), \dot{y}(t) \equiv y'(t)$, and t is often referred to as time. For example, for the solution determined by (4.45) and (4.46), if g and u take real values, we can solve for λ from (4.45), $\lambda = -f_u/g_u$ and substitute it into (4.46) to yield

$$\frac{d}{dt}\left(\frac{f_u}{g_u}\right) = H_x\left(x, y, \frac{f_u}{g_u}\right).$$

This equation and the motion equation in (4.44) form a system of the form shown in (4.69).

Phase diagrams can handle the following autonomous system with $f = f(x, y)$ and $g = g(x, y)$:

$$\begin{cases} \dot{x} = f(x, y), \\ \dot{y} = g(x, y). \end{cases}$$

We may be able to solve this equation system directly if f and g are simple enough. For complicated cases, we can use a phase diagram to illustrate the solution.

Example 4.13. From Example 4.10, we have

$$\dot{A} = rA - c,$$
$$\dot{c} = (r - p)\frac{c}{\alpha(c)}.$$

It is an autonomous system for $c(t)$ and $A(t)$. ■

3.1. *The Linear System*

By analyzing a linear system, we can gain a good understanding of phase diagrams.

The General Solution

Consider a linear system for $(x(t), y(t))$[13]:

$$\dot{x} = d_1(x - \bar{x}) + a_1(y - \bar{y}),$$
$$\dot{y} = a_2(x - \bar{x}) + d_2(y - \bar{y}), \tag{4.70}$$

where $a_1, a_2, d_1, d_2 \in \mathbb{R}$. Here, t is called time and $(\bar{x}, \bar{y})$ is called the steady state. Once it reaches the steady state, the solution no longer changes over time. The following two lines in $\mathbb{R}^2$ for (x, y) are called demarcation lines:

$$\dot{x} = 0 \Rightarrow d_1(x - \bar{x}) + a_1(y - \bar{y}) = 0;$$
$$\dot{y} = 0 \Rightarrow a_2(x - \bar{x}) + d_2(y - \bar{y}) = 0.$$

The intersection point of the demarcation lines is the steady state. These two lines divide the space into four regions. Equation system (4.70) can be written in a matrix form:

$$\begin{pmatrix} \dot{x} \\ \dot{y} \end{pmatrix} = \begin{pmatrix} x - \bar{x} \\ y - \bar{y} \end{pmatrix}, \tag{4.71}$$

where

$$A = \begin{pmatrix} d_1 & a_1 \\ a_2 & d_2 \end{pmatrix}.$$

---

[13]See Chiang (1984, p. 641).

The eigenvalues are determined by the following characteristic equation:

$$0 = |\lambda I - A| = \lambda^2 - (d_1 + d_2)\lambda + |A|,$$

implying two eigenvalues

$$\lambda_1 = \frac{1}{2}[d_1 + d_2 - \sqrt{(d_1 + d_2)^2 - 4|A|}],$$

$$\lambda_2 = \frac{1}{2}[d_1 + d_2 + \sqrt{(d_1 + d_2)^2 - 4|A|}].$$

We have $\lambda_1 \leq \lambda_2$ if they are real numbers. Let ξ_1 and ξ_2 be eigenvectors of λ_1 and λ_2 respectively. The general solution of (4.71) is

$$\begin{pmatrix} x(t) \\ y(t) \end{pmatrix} = \begin{pmatrix} \bar{x} \\ \bar{y} \end{pmatrix} + c_1 \xi_1 e^{\lambda_1 t} + c_2 \xi_2 e^{\lambda_2 t}, \tag{4.72}$$

where c_1 and c_2 are arbitrary constants.

Saddle-Point Stability with $|A| < 0$

If $|A| < 0$, then $\lambda_1 < 0$ and $\lambda_2 > 0$. Such a system is said to be saddle-point stable. From (4.72), we can see that a convergent solution must have $c_2 = 0$. Thus, the starting point (x_0, y_0) of a convergent solution, the initial condition, must satisfy

$$\begin{pmatrix} x_0 \\ y_0 \end{pmatrix} = \begin{pmatrix} \bar{x} \\ \bar{y} \end{pmatrix} + c_1 \xi_1,$$

for some constant $c_1 \in \mathbb{R}$. This condition restricts the initial point to a line. We call this line the convergence line, which is defined by

$$\begin{pmatrix} x \\ y \end{pmatrix} = \begin{pmatrix} \bar{x} \\ \bar{y} \end{pmatrix} + \tau \xi_1, \quad \text{for } \tau \in \mathbb{R}.$$

Besides the two demarcation lines, the convergence line is shown in Figure 4.4. Given the initial point (x_0, y_0) on the convergence line, the solution can be derived from (4.72), which is

$$\begin{pmatrix} x(t) \\ y(t) \end{pmatrix} = \begin{pmatrix} \bar{x} \\ \bar{y} \end{pmatrix} + \begin{pmatrix} x_0 - \bar{x} \\ y_0 - \bar{y} \end{pmatrix} e^{\lambda_1 t}.$$

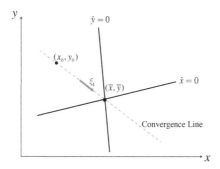

Figure 4.4. The Convergence Line

This solution converges to $(\bar{x}, \bar{y})$. On the other hand, the line determined by the other eigenvector is called the divergence line, which is defined by

$$\begin{pmatrix} x \\ y \end{pmatrix} = \begin{pmatrix} \bar{x} \\ \bar{y} \end{pmatrix} + \tau \xi_2, \quad \text{for } \tau \in \mathbb{R}.$$

We summarize our analysis in the following theorem.

Theorem 4.10. *For the linear system*

$$\dot{x} = A(x - \bar{x}),$$

where $x \in \mathbb{R}^2$ and $A \in \mathbb{R}^{2\times 2}$, suppose that the system is saddle-point stable with $|A| < 0$. Then, it has a negative eigenvalue $\lambda < 0$ and a positive eigenvalue $\mu > 0$. Let ξ and ζ be eigenvectors of λ and μ, respectively. Then, the convergence line is

$$x = \bar{x} + \tau \xi, \quad \tau \in \mathbb{R},$$

and the divergence line is

$$x = \bar{x} + \tau \zeta, \quad \tau \in \mathbb{R}.$$

If the initial point x_0 is on the convergence line, the solution is

$$x(t) = \bar{x} + (x_0 - \bar{x})e^{\lambda t};$$

and if the initial point x_0 is on the divergence line, the solution is

$$x(t) = \bar{x} + (x_0 - \bar{x})e^{\mu t}. \quad \blacksquare$$

Example 4.14. Draw the phase diagram for the following system:

$$\dot{x} = -(x - \bar{x}) + 10(y - \bar{y}),$$
$$\dot{y} = 20(x - \bar{x}) + 3(y - \bar{y}).$$

Starting from a point on the line defined by $\dot{x} = 0$, if we increase the value of y while keeping x fixed, then the first equation above implies $\dot{x} > 0$, indicating that $x(t)$ will move to the right when it is above the line defined by $\dot{x} = 0$ and will move to the left when it is below the line defined by $\dot{x} = 0$. Similarly, starting from a point on the line defined by $\dot{y} = 0$, if we increase the value of y while keeping x fixed, then the second equation above implies $\dot{y} > 0$, indicating that $y(t)$ will move up when it is above the line defined by $\dot{y} = 0$ and will move down when it is below the line defined by $\dot{y} = 0$.

From the above analysis, as shown in Figure 4.5, we now have a clear idea about the directions of movement of a solution in all four parts of the diagram. We can see that the diagram indeed looks like a saddle. Given any point on the phase diagram, for a solution starting from that point, we know roughly how the solution moves over time. ∎

Example 4.15. By the same approach as in the above example, we can draw the phase diagram in Figure 4.6 for the problem in Example 4.3 with $r < \rho$.

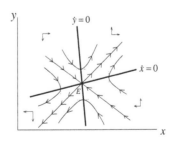

Figure 4.5. Phase Diagram

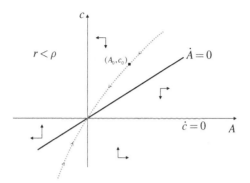

Figure 4.6. Phase Diagram

Cyclical Stability with $|A| > 0$ and $(d_1 + d_1)^2 < 4|A|$

In this case, the two eigenvalues are

$$\lambda_1 = \frac{d_1 + d_2}{2} - i\theta, \quad \lambda_2 = \frac{d_1 + d_2}{2} + i\theta$$

where $i \equiv \sqrt{-1}$ and $\theta \equiv \sqrt{|A| - (\frac{d_1 + d_1}{2})^2}$. By (4.72), the general solution can be expressed as

$$\begin{pmatrix} x(t) \\ y(t) \end{pmatrix} = \begin{pmatrix} \bar{x} \\ \bar{y} \end{pmatrix} + (\xi_1 e^{\lambda_1 t}, \xi_2 e^{\lambda_2 t}) \begin{pmatrix} c_1 \\ c_2 \end{pmatrix}.$$

The initial condition is

$$\begin{pmatrix} x_0 \\ y_0 \end{pmatrix} = \begin{pmatrix} \bar{x} \\ \bar{y} \end{pmatrix} + (\xi_1, \xi_2) \begin{pmatrix} c_1 \\ c_2 \end{pmatrix}.$$

Hence, the solution is

$$\begin{pmatrix} x(t) \\ y(t) \end{pmatrix} = \begin{pmatrix} \bar{x} \\ \bar{y} \end{pmatrix} + (\xi_1 e^{\lambda_1 t}, \xi_2 e^{\lambda_2 t})(\xi_1, \xi_2)^{-1} \begin{pmatrix} x_0 - \bar{x} \\ y_0 - \bar{y} \end{pmatrix}.$$

Since

$$e^{\lambda_1 t} = e^{\frac{d_1 + d_1}{2} t}[\cos(\theta t) - i\sin(\theta t)], \quad e^{\lambda_2 t} = e^{\frac{d_1 + d_1}{2} t}[\cos(\theta t) + i\sin(\theta t)],$$

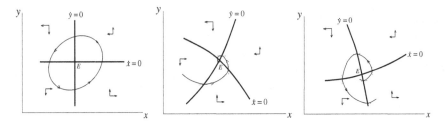

Figure 4.7. Cyclical, Globally Stable, and Unstable Solutions[14]

the convergence is totally determined by $d_1 + d_1$ with $\sin(\theta t)$ and $\cos(\theta t)$ indicating fluctuations. Hence, as shown in Figure 4.7, we have three possible cases:

1. If $d_1 + d_1 = 0$, the solution is a cycle (uniform fluctuations or a vortex).
2. If $d_1 + d_1 < 0$, the solution is convergent but with cycles (damped fluctuations).
3. If $d_1 + d_1 > 0$, the solution is divergent and with cycles (explosive fluctuations).

In particular, for the case with $d_1 + d_1 = 0$, we have

$$\begin{pmatrix} x(t) \\ y(t) \end{pmatrix} = \begin{pmatrix} \hat{x} \\ \hat{y} \end{pmatrix} + \begin{pmatrix} \alpha_1 & \beta_1 \\ \alpha_2 & \beta_2 \end{pmatrix} \begin{pmatrix} \sin(\theta t) \\ \cos(\theta t) \end{pmatrix},$$

where α_i and β_i are some constants. Then,

$$\begin{pmatrix} \sin(\theta t) \\ \cos(\theta t) \end{pmatrix} = B^{-1} \begin{pmatrix} x(t) - \hat{x} \\ y(t) - \hat{y} \end{pmatrix},$$

where $B \equiv \begin{pmatrix} \alpha_1 & \beta_1 \\ \alpha_2 & \beta_2 \end{pmatrix}$. Since $[\sin(\theta t)]^2 + [\cos(\theta t)]^2 = 1$, we have

$$(x(t) - \hat{x}, y(t) - \hat{y})(B')^{-1}B^{-1} \begin{pmatrix} x(t) - \hat{x} \\ y(t) - \hat{y} \end{pmatrix} = 1.$$

---

[14]When drawing phase diagrams, we should keep two things in mind. First, the directions should be consistent. If $\dot{x} > 0$ is above the curve defined by $\dot{x} = 0$, then $\dot{x} < 0$ is below it. Second, when talking about the curve defined by $\dot{x} = 0$, we are referring to the directions of $x(t)$, not about that of $y(t)$.

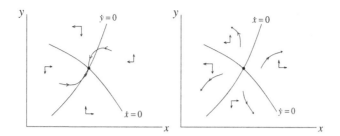

Figure 4.8. Convergent and Divergent Solutions

Since $(B')^{-1}B^{-1} = (BB')^{-1}$ is positive definite, the above equation defines a vortex.

Global Stability with $|A| > 0$ and $(d_1 + d_1)^2 \geq 4|A|$

In this case, since $|A| > 0$, λ_1 and λ_2 have the same sign as $d_1 + d_1$. Hence, as shown in Figure 4.8, we have two possible cases:

1. If $d_1 + d_1 > 0$, a solution starting from any point, except the steady state, is divergent.
2. If $d_1 + d_1 < 0$, a solution starting from any point is convergent.

Stable Path with $|A| = 0$

If $|A| = 0$, one of the eigenvalues must be zero and the two demarcation lines are the same. In other words, the two demarcation lines merge into one.[15] Let

$$A = \begin{pmatrix} \alpha^T \\ k\alpha^T \end{pmatrix},$$

where k is a constant and α is a vertical vector. Then, the demarcation line is defined by $\alpha \cdot (x - \bar{x}, y - \bar{y}) = 0$, and (4.71) becomes

$$\dot{x} = \alpha \cdot (x - \bar{x}, y - \bar{y}),$$
$$\dot{y} = k\alpha \cdot (x - \bar{x}, y - \bar{y}).$$

---

[15]Imagine that you can rotate the two axes so that the system becomes $\begin{pmatrix} \dot{x} \\ \dot{y} \end{pmatrix}$ $= \begin{pmatrix} d_1 + d_2 & 0 \\ 0 & 0 \end{pmatrix} \begin{pmatrix} x - \bar{x} \\ y - \bar{y} \end{pmatrix}$ under the new axes. We can easily draw the phase diagram for this system.

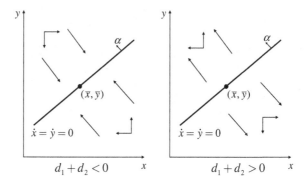

Figure 4.9. The Phase Diagrams when One of the Eigenvalues is Zero

All the points on the demarcation line are steady states, as shown in Figure 4.9.[16]

If $d_1 + d_1 > 0$, then $\lambda_1 = 0$ and $\lambda_2 = d_1 + d_1$. In this case, a stable solution must satisfy $c_2 = 0$. Hence, the initial condition is

$$\begin{pmatrix} x_0 \\ y_0 \end{pmatrix} = \begin{pmatrix} \bar{x} \\ \bar{y} \end{pmatrix} + c_1 \xi_1,$$

implying the following convergence line:

$$\begin{pmatrix} x \\ y \end{pmatrix} = \begin{pmatrix} \bar{x} \\ \bar{y} \end{pmatrix} + c \xi_1, \quad c \in \mathbb{R}.$$

Thus, a convergent solution satisfies

$$\begin{pmatrix} x(t) \\ y(t) \end{pmatrix} = \begin{pmatrix} \bar{x} \\ \bar{y} \end{pmatrix} + c_1 \xi = \begin{pmatrix} x_0 \\ y_0 \end{pmatrix},$$

indicating that the solution stays at the initial point forever and the initial point must be on the demarcation line. In fact, since $\lambda_1 = 0$, we have

$$A\xi_1 = \lambda_1 \xi_1 = 0,$$

implying $\alpha \cdot \xi_1 = 0$. Thus,

$$\alpha^T \begin{pmatrix} x_0 - \bar{x} \\ y_0 - \bar{y} \end{pmatrix} = c_1 \alpha^T \xi_1 = 0,$$

---

[16]The directions in Figure 4.9 are arbitrary.

implying that (x_0, y_0) must be on the demarcation line. Therefore, a stable solution must start from a point on the demarcation line and stays at that point forever. Hence, the convergence line is the same as the demarcation line.

If $d_1 + d_1 < 0,,$ then $\lambda_1 = d_1 + d_1$ and $\lambda_2 = 0$. In this case, any solution is convergent. The initial condition is

$$\begin{pmatrix} x_0 \\ y_0 \end{pmatrix} = \begin{pmatrix} \bar{x} \\ \bar{y} \end{pmatrix} + c_1\xi_1 + c_2\xi_2 = \begin{pmatrix} \bar{x} \\ \bar{y} \end{pmatrix} + (\xi_1, \xi_2)\begin{pmatrix} c_1 \\ c_2 \end{pmatrix}.$$

implying

$$\begin{pmatrix} c_1 \\ c_2 \end{pmatrix} = (\xi_1, \xi_2)^{-1}\begin{pmatrix} x_0 - \bar{x} \\ y_0 - \bar{y} \end{pmatrix}.$$

That is, the initial point can be anywhere. In fact, given any initial point $(x_0, y_0) \in \mathbb{R}^2$ the solution is

$$\begin{pmatrix} x(t) \\ y(t) \end{pmatrix} = \begin{pmatrix} \bar{x} \\ \bar{y} \end{pmatrix} + (\xi e^{\lambda t}, \varsigma)\begin{pmatrix} c_1 \\ c_2 \end{pmatrix} = \begin{pmatrix} \bar{x} \\ \bar{y} \end{pmatrix} + (\xi e^{\lambda t}, \varsigma)(\xi, \varsigma)^{-1}\begin{pmatrix} x_0 - \bar{x} \\ y_0 - \bar{y} \end{pmatrix},$$

which is convergent. The limit is

$$\begin{pmatrix} \hat{x} \\ \hat{y} \end{pmatrix} \equiv \begin{pmatrix} \bar{x} \\ \bar{y} \end{pmatrix} + (0, \varsigma)(\xi, \varsigma)^{-1}\begin{pmatrix} x_0 - \bar{x} \\ y_0 - \bar{y} \end{pmatrix},$$

which is generally not $(\bar{x}, \bar{y})$. We find

$$\alpha^T \begin{pmatrix} \hat{x} - \bar{x} \\ \hat{y} - \bar{y} \end{pmatrix} = (\alpha^T 0, \alpha^T \varsigma)(\xi, \varsigma)^{-1}\begin{pmatrix} x_0 - \bar{x} \\ y_0 - \bar{y} \end{pmatrix}$$

$$= (0, 0)(\xi, \varsigma)^{-1}\begin{pmatrix} x_0 - \bar{x} \\ y_0 - \bar{y} \end{pmatrix} = 0,$$

indicating that the limit $(\hat{x}, \hat{y})$ is on the demarcation line.

3.2. *Linearization*

For a general nonlinear system

$$\begin{cases} \dot{x} = f(x, y), \\ \dot{y} = g(x, y), \end{cases} \tag{4.73}$$

we can convert it into a linear system by linearization. Define the steady state as the point at which $\dot{x} = 0$ and $\dot{y} = 0$. That is, the steady state $(\bar{x}, \bar{y})$ is the point where

$$f(\bar{x}, \bar{y}) = 0, \quad g(\bar{x}, \bar{y}) = 0.$$

By Taylor's expansion, there exist $\xi \in (x, \bar{x})$ and $\eta \in (y, \bar{y})$ such that

$$
\begin{aligned}
f(x, y) &= f(\bar{x}, \bar{y}) + f_x(\xi, \eta)(x - \bar{x}) + f_y(\xi, \eta)(y - \bar{y}) \\
&= f_x(\xi, \eta)(x - \bar{x}) + f_y(\xi, \eta)(y - \bar{y}), \\
g(x, y) &= g(\bar{x}, \bar{y}) + g_x(\xi, \eta)(x - \bar{x}) + g_y(\xi, \eta)(y - \bar{y}) \\
&= g_x(\xi, \eta)(x - \bar{x}) + g_y(\xi, \eta)(y - \bar{y}).
\end{aligned}
$$

If (x, y) is near $(\bar{x}, \bar{y})$, then

$$
\begin{aligned}
f_x(\xi, \eta) &\approx f_x(\bar{x}, \bar{y}), \quad f_y(\xi, \eta) \approx f_y(\bar{x}, \bar{y}), \\
g_x(\xi, \eta) &\approx g_x(\bar{x}, \bar{y}), \quad g_y(\xi, \eta) \approx g_y(\bar{x}, \bar{y}).
\end{aligned}
$$

Thus, (4.73) can be approximated by

$$
\begin{cases}
\dot{x} = f_x(\bar{x}, \bar{y})(x - \bar{x}) + f_y(\bar{x}, \bar{y})(y - \bar{y}), \\
\dot{y} = g_x(\bar{x}, \bar{y})(x - \bar{x}) + g_y(\bar{x}, \bar{y})(y - \bar{y}).
\end{cases}
$$

This is a linear system, which has been analyzed in the previous section.

3.3. *Dynamic Path*

What is the dynamic adjustment path after a change in the system? There are two possible situations: the dynamic system may or may not be derived from an optimization problem. This is relevant since a two-variable dynamic system has two degrees of freedom or two free parameters in it. These two free parameters can be pinned down by optimization or by assumptions. Specifically, for a system

$$
\begin{cases}
\dot{x} = f(x, y), \\
\dot{y} = g(x, y),
\end{cases}
$$

when there is a change in f and/or g, the steady state may change. How can we determine the two free parameters or equivalently the starting point? For a system derived from an optimization problem, two boundary conditions (initial and terminal conditions) or two transversality conditions can determine the starting point of the optimal adjustment path. For a system that is not derived from an optimization problem, two assumptions are needed in order to pin down the adjustment path. The following two assumptions are typically made in economics.

Assumption 1. Either x or y cannot jump, but the other can.

Assumption 2. Any adjustment path can only jump at the beginning; it must move continuously afterwards. The size of the jump is determined by the fact that the path eventually converges to the steady state.

If x cannot jump, it means that we have an initial condition $x(0) = x_0$ imposed on x, where x_0 is the value of x before a change. Since the path eventually converges to the steady state, it is like a terminal condition (or a transversality condition) imposed on (x, y). For a dynamic system derived from an optimization problem, Assumption 1 generally has to be imposed arbitrarily; but in most cases (not always), Assumption 2 turns out to be an optimal behavior.

We now show in an example how to use these two assumptions to pin down the adjustment path after a change in the system. This example is borrowed from Blanchard and Fischer (1989, p. 529).

The Model

First, assume investment and consumption are affected by the long-term real interest rate $r(t)$, rather than by the short-term real interest rate $r_s(t)$. Let $A(t)$ be the aggregate demand, defined by

$$A = C + I + G = a + b(Y - T) + \alpha - \beta r + G$$
$$= bY - \beta r + a + \alpha - bT + G,$$

where $C(t)$ is aggregate consumption, $I(t)$ is aggregate investment, $Y(t)$ is aggregate output, T is income tax, G is government spending, and a, b, α and β are positive constants.

Second, assume that the adjustment of output takes time; that is,

$$\dot{Y} = \phi(A - Y) = \phi[-(1 - b)Y - \beta r + a + \alpha - bT + G],$$

where ϕ is a strictly increasing function with $\phi(0) = 0$.

Third, assume that there are two types of financial assets in the economy, a short-term bond that pays a nominal interest rate $i(t)$, and a real consol that pays one unit of good in each period. Let $Q(t)$ be the real price of the consol. The long-term return from the consol is then $r = 1/Q$ (the investor earns this much in each period), which can be derived from

$$Q = \sum_{t=1}^{\infty} \frac{1}{(1+r)^t} = \frac{1}{r}.$$

Hence, the short-term return from the consol is

$$\frac{1}{Q} + \frac{\dot{Q}}{Q} = r - \frac{\dot{r}}{r}.$$

Assume that asset holders equalize rates of return on both assets up to a constant risk premium η, i.e.,

$$r - \frac{\dot{r}}{r} = i - \pi^e + \eta,$$

where π^e is the expected inflation rate. If we have a fairly good idea of what π^e might be, there is little risk in the short bond. But, the consol is risky since part of the return is derived from capital gains.

Finally, the money demand function takes the standard form

$$\frac{M^d}{P} = L(i, Y).$$

Let $L(iY) = i^{-\delta}Y^k$, with constant elasticities $\delta > 0$ and $k > 0$. Then,

$$i = Y^{\frac{k}{\delta}} \left(\frac{M}{P}\right)^{-\frac{1}{\delta}}. \tag{4.74}$$

We then have two equations that determine the short-term dynamics and the long-run steady state:

$$\dot{Y} = \phi[-(1-b)Y - \beta r + a + \alpha - bT + G],$$

$$\dot{r} = r\left[r - Y^{\frac{k}{\delta}}\left(\frac{M}{P}\right)^{-\frac{1}{\delta}} + \pi^e - \eta\right]. \tag{4.75}$$

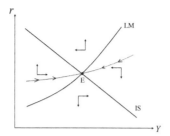

Figure 4.10. Phase Diagram

We further assume that money supply M, lump-sum tax T and government spending G are chosen by the government and are exogenous positive constants in the model. Also, risk premium η and expected inflation rate π^e are exogenous constants. Finally, P is also given — the key feature of a Keynesian model. Then, the two demarcation curves are

$$\text{IS curve:} \quad \dot{Y} = 0 \quad \text{or} \quad r = \frac{1}{\beta}[\alpha + \alpha - bT + G - (1-b)Y],$$

$$\text{LM curve:} \quad \dot{r} = 0 \quad \text{or} \quad r = Y^{\frac{k}{\delta}}\left(\frac{M}{P}\right)^{-\frac{1}{\delta}} + \eta - \pi^e. \tag{4.76}$$

The phase diagram defined by this set of equations is drawn in Figure 4.10.

The dynamic system in (4.75) is derived from equilibrium conditions, not from optimization. We impose two assumptions:

1. Y cannot jump, but r can.
2. An adjustment path can only jump at the beginning; it must move continuously afterwards.

The general solution of (4.76) has two arbitrary constants. The two assumptions above pin down these two constants. The model is now well defined. In the following, we use this model to analyze two policy changes.

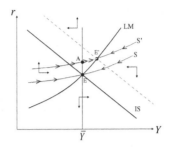

Figure 4.11. An Unexpected Tax Cut

The Dynamic Path for an Unexpected Change

Suppose that there is an unexpected tax cut and this tax cut does not affect government spending G and money supply M, implying that the tax cut is financed by debt.

This tax cut causes the IS curve to shift to the right, resulting in a new steady state E' in Figure 4.11. Since Y cannot jump, as soon as the tax cut is announced, the economy immediately jumps to point A and then moves along the convergence curve S' towards the new steady state E'.

During the adjustment period, the long rate r jumps up and then rises continuously. By (4.74), the short rate i remains unchanged initially and then rises with output Y.

The Dynamic Path for an Expected Change

Suppose now that the tax cut is announced beforehand at t_0 and then implemented later at t_1. Assume that this tax cut is credible.

Since Y cannot jump, as soon as the tax cut is announced at t_0, the economy will immediately jump to point A in Figure 4.12. Since at this point of time the system is still governed by the original system, the economy will move from A towards B. And, when t_1 arrives, the economy will reach point B on the new convergence curve S', and then move continuously towards E' along the convergence curve S'.

During the adjustment period, output decreases before the implementation of the tax cut, and then increases continuously after

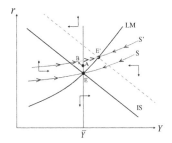

Figure 4.12. An Expected Tax Cut

the tax cut is implemented. By (4.74), the short rate i follows output. The long rate r initially jumps up and then increases continuously.

In this case, the anticipation of an expansionary fiscal policy has a contractionary effect on output. Interestingly also, from t_0 to t_1 the term structure of interest rates twists, with the long rate increasing and the short rate decreasing.

Finally, we present an example below for the linear model in (4.71), by which we can derive the equations that determine the specific turning points of the adjustment path.

Example 4.16 (An Expected Change). Given the system in (4.71) with $|A| < 0$, the system is initially in the steady state $(\bar{x}, \bar{y})$. Now, at time $t_0 = 0$, the system is expected to switch to the new steady state $(\bar{x}', \bar{y}')$ at a future time t_1. What is the adjustment path?

Assume that x cannot jump, but y can (Assumption 1). Let (x_0, y_0) be the initial point at A in Figure 4.13 with $x_0 = \bar{x}$. Before t_1, the system is under the old system defined by (4.72). Thus, the initial condition implies

$$\begin{pmatrix} \bar{x} \\ y_0 \end{pmatrix} = \begin{pmatrix} \bar{x} \\ \bar{y} \end{pmatrix} + c_1 \xi + c_2 \zeta. \tag{4.77}$$

This equation system determines the free parameters c_1 and c_2 We assume the path can jump at the beginning but not afterwards (Assumption 2). Hence, in order to converge to the new steady

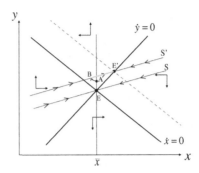

Figure 4.13. An Expected Change

state, the system must arrive at the new convergence line S' at time $t = t_1$, i.e.,

$$\begin{pmatrix} \bar{x} \\ \bar{y} \end{pmatrix} + c'\xi' = \begin{pmatrix} \bar{x} \\ \bar{y} \end{pmatrix} + c_1\xi e^{\lambda t_1} + c_2\zeta e^{\mu t_1}, \qquad (4.78)$$

for some constant $c' \in \mathbb{R}$, where the new eigenvectors are ξ' and ζ'. (4.77) is determined by Assumption 1 and (4.78) is determined by Assumption 2. Then, from (4.77), we have

$$\begin{pmatrix} c_1 \\ c_2 \end{pmatrix} = (\xi, \zeta)^{-1} \begin{pmatrix} 0 \\ y_0 - \bar{y} \end{pmatrix}.$$

Substituting this into (4.78) yields

$$\begin{pmatrix} \bar{x} \\ \bar{y} \end{pmatrix} + c'\xi' = \begin{pmatrix} \bar{x} \\ \bar{y} \end{pmatrix} + (\xi e^{\lambda t_1}, \zeta e^{\mu t_1})(\xi, \zeta)^{-1} \begin{pmatrix} 0 \\ y_0 - \bar{y} \end{pmatrix}.$$

This equation system determines y_0 and c', where y_0 indicates where point A is and c' indicates where point B is.

Notes

Chiang (1984, pp. 629–647), Turnovsky (1986), Stokey and Lucas (1989, pp. 239–259), Sargent (1987), Kamien and Schwartz (1991), and Chiang (1992) all serve as good references for this chapter.

Appendix

A.1. *Proof of Theorem 4.2*

Consider

$$V_{t+1}(x) \equiv \max_{u_{t+1},\dots} E_{t+1} \sum_{s=t+1}^{\infty} \beta^{s-t-1} f(x_s, u_s)$$

$$\text{s.t. } x_{s+1} = g(x_s, u_s, \varepsilon_{s+1}), \quad s \geq t+1,$$

$$\text{given } x_{t+1} = x.$$

Since $\{\varepsilon_t\}$ is an nth-order Markov process, we have

$$V_{t+1}(x, \varepsilon_{t+1}, \varepsilon_t, \dots, \varepsilon_{t-n+2})$$

$$\equiv \max_{u_{t+1},\dots} \left\{ \sum_{s=t+1}^{\infty} \beta^{s-t-1} f(x_s, u_s) \, \middle| \, x, \varepsilon_{t+1}, \varepsilon_t, \dots, \varepsilon_{t-n+2} \right\}$$

$$\text{s.t. } x_{s+1} = g(x_s, u_s, \varepsilon_{s+1}), \quad s \geq t+1,$$

$$\text{given } x_{t+1} = x.$$

Let $\tau = s - 1$. Then,

$$V_{t+1}(x, \varepsilon_{t+1}, \varepsilon_t, \dots, \varepsilon_{t-n+2})$$

$$\equiv \max_{u_{t+1},\dots} E \left\{ \sum_{\tau=t}^{\infty} \beta^{\tau-t} f(x_{\tau+1}, u_{\tau+1}) \, \middle| \, x, \varepsilon_{t+1}, \varepsilon_t, \dots, \varepsilon_{t-n+2} \right\}$$

$$\text{s.t. } x_{\tau+2} = g(x_{\tau+1}, u_{\tau+1}, \varepsilon_{\tau+2}), \quad \tau \geq t,$$

$$\text{given } x_{t+1} = x,$$

implying

$$V_{t+1}(x, \varepsilon'_t, \varepsilon'_{t-1}, \dots, \varepsilon'_{t-n+1})$$

$$\equiv \max_{u'_t,\dots} E \left\{ \sum_{\tau=t}^{\infty} \beta^{\tau-t} f(x'_\tau, u'_\tau) \, \middle| \, x, \varepsilon'_t, \varepsilon'_{t-1}, \dots, \varepsilon'_{t-n+1} \right\}$$

$$\text{s.t. } x'_{\tau+1} = g(x'_\tau, u'_\tau, \varepsilon'_\tau), \quad \tau \geq t,$$

$$\text{given } x'_t = x. \tag{4.79}$$

We also have

$$V_t(x, \varepsilon_t, \varepsilon_{t-1}, \ldots, \varepsilon_{t-n+1})$$

$$\equiv \max_{u_t, \ldots} E \left\{ \sum_{\tau=t}^{\infty} \beta^{\tau-t} f(x_\tau, u_\tau) \,\middle|\, x, \varepsilon_t, \varepsilon_{t-1}, \ldots, \varepsilon_{t-n+1} \right\}$$

$$\text{s.t. } x_{\tau+1} = g(x_\tau, u_\tau, \varepsilon_\tau), \quad \tau \geq t,$$

$$\text{given } x_t = x. \tag{4.80}$$

Comparing (4.79) with (4.80), we find that

$$V_{t+1}(x, \tau_1, \tau_2, \ldots, \tau_n) = V_t(x, \tau_1, \tau_2, \ldots, \tau_n),$$
$$\text{for any } (x, \tau_1, \tau_2, \ldots, \tau_n).$$

Hence, V_t is time invariant.

A.2. *Proof of Theorem 4.4*

This proof is from Kamien and Schwartz (1991). Suppose that $u^*(t), 0 \leq t \leq T$, is a solution of (4.34). Let $u(t)$ be some other admissible function satisfying the initial and terminal conditions. Denote

$$h(t) \equiv u(t) - u^*(t).$$

We have $h(0) = h(T) = 0$. For any constant $a \in \mathbb{R}$, function $y(t) \equiv u^*(t) + ah(t)$ will also be admissible and satisfy the initial and terminal conditions. Define

$$g(a) \equiv \int_0^T H[t, y(t), \dot{y}(t)] dt = \int_0^T H[t, u^*(t) + ah(t), \dot{u}^*(t) + a\dot{h}(t)] dt.$$

Since g takes the maximum when $a = 0$, we have $g'(0) = 0$, implying

$$0 = g'(0) = \int_0^T (H_u h + H_{\dot{u}} \dot{h}) dt = \int_0^T H_u h \, dt + \int_0^T H_{\dot{u}} dh$$

$$= \int_0^T H_u h \, dt + H_{\dot{u}} h \big|_0^T - \int_0^T h \left(\frac{d}{dt} H_{\dot{u}} \right) dt$$

$$= \int_0^T \left(H_u - \frac{d}{dt} H_{\dot{u}} \right) h \, dt. \tag{4.81}$$

Since h is an arbitrary continuously differentiable function taking zero at the endpoints, the above implies the Euler equation in (4.35).

For the sufficiency of the Euler equation, suppose that u^* satisfies the Euler equation and the initial and terminal conditions. For any admissible u satisfying the initial and terminal conditions, since H is concave in $(u, \dot{u})$, we have

$$H(t, u, \dot{u}) - H(t, u^* \dot{u}^*) \leq (u - u^*) H_u(t, u^* \dot{u}^*) + (\dot{u} - \dot{u}^*) H_{\dot{u}}(t, u^* \dot{u}^*),$$

which imply

$$\int_0^T \{H[t, u(t), \dot{u}(t)] - H[t, u^*(t), \dot{u}^*(t)]\} dt$$

$$\leq \int_0^{T'} [(u - u^*) H_u(t, u^*, \dot{u}^*) + (\dot{u} - \dot{u}^*) H_{\dot{u}}(t, u^*, \dot{u}^*)] dt$$

$$= \int_0^T (u - u^*) \left[H_u(t, u^*, \dot{u}^*) - \frac{d}{dt} H_{\dot{u}}(t, u^*, \dot{u}^*) \right] dt = 0.$$

That is, u^* is a solution of (4.34).

Finally, if the terminal value u_T is free, the corresponding version of problem (4.34) is

$$\max_{u \in A} \int_0^T H[t, u(t), \dot{u}(t)] dt \tag{4.82}$$
$$\text{s.t. } u(0) = u_0.$$

For this problem, (4.81) becomes

$$\int_0^T \left(H_u - \frac{d}{dt} H_{\dot{u}} \right) dt + [H_{\dot{u}} h]_{t=T} = 0. \tag{4.83}$$

Since (4.83) holds also for any h that has $h(T) = 0$, we still have the Euler equation. Then, (4.83) becomes $[H_{\dot{u}} h]_{t=T} = 0$. Since $h(T)$ is unrestricted and need not be zero, condition (4.37) must hold. The other two transversality conditions in (4.36) and (4.38) can be similarly proven.

A.3. *Proof of Theorem 4.5*

By the Lagrange theorem, there exists a function $\lambda \colon [0, T] \to \mathbb{R}^n$ such that u^* is a solution of

$$J(x_0) \equiv \max_{u,x} \int_0^T F[t, \lambda(t), x(t), u(t), \dot{x}(t)]dt$$
$$\text{s.t. } x(0) = x_0, x(T) \geq 0,$$

where F is defined by

$$F(t, \lambda, x, u, \dot{x}) \equiv f(x, u, t) + \lambda(t) \cdot [g(x, u, t) - \dot{x}].$$

By Theorem 4.5, the Euler equation for F is

$$\frac{d}{dt}\begin{pmatrix} F_{\dot{x}} \\ F_{\dot{u}} \end{pmatrix} = \begin{pmatrix} F_x \\ F_u \end{pmatrix},$$

implying

$$f_u + \lambda \cdot g_u = 0, \tag{4.84}$$
$$-\dot{\lambda} = f_x + \lambda \cdot g_x. \tag{4.85}$$

Let $H = f(x, u, t) + \lambda \cdot g(x, u, t)$. Then, (4.84)–(4.85) become (4.45)–(4.46). The transversality conditions come directly from (4.38).

A.4. *Proof of Theorem 4.6*

By Theorem 4.5, the Hamiltonian is

$$H = f(x, u)e^{-\rho t} + \mu(t) \cdot g(x, u, t).$$

The three conditions are

$$f_u(x, u)e^{-\rho t} + \mu \cdot g_u(x, u, t) = 0,$$
$$\dot{\mu} = -f_x(x, u)e^{-\rho t} - \mu \cdot g_x(x, u, t),$$
$$\lim_{t \to T} \mu x = 0, \quad \mu(T) \geq 0.$$

Let $\lambda(t) = \mu(t)e^{\rho t}$. Then, the three conditions become

$$f_u(x, u) + \lambda \cdot g_u(x, u, t) = 0,$$
$$\dot{\mu}e^{\rho t} = -f_x(x, u) - \lambda \cdot g_x(x, u, t),$$
$$\lim_{t \to T} \lambda e^{-\rho t} x = 0, \quad \mu(T)e^{-\rho t} \geq 0.$$

We have

$$\dot{\lambda} = \dot{\mu}e^{\rho t} + \rho\mu e^{\rho t} = \dot{\mu}e^{\rho t} + \rho\lambda.$$

Thus, the three conditions become

$$f_u(x, u) + \lambda \cdot g_u(x, u, t) = 0,$$
$$\dot{\mu} = \rho\lambda - f_x(x, u) - \lambda \cdot g_x(x, u, t),$$
$$\lim_{t \to T} \lambda e^{-\rho t} x = 0, \quad \lambda(T) \geq 0.$$

By choosing $H = f(x, u) + \lambda \cdot g(x, u, t)$, these three conditions become (4.48)–(4.50).

A.5. *Proof of Theorem 4.7*

Redefine the state variable as $y(t) \equiv (x(t), a)$.[17] We rewrite the problem as

$$J(x_0, x_T) \equiv \max_{u \in \mathcal{U}} \int_0^T f[y(t), u(t), t]dt$$
$$\text{s.t. } \dot{y}(t) = \begin{pmatrix} g[y(t), u(t), t] \\ 0 \end{pmatrix}$$
$$x(0) = x_0, x(T) = x_T, \quad y_{n+j}(0) \quad \text{and}$$
$$y_{n+j}(T) \text{ are free for } j = 1, \ldots, m.$$

Define

$$H = f(y, u, t) + \sum_{i=1}^{n} \lambda_i(t)g(y, u, t) + \sum_{j=1}^{m} \mu_j(t)0.$$

---

[17]Alternatively, we may treat the choice variables as a control vector and define a new set of admissible controls as $A = \{v \colon \mathbb{R} \to \mathbb{R}^m | v \text{ is a fixed vector}\}$. However, this will not work since the admissible set A has no interior point. The Euler equation works for an interior solution only.

By Theorem 4.5, we have (4.54), (4.55) and also

$$\dot{\mu} = -H_a. \tag{4.86}$$

The additional transversality conditions are

$$\mu(t_0) = \mu(T) = 0. \tag{4.87}$$

The expressions in (4.86) and (4.87) imply (4.56).

Chapter 5

Ordinary Differential Equations

In this chapter, we present a short introduction to ordinary differential equations. As we are aiming for a basic understanding, we will limit ourselves to linear equations, first-order differential equations, and some simple ways of solving them.

1. An Example

In this section, we demonstrate the usefulness of differential equations in economic analysis through an example. In a general equilibrium, prices are determined in equilibrium. However, when a change occurs in the economic system, it may take time for prices to adjust to the new equilibrium. Hence, a price is generally a function of time and it may adjust over time towards an equilibrium.

Suppose that the demand and supply functions are

$$x^d = a - bp, \quad x^s = \alpha + \beta p, \tag{5.1}$$

where a, b, α and β are constants, $b > 0$, $\beta > 0$, and p is the price. The equilibrium price is

$$p^* = \frac{a - \alpha}{b + \beta}.$$

Now, let $x^d = x^d(t)$ and $x^s = x^s(t)$ be functions of time and the adjustment process be defined by

$$\dot{x}^s = \delta(x^d - x^s), \tag{5.2}$$

187

where $\dot{x}^s = \frac{dx^s}{dt}$ and $\delta > 0$ is a constant. Substituting the expressions in (5.1) into (5.2) yields

$$\dot{p} = \frac{\delta}{\beta}(a - \alpha) - \frac{\delta}{\beta}(b + \beta)p. \tag{5.3}$$

This equation determines the price's path towards the equilibrium p^*. At the equilibrium, Equation (5.3) reaches the steady state with $\dot{p}(t) = 0$. This equation can be rewritten as

$$\frac{d(p - p^*)}{p - p^*} = -\frac{\delta}{\beta}(b + \beta)dt,$$

implying

$$p(t) = p^* + ce^{-\frac{\delta}{\beta}(b+\beta)t},$$

where c is an arbitrary constant. We can see that the price approaches the equilibrium price over time at speeds depending on factors b, β and δ. Let $p(0) = p_0$ be the initial price. Then,

$$p(t) = p^* + (p_0 - p^*)e^{-\frac{\delta}{\beta}(b+\beta)t}. \tag{5.4}$$

This example shows that a price's path towards an equilibrium can be described by a differential equation. By solving this differential equation, we can identify the factors that affect the adjustment path.

2. Introduction

A differential equation is an equation containing independent variables, unknown functions and their derivatives. If there is only one independent variable, then the differential equation is called an ordinary differential equation, otherwise it is called a partial differential equation. To put it more intuitively, a differential equation containing partial derivatives is called a partial differential equation, otherwise it is called an ordinary differential equation. For example, the following is an ordinary differential equation:

$$\left(\frac{dy}{dx}\right)^2 + x\frac{dy}{dx} + y = 0,$$

and the following is a partial differential equation:

$$\frac{\partial^2 z}{\partial x^2} + \frac{\partial^2 z}{\partial y^2} = 0.$$

We will only discuss ordinary differential equations.

A typical ordinary differential equation has the form

$$F\left(x, y, \frac{dy}{dx}, \cdots, \frac{d^n y}{dx^n}\right) = 0, \tag{5.5}$$

where F is a real-valued function. A differential equation involves derivatives. The highest order of the derivatives is the order of the equation. Hence, the order of equation (5.5) is n. If an ordinary differential equation (5.5) can be written as

$$\frac{d^n y}{dx^n} + a_1(x)\frac{d^{n-1}y}{dx^{n-1}} + \cdots + a_{n-1}(x)\frac{dy}{dx} + a_n(x)y = f(x), \tag{5.6}$$

with known functions $a_1, \ldots, a_n$ and f, then it is called a linear equation, otherwise it is called a nonlinear equation.

A solution of (5.5) in the form $y = \varphi(x)$ is called an (explicit) solution, and a solution in the form $\Phi(x, y) = 0$ is called an implicit solution. A solution of an nth-order equation typically contains n free parameters. That is, a solution of (5.5) can be written as

$$y = \varphi(x, c_1, c_2, \ldots, c_n) \quad \text{or} \quad \Phi(x, y, c_1, c_2, \ldots, c_n) = 0,$$

with n free constants $c_1, c_2, \ldots, c_n$. A solution in this form is called the general solution. To determine the arbitrary constants in the general solution, we need n additional conditions. We call conditions of the following type the initial conditions:

$$y(x_0) = y_0, \quad \frac{dy(x_0)}{dx} = y_1, \ldots, \quad \frac{d^{n-1}y(x_0)}{dx^{n-1}} = y_{n-1},$$

where $x_0, y_0, y_1, \ldots, y_{n-1}$ are given constants. A solution of a differential equation satisfying its initial conditions is called a particular solution.

For example, we have $(x+c)'_x = 1$ for any c, and $(ax^2+bx+c)''_x = 2a$. That is, $y(x) = x+c$ is a solution of $y' = 1$ for any c, and $y(x) = ax^2 + bx + c$ is a solution of $y'' = 2a$ for any b and c. This suggests that, after taking a first derivative, one free parameter is lost; after taking a second derivative, two free parameters are lost, and so on. Hence, the general solution of a differential equation of order n has n free parameters. We therefore generally need n additional conditions to pin down a particular solution.

3. First-Order Differential Equations

There is no general way to solve differential equations. Only to certain types, we have certain ways to solve them. In this section, we present a few ways of solving those types of first-order equations.

3.1. *Equations of Separable Variables*

An equation of the following form is called an equation of separable variables:

$$\frac{dy}{dx} = f(x)g(y). \tag{5.7}$$

If $g(y) \neq 0$ for all y, we can first transform it to

$$\frac{dy}{g(y)} = f(x)dx,$$

and then take integration on both sides to get

$$\int \frac{dy}{g(y)} = \int f(x)dx.$$

This is an implicit solution of (5.7).

Note that $\int f(x)dx$ is an indefinite integral of f, which is defined to be the general solution of equation $y' = f(x)$. For convenience, we often denote $F(x) \equiv \int f(x)dx$ to indicate the logical relation between f and F. Since $F(x)$ is the general solution of a first-order differential equation, F contains a free parameter.

Example 5.1. Given equation

$$\frac{dy}{dx} = \frac{x}{y},$$

we can rewrite it to

$$ydy = xdx.$$

Take integration on both sides to get

$$\frac{1}{2}y^2 = \frac{1}{2}x^2 + c,$$

where c is an arbitrary constant. The general solution is therefore

$$y^2 = x^2 + c, \tag{5.8}$$

where c is again an arbitrary constant. Suppose now that the initial condition is

$$y(1) = 2.$$

Applying this condition to the general solution in (5.8), we immediately find the constant to be $c = 3$, and hence the particular solution is

$$y^2 = x^2 + 3.$$

When c takes arbitrary values in $\mathbb{R}$, (5.8) is a family of curves in $\mathbb{R}^2$. The initial condition picks up a particular curve for $c = 3$ that goes through the point $(1,2) \in \mathbb{R}^2$. ∎

3.2. *Homogeneous Equations*

An equation of the following form is called a homogeneous equation:

$$\frac{dy}{dx} = f\left(\frac{y}{x}\right). \tag{5.9}$$

Define another variable by

$$w \equiv \frac{y}{x}.$$

Then, by $y = wx$, we have

$$\frac{dy}{dx} = w + x\frac{dw}{dx}.$$

(5.9) then becomes

$$\frac{dw}{dx} = \frac{f(w) - w}{x}.$$

This is an equation of separable variables, which we know how to solve.

Example 5.2. Consider

$$\frac{dy}{dx} = -\frac{2y}{x} + 1.$$

Let $w = y/x$. Then, by $y = xw$, we find

$$2w + 1 = \frac{dy}{dx} = x\frac{dw}{dx} + w,$$

implying

$$\frac{dw}{1 + w} = \frac{dx}{x}.$$

A solution to this equation is

$$\ln|1 + w| = \ln|x| + c,$$

implying

$$|1 + w| = c|x|,$$

where $c \geq 0$ is a free constant. Then, multiplying $|x|$ on both sides gives

$$|x + xw| = cx^2,$$

implying the general solution to the original equation:

$$|x + y| = cx^2. \quad \blacksquare$$

3.3. *Linear Equations*

A first-order linear equation can be written as

$$\frac{dy}{dx} = P(x)y + Q(x). \tag{5.10}$$

When $Q = 0$, (5.10) is an equation of separable variables. We know how to solve for its general solution in this case, which is

$$y = ce^{\int P(x)dx},$$

where c is an arbitrary constant. Now, assume that c is a function of x, and assume that the solution of (5.10) is

$$y = c(x)e^{\int P(x)dx}. \tag{5.11}$$

Substituting (5.11) into (5.10) yields

$$\frac{dc(x)}{dx} = Q(x)e^{-\int P(x)dx},$$

implying

$$c(x) = \int Q(x)e^{-\int P(x)dx}dx + \tilde{c},$$

where $\tilde{c}$ is a free constant. Substitute this back into (5.11) to obtain the general solution of (5.10):

$$y = e^{\int P(x)dx}\left(\int Q(x)e^{-\int P(x)dx}dx + \bar{c}\right).$$

The above solution process is called the method of changing parameters .

Example 5.3. Consider

$$\frac{dy}{dx} = \frac{n}{1+x}y + e^x(1+x)^n.$$

The linear part of the equation is

$$\frac{dy}{dx} = \frac{n}{1+x}y,$$

which has the following general solution:

$$y = c(1+x)^n.$$

Suppose now that the solution of the original equation has the form

$$y = c(x)(1+x)^n.$$

Substituting this into the original equation yields

$$c'(x) = e^x.$$

Then,

$$c(x) = e^x + \tilde{c},$$

where $\tilde{c}$ is a free parameter. Hence, the general solution of the original equation is

$$y = (e^x + \tilde{c})(1 + x)^n. \quad \blacksquare$$

3.4. *Exact Equations*

A first-order differential equation may be written in the following form:

$$M(x, y)dx + N(x, y)dy = 0. \tag{5.12}$$

If there is a function F such that

$$dF = Mdx + Ndy, \tag{5.13}$$

then (5.12) is called an exact equation. In this case, it is obvious that an implicit solution of (5.12) is

$$F(x, y) = c,$$

where c is a free parameter.

Theorem 5.1. *Equation* (5.12) *is exact iff* $M_y = N_x$. $\quad \blacksquare$

To find the general solution of an exact equation, the so-called method of dividing and combining is adopted. The basic idea is to divide M and N into several recognizable groups, move them to the right-hand side of the derivative operator, and then combine them into one term. Let us illustrate this method through an example.

Example 5.4. Consider

$$3x^2 dx + 4y^3 dy + 6xy^2 dx + 6x^2 ydy = 0.$$

With $M = 3x^2 + 6xy^2$ and $N = 4y^3 + 6x^2y$, one can easily verify that the above is an exact equation. To solve it, we first divide M and N into three groups:

$$dx^3 + dy^4 + (3y^2dx^2 + 3x^2dy^2) = 0.$$

Then, we move each group to the right-hand side of the derivative operator and obtain

$$dx^3 + dy^4 + 3d(x^2y^2) = 0.$$

Finally, we combine the three groups into one:

$$d(x^3 + y^4 + 3x^2y^2) - 0.$$

The general solution is therefore

$$x^3 + y^4 + 3x^2y^2 = c,$$

where c is an arbitrary constant. ∎

The following are some formulas that may be used with this method:

$$ydx + xdy = d(xy),$$
$$\varphi(x)d\psi(y) + \psi(y)d\varphi(x) = d[\varphi(x)\psi(y)],$$
$$\frac{ydx - xdy}{y^2} = d\left(\frac{x}{y}\right),$$
$$\frac{ydx - xdy}{xy} = d\left(\ln\frac{x}{y}\right),$$
$$\frac{ydx - xdy}{x^2 + y^2} = d\left(arc\ tg\frac{x}{y}\right),$$
$$\frac{ydx - xdy}{x^2 - y^2} = \frac{1}{2}d\ln\left(\frac{x - y}{x + y}\right).$$

We can solve an equation of type (5.12) if it is exact. What if the equation is not exact? For a non-exact equation, one obvious strategy is to convert it into an exact equation, if that is possible. An integrating factor is precisely for this purpose. A function $\mu(x, y)$ is called an integrating factor for (5.12) if the following equation is exact:

$$\mu M dx + \mu N dy = 0. \tag{5.14}$$

Since (5.14) is actually the same as (5.12), the general solution of (5.14) is also the general solution of (5.12).

The problem now is how to find such an integrating factor. Since finding an integrating factor generally involves a partial differential equation, which is very difficult to handle, we will restrict ourselves to integrating factors of the forms $\mu(x)$ and $\mu(y)$. By the exact condition $(\mu M)_y = (\mu N)_x$, we find that $\mu(x)$ is an integrating factor iff it is the solution of

$$\frac{d\mu}{\mu} = \frac{M_y - N_x}{N} dx. \tag{5.15}$$

This means that $\frac{M_y - N_x}{N}$ must be dependent on x only. If that is the case, we can then find $\mu(x)$ from (5.15). Similarly, $\mu(y)$ is an integrating factor iff it is the solution of

$$\frac{d\mu}{\mu} = \frac{N_x - M_y}{M} dy. \tag{5.16}$$

This means that $\frac{M_y - N_x}{M}$ must be dependent on y only. If that is the case, we can then find $\mu(y)$ from (5.16).

Example 5.5. Consider

$$y dx + (y - x) dy = 0.$$

It is not an exact equation. We find

$$\frac{M_y - N_x}{N} = \frac{2}{y - x}, \quad -\frac{M_y - N_x}{M} = -\frac{2}{y}.$$

From these expressions, we know that we can use (5.16) to solve for $\mu(y)$ from

$$\frac{d\mu}{\mu} = -\frac{2}{y} dy,$$

which gives a solution

$$\mu(y) = y^{-2}.$$

Multiplying the original equation by $\mu(y)$ yields

$$\frac{1}{y}dx + \left(\frac{1}{y} - \frac{x}{y^2}\right) dy = 0. \tag{5.17}$$

Since this is an exact equation, we can use the method of dividing and combining to solve it. We have

$$\frac{1}{y}dx + \left(\frac{1}{y} - \frac{x}{y^2}\right) dy = \frac{1}{y}dx + d\ln|y| + xd\frac{1}{y} = d\left(\frac{x}{y} + \ln|y|\right).$$

Hence, the general solution of (5.17), which is also the general solution of the original equation, is

$$\frac{x}{y} + \ln|y| = c,$$

where c is a free parameters. ∎

3.5. The Method of Power Series

We illustrate this method through an example.

Example 5.6. Consider

$$\frac{dy}{dx} = y - x, \quad \text{with} \quad y(0) = 0. \tag{5.18}$$

Assume that the solution can be expressed as

$$y(x) = \sum_{i=0}^{\infty} a_i x^i, \tag{5.19}$$

where $\{a_i\}$ are constants. Then,

$$y' = \sum_{i=1}^{\infty} i a_i x^{i-1}. \tag{5.20}$$

Substituting (5.19) and (5.20) into (5.18) yields

$$a_1 = a_0, \quad 2a_2 = a_1 - 1, \quad ka_k = a_{k-1}, \quad \text{for} \quad k \geq 3.$$

Using condition $y(0) = 0$, we find

$$a_1 = a_0 = 0, \quad a_2 = -\frac{1}{2}, \quad a_3 = -\frac{1}{3!}, \quad a_n = -\frac{1}{n!}.$$

Hence, the solution is

$$y = 1 + x - \left(1 + x + \frac{x^2}{2!} + \frac{x^3}{3!} + \cdots\right) = 1 + x - e^x. \quad \blacksquare$$

4. The Method of Laplace Transform

We now deal with differential equations of higher orders, but we limit ourselves to linear equations only. The Laplace transform is a convenient method for solving a linear equation with constant coefficients of the following form:

$$\frac{d^n x}{dt^n} + a_1 \frac{d^{n-1}x}{dt^{n-1}} + \cdots + a_{n-1}\frac{dx}{dt} + a_n x = f(t), \qquad (5.21)$$

where $a_1, \ldots, a_n$ are constants. This method can also handle a system of multiple linear equations of the form in (5.21).

Given a function $g(t)$, we can apply the Laplace transform L to it:

$$\mathcal{L}(g) \equiv \int_0^\infty e^{-st} g(t) dt.$$

Here, $\mathcal{L}(g)$ is a function of s, for $s > 0$, We denote $G(s) = \mathcal{L}(g)$. We call g the original function and G the image function. It is obvious that $\mathcal{L}$ is a linear mapping. The inverse Laplace transform $\mathcal{L}^{-1}$, which maps the image function back to its original function, is also linear. We find

$$\mathcal{L}[g'(t)] = \int_0^\infty e^{-st} g'(t) dt = e^{-st} g(t)|_{t=0}^{t=\infty} + s \int_0^\infty e^{-st} g(t) dt$$

$$= s\mathcal{L}[g(t)] - g(0),$$

where we assume $\lim_{t\to\infty} e^{-st} g(t) = 0$ for any $s > 0$. The above further implies

$$\mathcal{L}[g''(t)] = s\mathcal{L}[g'(t)] - g'(0)$$

$$= s\{s\mathcal{L}[g(t)] - g(0)\} - g'(0) = s^2 \mathcal{L}[g(t)] - sg(0) - g'(0).$$

Hence, in general,

$$\mathcal{L}[g^{(k)}(t)] = s^k G(s) - s^{k-1}g(0) - s^{k-2}g'(0) - \cdots - g^{(k-1)}(0). \quad (5.22)$$

Denote

$$F(s) = \mathcal{L}[f(t)] \equiv \int_0^\infty e^{-st} f(t)dt, \quad X(s) = \mathcal{L}[x(t)] \equiv \int_0^\infty e^{-st} x(t)dt.$$

Let $x^{(k)}(0) = x_k$ for $k = 0, \ldots, n-1$. Then, by taking the Laplace transform of Equation (5.21) and using (5.22), we get

$$X(s) = \frac{F(s) + x_0 \sum_{i=1}^n a_{i-1}s^{n-i} + x_1 \sum_{i=2}^n a_{i-2}s^{n-i} + \cdots + x_{n-1}}{s^n + a_1 s^{n-1} + \cdots + a_{n-1}s + a_n}. \quad (5.23)$$

Once we have calculated $F(s)$ and properly arranged the right-hand side of (5.23), we can then take the inverse Laplace transform to find $x(t)$ from $X(s)$. This $x(t)$ is a solution of (5.21).

The following proposition lists a few useful formulas used in the Laplace transform.

Proposition 5.1. *For $a \in \mathbb{R}$ and integer $n \geq 0$.*

(a) $\mathcal{L}^{-1}\left(\frac{1}{s-a}\right) = e^{at}, \quad \mathcal{L}^{-1}\left[\frac{1}{(s-a)^{n+1}}\right] = \frac{t^n e^{at}}{n!},$

(b) $\mathcal{L}^{-1}\left(\frac{a}{s^2+a^2}\right) = \sin(at), \quad \mathcal{L}^{-1}\left(\frac{s}{s^2+a^2}\right) = \cos(at).$

(c) $\mathcal{L}^{-1}[F(s)] = e^{at}\mathcal{L}^{-1}[F(s+a)].$ ■

Property (c) is very useful. For example, since

$$\mathcal{L}(1) = \int_0^\infty e^{-st} dt = \frac{1}{s},$$

we have

$$\mathcal{L}^{-1}\left(\frac{1}{s}\right) = 1.$$

Hence,

$$\mathcal{L}^{-1}\left(\frac{1}{s-a}\right) = e^{at}\mathcal{L}^{-1}\left(\frac{1}{s}\right) = e^{at}.$$

The following example shows how to apply the Laplace transform to solve a linear equation with constant coefficients.

Example 5.7. Consider equation

$$\frac{dx}{dt} - x = e^{2t}. \tag{5.24}$$

By taking the Laplace transform on both sides of the above equation, we find

$$sX(s) - x_0 - X(s) = \frac{1}{s-2},$$

where x_0 is an arbitrary constant. Then,

$$X(s) = \frac{1}{(s-1)(s-2)} + \frac{x_0}{s-1} = \frac{1}{s-2} + \frac{x_0 - 1}{s-1}.$$

By Proposition 5.1(a), we then find

$$x(t) = \mathcal{L}^{-1}\left(\frac{1}{s-2} + \frac{x_0^{-1}}{s-1}\right)$$

$$= \mathcal{L}^{-1}\left(\frac{1}{s-2}\right) + (x_0 - 1)\mathcal{L}^{-1}\left(\frac{1}{s-2}\right)$$

$$= e^{2t} + (x_0 - 1)e^t.$$

This is the general solution of (5.24).   ∎

Example 5.8. We can also solve (5.3) using the Laplace transform. By the Laplace transform, (5.3) becomes

$$sP(s) - p_0 = \frac{\delta}{\beta}(a - \alpha)\frac{1}{s} - \frac{\delta}{\beta}(b + \beta)P(s),$$

implying

$$P(s) = \frac{\frac{\delta}{\beta}(a-\alpha)\frac{1}{s} + p_0}{s + \frac{\delta}{\beta}(b+\beta)} = \frac{p^*}{s} + \frac{p_0 - p^*}{s + \frac{\delta}{\beta}(b+\beta)},$$

where $p^* = \frac{a-\alpha}{b+\beta}$. Hence,

$$p(t) = \mathcal{L}^{-1}\left[\frac{p^*}{s} + \frac{p_0 - p^*}{s + \frac{\delta}{\beta}(b+\beta)}\right]$$

$$= p^* \mathcal{L}^{-1}\left(\frac{1}{s}\right) + (p_0 - p^*)\mathcal{L}^{-1}\left(\frac{1}{s + \frac{\delta}{\beta}(b + \beta)}\right)$$

$$= p^* + (p_0 - p^*)e^{-\frac{\delta}{\beta}(b+\beta)t},$$

which is the same as the solution in (5.4). ■

The following example shows how to apply the Laplace transform to solve a linear equation system with constant coefficients.

Example 5.9. Consider an equation system for two functions $x_1(t)$ and $x_2(t)$

$$\begin{cases} x_1'' - 2x_1' - x_2' + 2x_2 = 0, \\ x_1' - 2x_1 + x_2' = -2x^{-t}, \end{cases}$$

with initial conditions

$$x_1(0) = 3, \quad x_1'(0) = 2, \quad x_2(0) = 0.$$

Let $X_1(s) \equiv \mathcal{L}(x_1)$ and $X_2(s) \equiv \mathcal{L}(x_2)$. Then,

$$\begin{cases} [s^2 X_1(s) - 3s - 2] - 2[sX_1(s) - 3] - sX_2(s) + 2X_2(s) = 0, \\ [sX_1(s) - 3] - 2X_1(s) + sX_2(s) = -\dfrac{2}{s+1}, \end{cases}$$

implying

$$\begin{pmatrix} s^2 - 2s & 2 - s \\ s - 2 & s \end{pmatrix} \begin{pmatrix} X_1(s) \\ X_2(s) \end{pmatrix} = \begin{pmatrix} 3s - 4 \\ 3 - \frac{2}{s+1} \end{pmatrix},$$

which immediately implies

$$X_1(s) = \frac{3s^2 - 4s - 1}{(s+1)(s-1)(s-2)} = \frac{1}{s-1} + \frac{1}{s+1} + \frac{1}{s-2},$$

$$X_2(s) = \frac{2}{(s+1)(s-1)} = \frac{1}{s-1} - \frac{1}{s+1}.$$

Then, using the inverse Laplace transform, we immediately find the solution

$$x_1(t) = e^t + e^{-t} + e^{2t}, \qquad x_2(t) = e^t - e^{-t}. \quad ■$$

5. Linear Equation Systems

We now consider a system of multiple equations, but we limit ourselves to linear equations only. Since a linear equation system can always be expressed as a first-order linear equation system, we restrict ourselves to first-order linear equation systems.

5.1. *Existence and Uniqueness*

Any vector-valued function $G: \mathbb{R} \to \mathbb{R}^n$ can be expressed as

$$G(t) \equiv \begin{pmatrix} g_1(t) \\ g_2(t) \\ \vdots \\ g_n(t) \end{pmatrix},$$

where $g_i(t)$ is a real-valued function. We define the derivative and integral of $G(t)$ as

$$G'(t) = \begin{pmatrix} g_1'(t) \\ g_2'(t) \\ \vdots \\ g_n'(t) \end{pmatrix}, \qquad \int G(t)dt \equiv \begin{pmatrix} \int g_1(t)dt \\ \int g_2(t)dt \\ \vdots \\ \int g_n(t)dt \end{pmatrix}.$$

The same notation applies to matrix-valued functions. Then, a first-order linear equation system can be expressed as

$$X'(t) = A(t)X(t) + F(t), \tag{5.25}$$

where

$$X(t) = \begin{pmatrix} x_1(t) \\ x_2(t) \\ \vdots \\ x_n(t) \end{pmatrix}, \quad A(t) = \begin{pmatrix} a_{11}(t) & a_{12}(t) & \cdots & a_{1n}(t) \\ a_{21}(t) & a_{22}(t) & \cdots & a_{2n}(t) \\ \vdots & \vdots & & \vdots \\ a_{n1}(t) & a_{n2}(t) & \cdots & a_{nn}(t) \end{pmatrix},$$

$$F(t) = \begin{pmatrix} f_1(t) \\ f_2(t) \\ \vdots \\ f_n(t) \end{pmatrix}.$$

When $F = 0$, the equation system becomes

$$X'(t) = A(t)X(t), \tag{5.26}$$

which is called a homogeneous linear system.

Example 5.10. The linear equation in (5.6) can be rewritten as a special case of (5.26). Let

$$y_1 = y, \quad y_2 = y', \quad y_3 = y'', \ldots, \quad y_n = y^{(n-1)}.$$

Then,

$$
\begin{pmatrix} y_1' \\ y_2' \\ \vdots \\ y_n' \end{pmatrix} = \begin{pmatrix} y_2 \\ y_3 \\ \vdots \\ y^{(n)} \end{pmatrix}
$$

$$
= \begin{pmatrix} 0 & 1 & & & \\ & 0 & 1 & & \\ & & \ddots & \ddots & \\ & & & 0 & 1 \\ -a_n & -a_{n-1} & \cdots & -a_2 & -a_1 \end{pmatrix} \begin{pmatrix} y_1 \\ y_2 \\ \vdots \\ y_n \end{pmatrix} + \begin{pmatrix} 0 \\ 0 \\ \vdots \\ f(x) \end{pmatrix}. \quad \blacksquare
$$

Proposition 5.2. *If $A(t)$ and $F(t)$ are continuous on an interval $[a, b]$, then, for any $t_0 \in [a, b]$ and vector X_0, Equation (5.25) has a unique solution $X(t)$ defined on $[a, b]$ such that $X(t_0) = X_0$.* $\blacksquare$

5.2. *Homogeneous Equations*

Functions $x_1(t), x_2(t), \ldots, x_k(t)$ defined on $[a, b]$ are said to be (linearly) dependent if there exist constants $c_1, c_2, \ldots, c_k$, not all zero, such that

$$c_1 x_1(t) + c_2 x_2(t) + \cdots + c_k x_k(t) = 0, \quad \forall t \in [a, b],$$

otherwise they are said to be (linearly) independent.

Example 5.11. Let us show that functions $x_1(t) = t, x_2(t) = t^2$ and $x_3(t) = t^3$ defined on $[0, 1]$ are linearly independent. Suppose

$$c_1 x_1(t) + c_2 x_2(t) + c_3 x_3(t) = 0, \quad \forall t \in [0, 1]. \qquad (5.27)$$

Then, for any three values t_1, t_2 and t_3 in $[0, 1]$, (5.27) implies

$$\begin{pmatrix} t_1 & t_1^2 & t_1^3 \\ t_2 & t_2^2 & t_2^3 \\ t_3 & t_3^2 & t_3^3 \end{pmatrix} \begin{pmatrix} c_1 \\ c_2 \\ c_3 \end{pmatrix} = \begin{pmatrix} 0 \\ 0 \\ 0 \end{pmatrix}. \qquad (5.28)$$

Consider a polynomial of t:

$$\begin{vmatrix} t & t^2 & t^3 \\ t_2 & t_2^2 & t_2^3 \\ t_3 & t_3^2 & t_3^3 \end{vmatrix} = 0.$$

Since t_2 and t_3 are obviously roots of this polynomial, there is some $a \in \mathbb{R}$ such that

$$\begin{vmatrix} t & t^2 & t^3 \\ t_2 & t_2^2 & t_2^3 \\ t_3 & t_3^2 & t_3^3 \end{vmatrix} = (t - t_2)(t - t_3)(t - a).$$

Thus, if $t_1 \neq a$, equation (5.28) implies $c_1 = c_2 = c_3 = 0$. Hence, (5.27) implies $c_1 = c_2 = c_3 = 0$. Therefore, $x_1(t), x_2(t)$ and $x_3(t)$ are linearly independent. ∎

Proposition 5.3. *Equation (5.26) has n independent solutions X_1, $\ldots, X_n$. And, given any set of n independent solutions $X_1, \ldots, X_n$, any solution of (5.26) can be expressed as*

$$X(t) = c_1 X_1(t) + c_2 X_2(t) + \cdots + c_n X_n(t),$$

for some constants $c_1 c_2, \ldots, c_n$. ∎

Given a set of solutions $X_1, \ldots, X_n$, we call $\Phi(t) \equiv [X_1(t), X_2(t), \ldots, X_n(t)]$ a solution matrix. When the solutions are independent, we call $\Phi(t)$ a base matrix and $X_1, \ldots, X_n$ a solution basis. By Proposition 5.3, the set of solutions of (5.26) forms a vector space of dimension n. Hence, Proposition 5.3 can be stated in another way as follows.

Theorem 5.2.

- *Equation* (5.26) *has a base matrix.*
- *Given a base matrix* $\Phi(t)$, *the general solution of* (5.26) *is* $X(t) = \Phi(t)C$, *where* C *is an arbitrary constant vector.* ∎

Proposition 5.4.

(a) *A solution matrix* $\Phi(t)$ *is a base matrix iff* $|\Phi(t_0)| \neq 0$ *for some* $t_0 \in [a, b]$.

(b) *If there exists a* $t_0 \in [a, b]$ *such that* $|\Phi(t_0)| \neq 0$, *then* $|\Phi(t)| \neq 0$ *for all* $t \in [a, b]$. ∎

Example 5.12. Consider

$$X' = \begin{pmatrix} 1 & 1 \\ 0 & 1 \end{pmatrix} X. \tag{5.29}$$

We can easily verify that the following is a base matrix:

$$\Phi(t) \equiv \begin{pmatrix} e^t & te^t \\ 0 & e_t \end{pmatrix}.$$

Therefore, the general solution is

$$X = \begin{pmatrix} e^t & te^t \\ 0 & e^t \end{pmatrix} C,$$

where $C \in \mathbb{R}^2$ is a free constant vector. ∎

5.3. *Linear Equation Systems*

Equipped with knowledge on the homogenous equation system (5.26) in the last section, we can now discuss the linear equation system in (5.25).

Proposition 5.5. *Let* $\Phi(t)$ *be a base matrix for the homogeneous equation system in* (5.26) *and* $\bar{X}(t)$ *be a solution of* (5.25). *Then, the general solution of* (5.25) *is*

$$X(t) = \Phi(t)C + \bar{X}(t),$$

where C *is an arbitrary constant vector.* ∎

Now consider a general way to solve an equation system. We first look at how to find a particular solution of the linear equation system in (5.25), given a base matrix $\Phi(t)$. One method is called the method of changing constant. As we know, $X(t) = \Phi(t)C$ is a solution of (5.26) if C is a constant vector. Assume that a solution of (5.25) is of the form:

$$X(t) = \Phi(t)C(t).$$

Substituting it into (5.25) gives

$$C(t) = \tilde{C} + \int_0^t \Phi^{-1}(s)F(s)ds,$$

for an arbitrary constant vector $\tilde{C} \in \mathbb{R}^n$. We hence have the following theorem.

Theorem 5.3. *Given a base matrix $\Phi(t)$, the general solution of* (5.25) *is*

$$X(t) = \Phi(t)\left[C + \int_0^t \Phi^{-1}(s)F(s)ds\right]. \quad \blacksquare \qquad (5.30)$$

Example 5.13. Consider

$$X' = \begin{pmatrix} 1 & 1 \\ 0 & 1 \end{pmatrix} X + \begin{pmatrix} e^{-t} \\ 0 \end{pmatrix}.$$

A base matrix is

$$\Phi(t) \equiv \begin{pmatrix} e^t & te^t \\ 0 & e^t \end{pmatrix}.$$

We have

$$\int_0^t \Phi^{-1}(s)F(s)ds = \int_0^t e^{-s}\begin{pmatrix} 1 & -s \\ 0 & 1 \end{pmatrix}\begin{pmatrix} e^{-s} \\ 0 \end{pmatrix}ds$$

$$= \int_0^t \begin{pmatrix} e^{-2s} \\ 0 \end{pmatrix}ds = \begin{pmatrix} \frac{e^t-e^{-t}}{2} \\ 0 \end{pmatrix}.$$

Hence, by (5.30), the general solution is

$$X = e^t \begin{pmatrix} 1 & t \\ 0 & 1 \end{pmatrix} \left[c + \begin{pmatrix} \frac{e^t - e^{-t}}{2} \\ 0 \end{pmatrix} \right]. \quad \blacksquare$$

5.4. *Linear Equation Systems with Constant Coefficients*

By Theorem 5.3, we now know that the key to solving a linear equation system is to find a base matrix. When the coefficients of (5.26) are constants, that is,

$$X'(t) = AX(t), \tag{5.31}$$

where A is a constant matrix, we have a general method of finding a base matrix based on eigenvalues.

Define matrix e^A by

$$e^A \equiv \sum_{k=0}^{\infty} \frac{A^k}{k!} = I + A + \frac{A^2}{2!} + \cdots \frac{A^m}{m!} + \cdots,$$

where we assume $A^0 = I$ and $0! = 1$. Note that the above matrix series is convergent for any matrix $A \in \mathbb{R}^{n \times n}$. Hence, for any $A \in \mathbb{R}^{n \times n}$, e^A is a well-defined matrix in $\mathbb{R}^{n \times n}$.

Proposition 5.6.

- *If A and B are commutative such that $AB = BA$, then $e^{A+B} = e^A e^B$.*
- $(e^A)^{-1} = e^{-A}$.
- $e^{T^{-1}AT} = T^{-1}e^A T$. $\quad \blacksquare$

Theorem 5.4. $\Phi(t) \equiv e^{At}$ *is a base matrix for* (5.13). *It is called the standard base matrix since* $\Phi(0) = 1$. $\quad \blacksquare$

Example 5.14. Consider

$$A = \begin{pmatrix} 2 & 1 \\ 0 & 2 \end{pmatrix}.$$

Since

$$A \equiv \begin{pmatrix} 2 & 1 \\ 0 & 2 \end{pmatrix} = 2I + \begin{pmatrix} 0 & 1 \\ 0 & 0 \end{pmatrix},$$

and since the two matrices on the right-hand side are commutative, by Proposition 5.6,

$$
\begin{aligned}
e^{At} &= e^{2It} e^{\begin{pmatrix} 0 & 1 \\ 0 & 0 \end{pmatrix} t} \\
&= \begin{pmatrix} e^{2t} & \\ & e^{2t} \end{pmatrix} \left\{ I + \begin{pmatrix} 0 & 1 \\ 0 & 0 \end{pmatrix} t + \frac{1}{2!} \begin{pmatrix} 0 & 1 \\ 0 & 0 \end{pmatrix}^2 t^2 + \cdots \right\} \\
&= e^{2t} \begin{pmatrix} 1 & t \\ 0 & 1 \end{pmatrix}. \quad \blacksquare
\end{aligned}
$$

Example 5.15. As in Example 5.14, we can show that the base matrix in example 5.12 is the standard base matrix for Equation (5.29). ∎

For a simple matrix A, we can use Theorem 5.4 to find a base matrix. However, when A is not simple, we will have difficulty in calculating e^{At}. We now introduce another method of finding a base matrix that is applicable to any matrix A. For this purpose, we present the following proposition, which can be easily verified.

Proposition 5.7. $\varphi(t) = e^{\lambda t} C$ *is a solution of* (5.31), $C \neq 0$, *if and only if* λ *is an eigenvalue of* A *and* C *is an eigenvector of* λ. ∎

Theorem 5.5. *If* A *has* n *linearly independent eigenvectors* $\xi_1, \xi_2, \ldots, \xi_n$ *corresponding to eigenvalues* $\lambda_1, \lambda_2, \ldots, \lambda_n$ *(not necessarily distinct), then* $\Phi(t) = [e^{\lambda_1 t} \xi_1, e^{\lambda_2 t} \xi_2, \ldots, e^{\lambda_n t} \xi_n]$ *is a base matrix of* (5.13) *and*

$$e^{At} = \Phi(t)\Phi^{-1}(0). \quad \blacksquare \tag{5.32}$$

Note that if A is real, e^{At} is real. Therefore, formula (5.32) also provides a way to convert a complex base matrix to a real one.

Example 5.16. Consider

$$X'(t) = \begin{pmatrix} 1 & 4 \\ 0 & 2 \end{pmatrix} X(t).$$

For

$$A = \begin{pmatrix} 1 & 4 \\ 0 & 2 \end{pmatrix},$$

the eigenvalues are $\lambda_1 = 1$ and $\lambda_2 = 2$. We can find a simple eigenvector for each eigenvalue:

$$(\lambda_1 I - A)\xi = \begin{pmatrix} 0 & -4 \\ 0 & -1 \end{pmatrix} \xi = 0 \quad \Rightarrow \quad \xi_1 = \begin{pmatrix} 1 \\ 0 \end{pmatrix},$$

and

$$(\lambda_2 I - A)\xi = \begin{pmatrix} 1 & -4 \\ 0 & 0 \end{pmatrix} \xi = 0 \quad \Rightarrow \quad \xi_1 = \begin{pmatrix} 4 \\ 1 \end{pmatrix}.$$

Hence, by Theorem 5.5, a base matrix is

$$\Phi(t) = (e^t \xi_1, \quad e^{2t} \xi_2) = \begin{pmatrix} e^t & 4e^{2t} \\ 0 & e^{2t} \end{pmatrix}. \quad \blacksquare$$

Example 5.17. We now solve the equation system in Example 5.9 using eigenvalues. Let $x_3 \equiv x_1'$. Then, the problem becomes

$$\begin{cases} x_1' = x_3, \\ x_3' - 2x_1' - x_2' + 2x_2 = 0, \\ x_1' - 2x_1 + x_2' = -2e^{-t}, \end{cases}$$

or

$$\begin{pmatrix} 1 & 0 & 0 \\ -2 & -1 & 1 \\ 1 & 1 & 0 \end{pmatrix} \begin{pmatrix} x_1' \\ x_2' \\ x_3' \end{pmatrix} = \begin{pmatrix} 0 & 0 & 1 \\ 0 & -2 & 0 \\ 2 & 0 & 0 \end{pmatrix} \begin{pmatrix} x_1 \\ x_2 \\ x_3 \end{pmatrix} + \begin{pmatrix} 0 \\ 0 \\ -2e^{-t} \end{pmatrix}.$$

Then,

$$
\begin{aligned}
X'(t) &= \begin{pmatrix} 1 & 0 & 0 \\ -2 & -1 & 1 \\ 1 & 1 & 0 \end{pmatrix}^{-1} \left[\begin{pmatrix} 0 & 0 & 1 \\ 0 & -2 & 0 \\ 2 & 0 & 0 \end{pmatrix} X(t) - 2e^{-t} \begin{pmatrix} 0 \\ 0 \\ 1 \end{pmatrix} \right] \\
&= \begin{pmatrix} 0 & 0 & 1 \\ 2 & 0 & -1 \\ 2 & -2 & 1 \end{pmatrix} X(t) - 2e^{-t} \begin{pmatrix} 0 \\ 1 \\ 1 \end{pmatrix}.
\end{aligned}
$$

From

$$0 = \begin{vmatrix} \lambda & 0 & -1 \\ -2 & \lambda & 1 \\ -2 & 2 & \lambda - 1 \end{vmatrix} = \lambda^3 - \lambda^2 - 4\lambda + 4 = (\lambda - 1)(\lambda - 2)(\lambda + 2),$$

we find three eigenvalues $\lambda_1 = 1$, $\lambda_2 = 2$ and $\lambda_3 = -2$ and a simple eigenvector for each:

$$\xi_1 = \begin{pmatrix} 1 \\ 1 \\ 1 \end{pmatrix}, \qquad \xi_2 = \begin{pmatrix} 1 \\ 0 \\ 2 \end{pmatrix}, \qquad \xi_3 = \begin{pmatrix} -1 \\ 2 \\ 2 \end{pmatrix}.$$

Hence, by Theorem 5.5, a base matrix is

$$\Phi(t) = \begin{pmatrix} e^t & e^{2t} & -e^{2t} \\ e^t & 0 & 2e^{-2t} \\ e^t & 2e^{2t} & 2e^{-2t} \end{pmatrix}.$$

By Theorem 5.3, the general solution is

$$X(t) = \Phi(t) \left[C + \int_0^t \Phi^{-1}(s)F(s)ds \right].$$

We have

$$\int_0^t \Phi^{-1}(s)F(s)ds = -\frac{1}{3} \int_0^t \begin{pmatrix} 4e^{-s} & 4e^{-s} & -2e^{-s} \\ 0 & -3e^{-2s} & 3e^{-2s} \\ -2e^{2s} & e^{2s} & e^{2s} \end{pmatrix} \begin{pmatrix} 0 \\ 1 \\ 1 \end{pmatrix} e^{-s} ds$$

$$= -\frac{2}{3} \int_0^t \begin{pmatrix} e^{-2s} \\ 0 \\ e^s \end{pmatrix} ds = -\frac{2}{3} \begin{pmatrix} \frac{1-e^{-2t}}{2} \\ 0 \\ e^t - 1 \end{pmatrix}.$$

By the initial conditions, we find

$$C = \begin{pmatrix} 1 & 1 & -1 \\ 1 & 0 & 2 \\ 1 & 2 & 2 \end{pmatrix}^{-1} \begin{pmatrix} 3 \\ 0 \\ 2 \end{pmatrix} = \frac{1}{3} \begin{pmatrix} 4 \\ 3 \\ -2 \end{pmatrix}.$$

Hence, the solution is

$$X(t) = \begin{pmatrix} e^t & e^{2t} & -e^{-2t} \\ e^t & 0 & 2e^{-2t} \\ e^t & 2e^{2t} & 2e^{-2t} \end{pmatrix} \left[\frac{1}{3} \begin{pmatrix} 4 \\ 3 \\ -2 \end{pmatrix} - \frac{2}{3} \begin{pmatrix} \frac{1-e^{-2t}}{2} \\ 0 \\ e^t - 1 \end{pmatrix} \right]$$

$$= \begin{pmatrix} e^t + e^{-t} + e^{2t} \\ e^t - e^{-t} \\ e^t - e^{-t} + 2e^{2t} \end{pmatrix},$$

which gives us the same solution as in Example 5.9. ∎

Notes

Chiang (1984, Chapter 14) and Chiang and Wainwright (2005, Chapters 15 and 19) are both good references.

Appendix

A.1. *Proof of Theorem 5.1*

If (5.12) is exact, then

$$M = \frac{\partial F}{\partial x}, \qquad N = \frac{\partial F}{\partial y}.$$

This immediately implies the exact condition: $M_y = N_x$. The exact condition is therefore necessary.

Conversely, when the exact condition is satisfied, we find

$$d \int M dx = M dx + \left(\int M_y dx \right) dy = M dx + \left(\int N_x dx \right) dy$$

$$= M dx + [N + C(y)] dy = M dx + N dy + C(y) dy,$$

where $C(y)$ is some function of y. This implies

$$d \int M dx - d \int C(y) dy = M dx + N dy.$$

That is, we find

$$F \equiv \int M dx - \int C(y) dy,$$

which satisfies (5.13). Hence, the exact condition is also sufficient.

A.2. *Proof of Proposition 5.1*

We prove property (c) only. We have

$$F(s+a) = \int_0^\infty e^{-(s+a)t} f(t)dt = \int_0^\infty e^{-st}[e^{-at}f(t)dt] = \mathcal{L}[e^{-at}f(t)],$$

which then implies

$$\mathcal{L}^{-1}[F(s+a)] = e^{-at}f(t) = e^{-at}\mathcal{L}^{-1}[F(s)].$$

A.3. *Proof of Proposition 5.4*

Part (a) can be proven in the same way as the proof in Example 5.11. We need to show Part (b) only. By (a), if $|\Phi(t_0)| \neq 0$ for some x_0, the solution matrix $\Phi(t)$ is a base matrix. Thus, for any t, its column vectors are linearly independent, implying $|\Phi(t)| \neq 0$ for any t.

A.4. *Proof of Theorem 5.4*

We have

$$\Phi'(t) = A + \frac{2A^2 t}{2!} + \cdots + \frac{mA^m t^{m-1}}{m!} + \cdots$$

$$= A\left(I + A + \frac{A^2}{2!} + \cdots + \frac{A^m}{m!} + \cdots\right) = A\Phi(t).$$

A.5. *Proof of Theorem 5.5*

By Proposition 5.7, $\Phi(t)$ is a solution matrix. Also, $|\Phi(0)| \neq 0$. Thus, it is a base matrix. Further, by Theorem 5.2, the dimension of the solution space of (5.26) is n. Hence, we must have a $B \in \mathbb{R}^{n \times n}$ such that $e^{At} = \Phi(t)B$, which immediately implies $B = \Phi^{-1}(0)$.

Chapter 6

Difference Equations

This chapter intends to give a short introduction to difference equations. We discuss linear equations only.

1. Introduction

A typical sequence $y_0, y_1, \ldots, y_t, \ldots$ can be denoted in short by $\{y_t\}$, or more precisely $\{y_t\}_0^\infty$. An ordinary difference equation of $\{y_t\}$ is a relation of the form

$$F(t, y_{t+n}, y_{t+n-1}, y_{t+n-2}, \ldots, y_t) = 0, \tag{6.1}$$

where F is a real-valued function and the index t takes integers. The order of a difference equation is the difference between the highest and lowest values of the index in the equation. The above equation has order n. A difference equation is linear if it has the form

$$y_{t+n} + a_{1,t} y_{t+n-1} + a_{2,t} y_{t+n-2} + \cdots + a_{n-1,t} y_{t+1} + a_{n,t} y_t = f_t,$$

where $a_{i,t}$ and f_t are given sequences. A solution of the form

$$y_t = f(t, c_1, c_2, \ldots, c_n), \tag{6.2}$$

with arbitrary constants $c_1, c_2, \ldots, c_n$ is called the general solution. If $y_0, y_1, \ldots, y_{n-1}$ are assigned values (called initial values), (6.1) has a unique solution, which is called a particular solution.

Define the (first) difference operator Δ as

$$\Delta y_t \equiv y_{t+1} - y_t,$$

which is called the difference of y_t. The second difference operator Δ^2 is defined as $\Delta^2 y_t \equiv \Delta(\Delta y_t)$. In general,

$$\Delta^n y_t \equiv \Delta \left(\Delta^{n-1} y_t\right),$$

where $\Delta^0 = 1$. The following proposition is obvious but quite useful.

Proposition 6.1. (*Properties of Δ*).

- $\Delta^n \Delta^m y_t = \Delta^m \Delta^n y_t$;
- $\Delta(ax_t + by_t) = a\Delta x_t + b\Delta y_t$, *for any $a, b \in \mathbb{R}$.* ∎

Denote by Δ^{-1} the inverse difference operator, defined by

$$\Delta(\Delta^{-1} y_t) = y_t,$$

for any sequence $\{y_t\}$.

Theorem 6.1. *For any sequence y_t,*

$$\Delta^{-1} y_t = c + \sum_{i=1}^{t-1} y_i,$$

where c is an arbitrary constant. ∎

2. First-Order Difference Equations

Given sequences p_t and q_t, a difference equation of the following form is called a first-order linear difference equation:

$$y_{t+1} - p_t y_t = q_t. \tag{6.3}$$

Theorem 6.2. *The general solution of (6.3) is*

$$y_t = \prod_{i=1}^{t-1} p_i \left(c + \sum_{i=1}^{t-1} \frac{q_i}{p_1 \cdots p_i} \right), \tag{6.4}$$

where c is an arbitrary constant. ∎

Proof. [1] Dividing both sides of (6.3) by $\prod_{i=1}^{t} p_i$ yields

$$\frac{y_{t+1}}{\prod_{i=1}^{t} p_i} - \frac{y_t}{\prod_{i=1}^{t-1} p_i} = \frac{q_t}{\prod_{i=1}^{t} p_i},$$

which can be written as

$$\Delta \left(\frac{y_t}{\prod_{i=1}^{t-1} p_i} \right) = \frac{q_t}{\prod_{i=1}^{t} p_i}.$$

Therefore,

$$\frac{y_t}{\prod_{i=1}^{t-1} p_i} = \Delta^{-1} \left(\frac{q_t}{\prod_{i=1}^{t} p_i} \right).$$

Then, by Theorem 6.1, we have the solution in (6.4). ■

3. The Iterative Method

There are some special methods to solve difference equations. For example, we can use the iterative method to solve (6.3). By using (6.3) repeatedly, we find

$$y_{t+1} = p_t y_t + q_t = p_t(p_{t-1}y_{t-1} + q_{t-1}) + q_t = p_t p_{t-1} y_{t-1} + p_t q_{t-1} + q_t$$

$$= p_t p_{t-1} p_{t-2} y_{t-2} + p_t p_{t-1} q_{t-2} + p_t q_{t-1} + q_t$$

$$= \cdots$$

$$= \left(\prod_{i=1}^{t} p_i \right) y_1 + \sum_{i=1}^{t} (p_{i+1} p_{i+2} \cdots p_t) q_i,$$

which gives us the same solution as in Theorem 6.2.

We can also solve (6.3) forward, rather than backward as above (the words "forward" and "backward" are self-explanatory). Again,

---

[1] A similar approach can be taken to solve the continuous-time version, $y' - p(t)y = q(t)$, of this difference equation.

by using (6.3) repeatedly, we find

$$y_1 = \frac{1}{p_t}y_{t+1} - \frac{q_t}{p_t} = \frac{1}{p_t}\left(\frac{1}{p_{t+1}}y_{t+2} - \frac{q_{t+1}}{p_{t+1}}\right) - \frac{q_t}{p_t}$$

$$= \frac{1}{p_t p_{t+1}}y_{t+2} - \frac{q_{t+1}}{p_t p_{t+1}} - \frac{q_t}{p_t}$$

$$= \frac{1}{p_t p_{t+1} p_{t+2}}y_{t+3} - \frac{q_{t+2}}{p_t p_{t+1} p_{t+2}} - \frac{q_{t+1}}{p_t p_{t+1}} - \frac{q_t}{p_t}$$

$$= \cdots$$

$$= \frac{y_T}{p_t \cdots p_{T-1}} - \sum_{i=t}^{T-1} \frac{q_i}{p_t p_{t+1} \cdots p_i}. \tag{6.5}$$

Instead of y_1 being arbitrary, y_T a value at a future time, is arbitrary in this solution. This is also a general solution of (6.3). Note that T can be infinity, in which case the infinite series involved needs to be convergent.

The general solutions in (6.4) and in (6.5) are actually the same. From (6.5), we find

$$y_t = \frac{y_T}{p_t \cdots p_{T-1}} \prod_{i=1}^{t-1} p_i - \sum_{i=1}^{T-1} \frac{q_i}{p_t p_{t+1} \cdots p_i} + \sum_{i=1}^{t-1} \frac{q_i}{p_t p_{t+1} \cdots p_i}$$

$$= \prod_{i=1}^{t-1} p_i \left(\frac{y_T}{p_t \cdots p_{T-1}} - \sum_{i=1}^{T-1} \frac{q_i}{p_1 \cdots p_i} + \sum_{i=1}^{t-1} \frac{q_i}{p_1 \cdots p_i} \right),$$

which is the same as (6.4).

The iterative method is popularly adopted for solving difference equations, since it is simple and applicable to many types of difference equations.

4. The z-Transformation Method

Whereas the Laplace transformation may be used to solve differential equations, the so-called z-transformation may be used to solve difference equations, including linear equations with constant coefficients.

Define the forward operator ζ by

$$\zeta^n y_t = y_{t+n},$$

for any positive or negative integer n. This transformation is called z-transformation. We have $\zeta = 1 + \Delta$.

Proposition 6.2. (*Properties of ζ*)

- $\zeta^n \zeta^m y_t = \zeta^m \zeta^n y_t$.
- $\zeta(ax_t + by_t) = a\zeta x_t + b\zeta y_t$, *for any $a, b \in \mathbb{R}$.* ∎

Consider a linear equation with constant coefficients:

$$y_{t+n} + a_1 y_{t+n-1} + a_2 y_{t+n-2} + \cdots + a_n y_t = f_t, \tag{6.6}$$

where a_i are constants. We call the following polynomial of λ the characteristic polynomial of (6.6):

$$f(\lambda) \equiv \lambda^n + a_1 \lambda^{n-1} + a_2 \lambda^{n-2} + \cdots + a_n. \tag{6.7}$$

Then, Equation (6.6) can be written as

$$f(\zeta)y_t = f_t. \tag{6.8}$$

This immediately implies a particular solution of (6.6):

$$\bar{y}_t = \frac{1}{f(\zeta)} f_t, \tag{6.9}$$

where $\frac{1}{f(\zeta)}$ is defined to be the operator such that $f(\zeta)\frac{1}{f(\zeta)}x_t = x_t$ for any series x_t.

Proposition 6.3.

(a) *If $f(a) \neq 0$, then $\frac{1}{f(\zeta)}a^t = \frac{a^t}{f(a)}$.*

(b) $\frac{1}{(\zeta-a)^m}a^t = \frac{t^m a^{t-m}}{m!}$.

(c) $\frac{1}{f(\zeta)}a^t t^m = a^t \frac{1}{f(a\zeta)}t^m$.

(d) *If $\frac{1}{f(\zeta)} = \frac{1}{f(1+\Delta)} = \sum_{i=0}^{\infty} b_i \Delta^i$, then $\frac{1}{f(\zeta)}t^m = (b_0 + b_1\Delta + \cdots + b_m\Delta^m)t^m$.* ∎

Proposition 6.3 tells us that if f_t is a linear combination of terms $a^t t^m$, we can use the z-transformation to solve for a particular solution quickly. Unlike the Laplace transformation, the z-transformation does not give us the general solution.

Example 6.1. For equation $y_{t+1} - a y_t - b = 0$, let $f(\zeta) = \zeta - a$. By Proposition 6.3(a), a particular solution is

$$y_t = \frac{1}{\zeta - a} b = b \frac{1}{\zeta - a} 1^t = \frac{b}{1 - a}. \quad \blacksquare$$

Notes

Chapter 16 of Chiang (1984) is a good reference for first-order difference equations. Chapters 17 and 18 of Chiang (1984) are good references for high-order difference equations and linear difference equation systems.

Chapter 7

Probability Theory

This chapter offers a concise review of probability theory. No proofs are provided since the results are well known and can be found easily in many books. Instead, we offer rich examples to help readers understand the theory.

1. Probability Space

Example 7.1. When we flip a coin, there are two possible outcomes — head or tail. We call the outcome a random event. Hence, there are two possible events: "head" and "tail". Denote $\Omega = \{$head, tail$\}$ and call it the sample space. Then, these two events are called basic events. If the coin is perfectly symmetric, the probability of each basic event occurring is 0.5. ■

Example 7.2. If we flip a coin twice, there are four possible basic events:

$$(\text{head}, \text{head}), \quad (\text{head}, \text{tail}), \quad (\text{tail}, \text{head}), \quad (\text{tail}, \text{tail}).$$

In this case, the sample space is

$$\Omega = \{(\text{head}, \text{head}), (\text{head}, \text{tail}), (\text{tail}, \text{head}), (\text{tail}, \text{tail})\}.$$

Each basic event has probability $1/4$ of occurring. A subset of Ω is called an event. For example, the event where at least one head is up is

$$A = \{(\text{head}, \text{head}), (\text{head}, \text{tail}), (\text{tail}, \text{head})\}.$$

The probability of this event occurring is $3/4$. ∎

We now formally define a probability space. Given a non-empty set Ω let $\mathcal{F}$ be a set of subsets of Ω. This $\mathcal{F}$ is called a σ-algebra if it is

— Closed under complementation: $A^c \equiv \Omega \backslash A \in \mathcal{F}$ for all $A \in \mathcal{F}$;
— Closed under countable unions: $\cup_{i=1}^{\infty} A_i \in \mathcal{F}$ if $A_i \in \mathcal{F}$ for all i.

These two conditions immediately imply that a σ-algebra is also closed under countable intersections. Then, Ω is called the sample space, members of Ω are called basic events, and members of $\mathcal{F}$ are called events.

Events $\{A_i\}_{i=1}^{\infty}$ are disjoint events if $A_i \cap A_j = \emptyset$ for any $i \neq j$.

Given a sample space Ω with σ-algebra $\mathcal{F}$, a function $P : \mathcal{F} \rightarrow [0, 1]$ is called a probability measure if

— $P(\Omega) = 1$,
— σ-additive: $P(\cup_{i=1}^{\infty} A_i) = \sum_{i=1}^{\infty} P(A_i)$ if A_i's are disjoint events.

Then, $(\Omega, \mathcal{F}, P)$ is called a probability space.

Theorem 7.1. *Given a probability space* $(\Omega, \mathcal{F}, P)$:

- $P(\emptyset) = 0$.
- *For any two events* $A_1, A_2 \in \mathcal{F}$, *we have*

$$P(A_1 \cup A_2) = P(A_1) + P(A_2) - P(A_1 \cap A_2).$$

- *For any events* $A_1, A_2, \ldots, A_n$, *we have*

$$P\left(\bigcup_{i=1}^{n} A_i\right) \leq \sum_{i=1}^{n} P(A_i).$$

- *For any two events* A *and* B, $A \supset B$, *we have*

$$P(A \backslash B) = P(A) - P(B), \quad P(A) \geq P(B).$$

- *For any event A, we have*

$$P(A^c) = 1 - P(A). \quad \blacksquare$$

Theorem 7.2 (Continuity). *Given a probability space* $(\Omega, \mathcal{F}, P)$,

- *For* $A_n \in \mathcal{F}, A_n \supset A_{n+i}$, *we have*

$$\lim_{n \to \infty} P(A_n) = P\left(\bigcap_{n=1}^{\infty} A_n\right).$$

- *For* $A_n \in \mathcal{F}, A_n \subset A_{n+i}$, *we have*

$$\lim_{n \to \infty} P(A_n) = P\left(\bigcup_{n=1}^{\infty} A_n\right). \quad \blacksquare$$

Example 7.3. Pick m items out of n given items $a_1, a_2, \ldots, a_n$, where $m \leq n$. How many combinations are there?

Solution 1: Suppose the order matters. The first item is picked from n available items; the second item is picked from $n - 1$ available items; ...; the mth item is picked from $n - m + 1$ available items. Hence, the number of ordered combination is

$$n(n-1)\cdots(n-m+1) = \frac{n!}{(n-m)!}.$$

We denote

$$A_n^m \equiv \frac{n!}{(n-m)!}.$$

Solution 2: Suppose the order does not matter. Given m items, there are $m!$ ordered combinations. But since the order does not matter, there is only one non-ordered combination. Hence, when we pick m items out of n given items, the number of non-ordered combinations is

$$C_n^m \equiv \frac{n!}{m!(n-m)!}. \quad \blacksquare$$

Obviously, we have

$$C_n^m = C_n^{n-m}, \quad A_n^m = nA_{n-1}^{m-1}. \tag{7.1}$$

Assume $A_n^0 = 1$ and $C_n^0 = 1$. ∎

Example 7.4. A box has n_1 different white balls and n_2 different black balls. We take out $m_1 + m_2$ balls, where $m_i \leq n_j$. what is the probability of event

$$A = \{\text{we have } m_1 \text{ white balls and } m_2 \text{ black balls}\}?$$

Solution: Obviously, we have a total of $C_{n_1+n_2}^{m_1+m_2}$ combinations. If we happen to have m_1 white balls and m_2 black balls, we have $C_{n_1}^{m_1}$ possible combinations of white balls and $C_{n_2}^{m_2}$ possible combinations of black balls. Hence, the probability that we have m_1 white balls and m_2 black balls is

$$P(A) = \frac{C_{n_1}^{m_1} C_{n_2}^{m_2}}{C_{n_1+n_2}^{m_1+m_2}}. \quad ∎$$

Example 7.5. A box has n_1 white balls and n_2 black balls. We take out k balls, where $k \leq n_1$. what is the probability of event

$$A = \{\text{we have } 0 \text{ white ball, } 1 \text{ white ball, } \dots, \text{ or } k \text{ white balls}\}?$$

Obviously, $P(A) = 1$. There are $k + 1$ possible scenarios: None of the k balls is white, one of the k balls is white, and so on. Hence, the probability is

$$P(A) = \frac{\sum_{i=0}^{k} C_{n_1}^{i} C_{n_2}^{k-i}}{C_{n_1+n_2}^{k}}.$$

Therefore, we have the well-known Vandermonde formula:

$$\sum_{i=0}^{k} C_{n_1}^{i} C_{n_2}^{k-i} = C_{n_1+n_2}^{k}. \quad ∎ \tag{7.2}$$

Example 7.6. A box has n different white balls and m different black balls. We take out k balls consecutively and do not replace them. What is the probability of event

$$A = \{\text{the last ball being taken out is white}\}?$$

Solution 1: Since the balls are not replaced once they are taken out, the set of balls removed from the box is an ordered combination. The order matters. Imagine that we have k holes, numbered from 1 to k. To fill these holes, we can take out a white ball first and put it into the kth hole and then continue to pick balls to fill the remaining holes. If we require a white ball in the kth hole, there are n white balls to choose from. But the remaining $k - 1$ balls can be arbitrary, giving A_{n+m-1}^{k-1} possible scenarios. In contrast, if it is not required that a white ball be placed in the kth hole, there are A_{n+m}^k possible scenarios. Hence,

$$P(A) = \frac{n A_{n+m-1}^{k-1}}{A_{n+m}^k} = \frac{n}{n+m}.$$

Interestingly, this probability is independent of k.

Solution 2: Let us derive this result using a more intuitive approach. If $k = 1$, we obviously have

$$P(A) = \frac{n}{n+m}.$$

If $k = 2$, the first ball is either a white or a black one. Hence,

$$P(A) = \frac{n}{n+m} \frac{n-1}{n+m-1} + \frac{m}{n+m} \frac{n}{n+m-1}$$
$$= \frac{n(n+m-1)}{(n+m)(n+m-1)} = \frac{n}{n+m}.$$

If $k = 3$, the first two balls can be (white, white), (white, black), (black, white), and (black, black). Hence,

$$P(A) = \frac{n}{n+m} \frac{n-1}{n+m-1} + \frac{n-2}{n+m-2}$$
$$+ \frac{n}{n+m} \frac{m}{n+m-1} \frac{n-1}{n+m-2} + \frac{m}{n+m} \frac{n}{n+m-1} \frac{n-1}{n+m-2}$$
$$= + \frac{m}{n+m} \frac{m-1}{n+m-1} \frac{n}{n+m-2} \frac{\sum_{i=1}^{3} C_{3-1}^{i-1} A_n^i A_m^{3-i}}{A_{n+m}^3}.$$

Hence, for an arbitrary k, we should have

$$P(A) = \frac{\sum_{i=1}^k C_{k-1}^{i-1} A_n^i A_m^{k-i}}{A_{n+m}^k}.$$

The denominator is obvious. In the numerator, the term $A_n^i A_m^{k-i}$ is also obvious. For the case of i white balls, $i-1$ of them may be in any of the $(k-1)$ holes (but not in the kth hole). In the kth hole there must be a white ball, and in the remaining holes there must be black balls, with C_{k-1}^{i-1} possibile scenarios. Using (7.1), we have

$$\sum_{i=1}^k C_{k-1}^{i-1} A_n^i A_m^{k-i} = \sum_{i=0}^{k-1} C_{k-1}^i A_n^{i+1} A_m^{k-i-1} = \sum_{i=0}^{k-1} C_{k-1}^i n A_{n-1}^i A_m^{k-i-1}$$

$$= n \sum_{i=0}^{k-1} \frac{(k-1)!}{i!(k-1-i)!} A_{n-1}^i A_m^{k-i-1}$$

$$= n(k-1)! \sum_{i=0}^{k-1} C_{n-1}^i C_m^{k-1-i}.$$

Using the Vandermonde formula in (7.2),

$$\sum_{i=1}^k C_{k-1}^{i-1} A_n^i A_m^{k-i} = n(k-1)! C_{n+m-1}^{k-1} = n A_{n+m-1}^{k-1}.$$

Hence, using (7.1) again,

$$P(A) = \frac{n A_{n+m-1}^{k-1}}{A_{n+m}^k} = \frac{n A_{n+m-1}^{k-1}}{(n+m) A_{n+m-1}^{k-1}} = \frac{n}{n+m}. \quad \blacksquare$$

Example 7.7. A box has n_1 white balls and n_2 black balls. We take out one ball at a time and put it back immediately. We do this n times. For $k \le n_1$, what is the probability of event

$$A = \{k \text{ balls are white}\}?$$

Solution: We have repeated the Bernoulli experiment n times. Hence,

$$P(A) = C_n^k \left(\frac{n_1}{n_1 + n_2} \right)^k \left(\frac{n_2}{n_1 + n_2} \right)^{n-k}. \quad \blacksquare$$

Example 7.8. This example repeats the last one, except that when a ball is taken out, it is not returned. We balls out n times. What is the probability of event

$$A = \{k \text{ balls are white}\}?$$

Solution: This is equivalent to removing n balls from the box once and for all. This case is the same as Example 7.4. Hence, the solution is

$$P(A) = \frac{C_{n_1}^k C_{n_2}^{n-k}}{C_{n_1+n_2}^n}. \quad \blacksquare$$

Example 7.9. m person are allocated to n rooms with equal probability, $m \leq n$. Consider the following three events:

$A = \{$there are m designated rooms and they turn out to have one person in each$\}$,

$B = \{$among the n rooms, there are m rooms with only one person in each$\}$,

$C = \{$a designated room has k persons, $k \leq m\}$.

Solution: For event A, the first person is allocated to a given room with probability m/n; the second person is allocated to another given room with probability $(m-1)/n$; ...; the last person is allocated to the remaining given room with probability $1/n$. Hence,

$$P(A) = \frac{m!}{n^m}.$$

For event B, we first select m rooms and then allocate the m persons to these rooms, one person to each room. In the first step, we have C_n^m choices. The second step is the same event as event A. Hence,

$$P(B) = C_n^m \frac{m!}{n^m} = \frac{n!}{n^m(n-m)!}$$

For event C, there are two steps. In the first step, we select k persons from the m persons. There are C_m^k choices. These persons are assigned to the given room. In the second step, the remaining $m - k$ persons are allocated arbitrarily to the remaining $n - 1$ rooms. Each of them can choose from $n - 1$ out of n rooms; there are $(n - 1)^{m-k}$ possible scenarios. Hence,

$$P(C) = C_m^k \frac{(n - 1)^{m-k}}{n^m}.$$

Example 7.10. Pick a number from 1 to 10 return it immediately. Do this seven times. Each number has the same probability of being picked. Consider

$A_1 = \{\text{the seven numbers are all different}\},$

$A_2 = \{\text{the seven numbers do not include 1 and 10}\},$

$A_3 = \{10 \text{ appears exactly twice}\},$

$A_4 = \{10 \text{ appears at least twice}\},$

$A_5 = \{\text{the sum of the seven numbers is 20}\}.$

Solution: For A_1, if the seven numbers can be arbitrary, there are total 10^7 possibilities; if the seven numbers must be different, we pick the first number from 10 available numbers, the second number from nine available numbers, and so on. Hence,

$$P(A_1) = \frac{10 \times 9 \times \cdots \times 4}{10^7} = \frac{A_{10}^7}{10^7}.$$

For A_2, since 1 and 10 are not allowed, we are left with eight numbers to choose from. Hence,

$$P(A_2) = \frac{8^7}{10^7} = \left(\frac{4}{5}\right)^7.$$

For A_3, two of the seven numbers we pick are a 10, giving C_7^2 possibilities. The remaining five numbers may be any number between 1 and 9, giving 9^5 possibilities. Hence,

$$P(A_3) = \frac{C_7^2 9^5}{10^7}.$$

For A_4, we only need to extend the last case to include the cases when 10 appears more than twice. Hence,

$$P(A_4) = \frac{\sum_{i=2}^{7} C_7^i 9^{7-i}}{10^7}.$$

For A_5, suppose that the seven numbers are $x_1, x_2, \ldots, x_7$, where x_i is the ith number we pick. The number of possibilities is

$$n = \sum_{x_1 + x_2 + \cdots + x_7 = 20} 1.$$

This n equals the coefficient of the x^{20} term in $(x + x^2 + \cdots + x^{10})^7$. Since

$$(x + x^2 + \cdots + x^{10})^7 = x^7 (1 + x + x^2 + \cdots + x^9)^7,$$

the coefficient of the x^{20} term in $(x + x^2 + \cdots + x^{10})^7$ equals the coefficient of the x^{13} term in $(x + x^2 + \cdots + x^9)^7$. We have

$$(x + x^2 + \cdots + x^9)^7 = \left(\frac{1 - x^{10}}{1 - x}\right)^7$$

$$= (1 - x^{10})^7 \frac{1}{\sum_{i=0}^{7} C_7^i (-1)^i x^i}$$

$$= (1 - 7x^{10} + \cdots)$$

$$\times (1 + \cdots + 84x^3 + \cdots + 27132x^{13} + \cdots),$$

from which we find that the coefficient of the x^{13} term is 26544. Hence,

$$P(A_5) = \frac{26544}{10^7}. \quad \blacksquare$$

Example 7.11. n balls fall into N boxes with equal probability. Consider

$$A = \{n \text{ given boxes each holding one of the } n \text{ balls}\}.$$

Solution 1 (Maxwell–Boltzmann): Suppose that the n balls are different and each box can hold an unlimited number of balls. Then,

$$P(A) = \frac{n!}{N^n}.$$

Solution 2 (Bose–Einstein): Suppose that the n balls are the same and each box can hold an unlimited number of balls. Consider a special case with $N = 3$ and $n = 2$. Denote the two balls by a and b. There are $3^2 = 9$ possibilities as follows:

$$
\begin{array}{lll}
1: ab| - | - & 2: - |ab| - & 3: - | - |ab \\
4: a\,|b| - & 5: b\,|a| - & 6: a| - |b \\
7: b| - |a & 8: - |a|b & 9: - |b|a
\end{array}
$$

where "$|$" separates boxes and "$-$" indicates an empty box. Cases 4 and 5 are two different events, so are Cases 6 and 7 and Cases 8 and 9. However, if $a = b$, there are only 6 possibilities and if boxes 1 and 3 are among the given boxes, there is one possibility, implying

$$P(A) = \frac{1}{6}.$$

In general, if all balls are denoted by a, we can indicate a basic event as

$$aa\,|a|\,aaaa| - | \cdots |aa \qquad\qquad (7.3)$$

in which there are n a's and $N - 1$ vertical bars. There are $n + N - 1$ positions in (7.3) for a and $|$ to fill. The n balls are free to occupy any combination of these positions (the rest are occupied by vertical bars). Hence, there are C_{n+N-1}^n basic events. But there is only one basic event in event A. Hence,

$$P(A) = \frac{1}{C_{n+N-1}^n}.$$

Solution 3 (Fermi–Dirac): Suppose that the n balls are identical and each box can hold at most one ball. There are N available boxes. Here, we have C_N^n basic events. Event A consists of only one basic event. Hence,

$$P(A) = \frac{1}{C_N^n}. \quad \blacksquare$$

2. Conditional Probability

We use an example to motivate the definition of conditional probability.

Example 7.12. There are 10 balls, numbered 1,2,...,10. Suppose that we randomly pick a ball with equal probability. Consider two events

$$A = \{\text{the ball is either 4 or 5}\}, \quad B = \{\text{the ball is even numbered}\}.$$

Given event B has happened, what is the probability of event A? Given B, ball 5 has not been picked for sure, and ball 4 will be picked with probability 1/5 since it is one of the five even-numbered balls. Hence, we have

$$P(A|B) = \frac{1}{5}.$$

Note that we have $P(A \cap B) = 1/10$ and $P(B) = 1/2$. Hence,

$$P(A|B) = \frac{P(A \cap B)}{P(B)}.$$

Notice here that $P(A|B) \neq \frac{P(A)}{P(B)}$. We now repeat the above n times. Let n_i be the number of times ball i is picked. Obviously we have $n = \sum_{i=1}^{10} n_i$. Then,

$$\text{frequency of } A = \frac{n_4 + n_5}{n}, \quad \text{frequency of } A|B = \frac{n_4}{\sum_{i=1}^{5} n_{2i}},$$

$$\text{frequency of } A \cap B = \frac{n_4}{n} \quad \text{frequency of } B = \frac{\sum_{i=1}^{5} n_{2i}}{n}.$$

We again have

$$P(A \cap B) = P(A|B)P(B). \tag{7.4}$$

Although frequency is not probability, it can offer a justification for the definition of conditional probability. $\quad \blacksquare$

Formula (7.4) is intuitive. To assess the probability of $A \cap B$, we can first calculate the probability of B, then conditional on B we can calculate the probability of A, and the probability of $A \cap B$ should be the product of these two probabilities. Using this formula, we can define the conditional probability of $A|B$.

Definition 7.1. For any two events A and B, with $P(B) > 0$, the conditional probability of event $A|B$ is defined as

$$P(A|B) = \frac{P(A \cap B)}{P(B)}.$$

This is called the Bayes rule. ∎

Theorem 7.3. *Given a probability space* (Ω, F, P)*, for any event B with $P(B) > 0$, $P(\cdot|B)$ is a probability measure on F, i.e.,*

— $P(\Omega|B) = 1$,
— *σ-additive:* $P(\cup_{i=1}^{\infty} A_i|B) = \sum_{i=1}^{\infty} P(A_i|B)$ *if A_i's are disjoint events.*

Theorem 7.4 (Product Formula). *For events A_i, we have*

$$P(A_1 \cap A_2 \cap \cdots \cap A_n) = P(A_1)P(A_2|A_1)P(A_3|A_1 \cap A_2)$$
$$\cdots P(A_n|A_1 \cap A_2 \cap \cdots \cap A_{n-1}).$$

A sequence of events $\{H_i\}_{i=1}^{n}$ *is called a partition of a probability space* (Ω, σ, P) *if they are disjoint events and* $P(\cup_{i=1}^{n} H_i) = 1$*, where n can be finite or infinite.*

Theorem 7.5 (Complete Probability Formula). *Let* $\{H_i\}_{i=1}^{n}$ *be a partition of a probability space* (Ω, F, P)*, and $p(H_i) > 0$ for all i, where n can be finite or infinite. Then, for any event A,*

$$P(A) = \sum_{i=1}^{n} P(A|H_i)P(H_i). \tag{7.5}$$

Example 7.13. There are n_1 white balls and m_1 black balls in box 1, and n_2 white balls and m_2 black balls in box 2. Take one ball out of box 1 and put it into box 2. Now, pick one ball out of box 2. What is the probability of $A = \{$the second ball is white$\}$?

Solution: Let

$$H_w = \{\text{the ball that moved from box 1 to box 2 is white}\},$$
$$H_b = \{\text{the ball that moved from box 1 to box 2 is black}\}.$$

We obviously have $H_w \cap H_b = \emptyset$ and $P(H_w \cup H_b) = 1$. Then,

$$P(A) = P(H_w)P(A|H_w) + P(H_b)P(A|H_b)$$
$$= \frac{n_1}{n_1 + m_1} \frac{n_2 + 1}{n_2 + m_2 + 1} + \frac{m_1}{n_1 + m_1} \frac{n_2}{n_2 + m_2 + 1}. \quad \blacksquare$$

Proposition 7.1 (Bayes). *Let $\{H_i\}_{i=1}^n$ be a partition of a probability space (Ω, σ, P), where n can be finite or infinite. Then, for any event A with $P(A) > 0$, we have*

$$P(H_j|A) = \frac{P(A|H_j)P(H_j)}{P(A)} = \frac{P(A|H_j)P(H_j)}{\sum_{i=1}^n P(A|H_i)P(H_i)},$$
$$\text{for } j = 1, \ldots, n. \quad \blacksquare \quad (7.6)$$

Example 7.14. There are three boxes:

$$\text{box } 1 : n_1 \text{ white balls and } m_1 \text{ black balls};$$
$$\text{box } 2 : n_2 \text{ white balls and } m_2 \text{ black balls};$$
$$\text{box } 3 : n_3 \text{ white balls and } m_3 \text{ black balls}.$$

We randomly pick one box and then take one ball from this box. Given event $A = \{\text{this ball is white}\}$, what is the probability of event $H_1 = \{\text{this ball is from box 1}\}$?

Solution: Let

$$H_i = \{\text{box } i \text{ was picked}\}.$$

By (7.5), we have

$$P(A) = P(H_1)P(A|H_1) + P(H_2)P(A|H_2) + P(H_3)P(A|H_3)$$
$$= \frac{1}{3}\frac{n_1}{n_1 + m_1} + \frac{1}{3}\frac{n_2}{n_2 + m_2} + \frac{1}{3}\frac{n_3}{n_3 + m_3}.$$

Then, by (7.6), we have

$$P(H_1|A) = \frac{P(A|H_1)P(H_1)}{P(A)} = \frac{\frac{1}{3}\frac{n_1}{n_1+m_1}}{\frac{1}{3}\frac{n_1}{n_1+m_1} + \frac{1}{3}\frac{n_2}{n_2+m_2}\frac{1}{3}\frac{n_3}{n_3+m_3}}$$

$$= \frac{\frac{n_1}{n_1+m_1}}{\frac{n_1}{n_1+m_1} + \frac{n_2}{n_2+m_2} + \frac{n_3}{n_3+m_3}}. \quad \blacksquare$$

Example 7.15. A visiting friend came by train, boat, bus or air with probability 3/10, 1/5, 1/10 or 2/5, respectively. The probability of his being late is 1/4, 1/3, 1/12 or zero if he came by train, boat, bus or air, respectively. Given event $A = \{$he is late$\}$, what is the probability that he took a train?

Solution: Let

$$H_1 = \{\text{by train}\}, H_2 = \{\text{by boat}\}, H_3 = \{\text{by bus}\}, H_4 = \{\text{by air}\}.$$

Then,

$$P(H_1|A) = \frac{P(H_1)P(A|H_1)}{\substack{P(H_1)P(A|H_1) + P(H_2)P(A|H_2) \\ + P(H_3)P(A|H_3) + P(H_4)P(A|H_4)}} = \frac{1}{2}. \quad \blacksquare$$

Example 7.16. Starting with P_1, two players P_1 and P_2 take turns to take a ball out of a box containing n white balls and m black balls. No ball is returned after it is taken out. Consider event $A = \{P_1$ takes out a white ball first$\}$.

Solution: Obviously, A contains the following basic events: (white), (black, black, white), and (black, black, black, black, white), etc. Hence,

$$P(A) = \frac{n}{n+m} + \frac{m}{n+m}\frac{m-1}{n+m-1}\frac{n}{n+m-2}$$

$$+ \frac{m}{n+m}\frac{m-1}{n+m-1}\frac{m-2}{n+m-2}\frac{m-3}{n+m-3}\frac{n}{n+m-4}$$

$$+ \cdots = \sum_{i=1}^{\infty} \frac{nA_m^{i-1}}{A_{n+m}^i}. \quad \blacksquare$$

Example 7.17. Take k balls once for all out of a box containing n white balls and m black balls. Consider event $A = \{$at least one white ball$\}$.

Solution 1: We have $A^c = \{$all balls are black$\}$ and

$$P(A^c) = \frac{C_m^k}{C_{n+m}^k}.$$

Hence,

$$P(A) = 1 - P(A^c) = 1 - \frac{C_m^k}{C_{n+m}^k}.$$

Solution 2: Taking k balls once for all is equivalent to taking k balls out in sequence, one at a time, without returning any to the box, until a white ball is obtained. Then, A consists of the following basic events: (white), (black, white), (black, black, white), etc. Hence,

$$P(A) = \frac{n}{n+m} + \frac{m}{n+m}\frac{n}{n+m-1}$$
$$+ \frac{m}{n+m}\frac{m-1}{n+m-1}\frac{n}{n+m-2} + \cdots$$
$$= \sum_{i=1}^{k} \frac{n A_m^{i-1}}{A_{n+m}^i}. \quad \blacksquare$$

Example 7.18. There are n envelopes, labeled $1, 2, \ldots, n$. There are also n letters, labeled $1, 2, \ldots, n$. We now arbitrarily put the n letters into the n envelopes, one letters for each envelope. Consider event $A = \{$none of them matches$\}$.

Solution: Let $A_i = \{$the ith letter is in the ith envelope$\}$. Then,

$$P(A) = P\left[\left(\bigcup_{i=1}^{n} A_i\right)^c\right] = 1 - P\left(\bigcup_{i=1}^{n} A_i\right).$$

We have

$$P\left(\bigcup_{i=1}^{n} A_i\right) = \sum_{i=1}^{n} P(A_i) - \sum_{i_1,i_2} P(A_{i_1} \cap A_{i_2})$$
$$+ \sum_{i_1,i_2,i_3} P(A_{i_1} \cap A_{i_2} \cap A_{i_3}) - \cdots \pm P(A_1 \cap \cdots \cap A_n).$$

We have

$$P(A_i) = \frac{1}{n}, P(A_i \cap A_j) = P(A_i)P(A_j|A_i) = \frac{1}{n}\frac{1}{n-1}.$$

Then,

$$s_2 \equiv \sum_{i_1,i_2} P(A_{i_1} \cap A_{i_2}) = C_n^2 \frac{1}{n}\frac{1}{n-1} = \frac{1}{2!}.$$

Similarly,

$$\sum_{i_1,i_2,i_3} P(A_{i_1} \cap A_{i_2} \cap A_{i_3}) = \frac{1}{3!}.$$

Hence,

$$P(A) = 1 - \sum_{i=1}^{n} \frac{(-1)^{i+1}}{i!} = \sum_{i=0}^{n} \frac{(-1)^i}{i!}. \quad \blacksquare$$

Intuitively, if two events A and B are independent, we expect to have $P(A) = P(A|B)$. This is equivalent to $P(A \cap B) = P(A)P(B)$. This leads to the following definition.

Definition 7.2. Two events A and B are independent if $P(A \cap B) = P(A)P(B)$. In general, n events $A_1, A_2, \ldots, A_n$ are independent if $P(A_1 \cap \ldots \cap A_n) = P(A_1) \ldots P(A_n)$.

Theorem 7.6. *If events $A_1, A_2, \ldots, A_n$ are independent, then for any combination $\{i_1, \ldots, i_n\}$ of $\{1, \ldots, n\}$, $A_{i_1}^c, \ldots, A_{i_m}^c$, $A_{i_{m+1}}, \ldots,$ A_{i_n} are also independent.* $\blacksquare$

Example 7.19. We flip two coins once. There are four basic events:

$$\omega_1 = (\text{head, head}), \quad \omega_2 = (\text{head, tail}),$$
$$\omega_3 = (\text{tail, head}), \quad \omega_4 = (\text{tail, tail}).$$

Each of these basic events has probability $1/4$. Consider two events:

$$A = \{\text{the first flip results in a head}\},$$
$$B = \{\text{the second flip results in a head}\}.$$

We have

$$A = \{\omega_1, \omega_2\}, \quad B = \{\omega_1, \omega_3\}.$$

Hence,

$$P(A) = \frac{1}{2}, \quad P(B) = \frac{1}{2}, \quad P(A \cap B) = \frac{1}{4}.$$

Since $P(A \cap B) = P(A)P(B)$, we find that A and B are independent. ∎

Example 7.20. Consider a shooting exercise. The probability of hitting the target is p in each shot. Assume that shots are independent of each other. Consider

$$A_k = \{\text{the target is hit in the } k\text{th shot;}$$
$$\text{it may or may not be hit a second time}\},$$
$$B_k = \{\text{during the first } k \text{ shots, the target is hit at least once}\},$$
$$C = \{\text{the target is hit at least once during the exercise}\}.$$

Solution: It is obvious that $P(A_k) = p$. For B_k, we have

$$P(B_k^c) = P(A_1^c \cap A_2^c \cap \cdots \cap A_k^c) = P(A_1^c)P(A_2^c) \cdots P(A_k^c) = (1-p)^k,$$

implying $P(B_k) = 1 - (1-p)^k$. For C, we have

$$C^c = \bigcap_{k=1}^{\infty} A_k^c = \bigcap_{k=1}^{\infty} B_k^c.$$

Since $B_{k+1}^c \subset B_k^c$, by Theorem 7.2, we have

$$P(C^c) = \lim_{k \to \infty} P(B_k^c) = \lim_{k \to \infty} (1-p)^k = 0.$$

Hence, $P(C) = 1$. ∎

Example 7.21. From numbers $1, 2, \ldots, 10$, pick a number each time and put it back right away. Do this K times independently. Consider $A_m = \{\text{the largest number is m}\}$, where $m \le 10$.

Solution: Let $B_m = \{$all k numbers $\leq m\}$ and $C_i = \{$the ith number picked $\leq m\}$. We have

$$P(B_m) = P(C_1 \cap C_2 \cap \cdots \cap C_k) = P(C_1)P(C_2) \cdots P(C_k) = \left(\frac{m}{10}\right)^k.$$

We have $A = B_m \backslash B_{m-1}$. Since $B_{m-1} \subset B_m$, we have

$$P(A_m) = P(B_m) - P(B_{m-1}) = \frac{m^k - (m-1)^k}{10^m}. \quad \blacksquare$$

Example 7.22. Consider an event A that happens with a small probability $\varepsilon > 0$ in an experiment. If we keep repeating the same experiment independently, then A will happen sooner or later.

Proof. Let

$$A_k = \{A \text{ happens in the } k\text{th experiment}\},$$
$$B_k = \{A \text{ happens in the first } k \text{ experiments}\}.$$

We have

$$P(B_k^c) = P(A_1^c \cap A_2^c \cap \cdots \cap A_k^c) = P(A_1^c)P(A_2^c) \cdots P(A_k^c) = (1-\varepsilon)^k.$$

Hence,

$$P(B_k) = 1 - (1-\varepsilon)^k \to 1 \quad \text{as } k \to \infty. \quad \blacksquare$$

Example 7.23. A particle is moving around points $0, 1, 2, \ldots, n$. If it is at $t, 0 < t < n$, it will move either toward $t+1$ with probability p or toward $t-1$ with probability $1-p$. If it is at 0 or n, it will stay there forever. If it is at t, let q_t be the probability that it will eventually arrive at 0. Find q_t.

Solution: Suppose that the particle is at t, where $0 < t < n$. If it moves toward $t+1$, it may eventually arrive at 0 with probability q_{t+1}; if it moves toward $t-1$, it may eventually arrive 0 at with probability q_{t-1}. Hence,

$$q_t = pq_{t+1} + (1-p)q_{t-1}, \quad \text{for } 0 < t < n. \tag{7.7}$$

Besides, we obviously have $q_0 = 1$ and $q_n = 0$. Equation (7.7) can be rewritten as

$$pq_t + (1-p)q_t = pq_{t+1} + (1-p)q_{t-1},$$

implying

$$q_{t+1} - q_t = \frac{1-p}{p}(q_t - q_{t-1}),$$

implying

$$q_t - q_{t-1} = \frac{1-p}{p}(q_{t-1} - q_{t-2}) = \left(\frac{1-p}{p}\right)^2 (q_{t-2} - q_{t-3})$$

$$= \cdots = \left(\frac{1-p}{p}\right)^{t-1} (q_1 - q_0).$$

If $p \neq 0.5$, we have

$$q_t = q_{t-1} + \left(\frac{1-p}{p}\right)^{t-1} (q_1 - q_0)$$

$$= q_{t-2} + \left(\frac{1-p}{p}\right)^{t-2} (q_1 - q_0) + \left(\frac{1-p}{p}\right)^{t-1} (q_1 - q_0)$$

$$= \cdots = q_0 + (q_1 - q_0) \sum_{i=0}^{t-1} \left(\frac{1-p}{p}\right)^i = q_0 + (q_1 - q_0)\frac{1 - \left(\frac{1-p}{p}\right)^t}{1 - \frac{1-p}{p}}$$

$$= q_0 - p(q_1 - q_0)\left[1 - \left(\frac{1-p}{p}\right)^t\right],$$

implying

$$q_t - q_0 = p(q_1 - q_0)\left[1 - \left(\frac{1-p}{p}\right)^t\right].$$

In particular,

$$q_n - q_0 = p(q_1 - q_0)\left[1 - (\frac{1-p}{p})^n\right].$$

Dividing the above two equations on both sides implies

$$\frac{q_t - q_0}{q_n - q_0} = \frac{1 - \left(\frac{1-p}{p}\right)^t}{1 - \left(\frac{1-p}{p}\right)^n},$$

implying

$$q_t = \frac{\left(\frac{1-p}{p}\right)^n - \left(\frac{1-p}{p}\right)^t}{\left(\frac{1-p}{p}\right)^n - 1}.$$

For the special case when $p = 0.5$, we can easily find $q_t = t$. Note that $q_1 \neq 1 - p$ since if the particle moves toward 2 in the next move, it may eventually move toward 0, implying $q_1 > 1 - p$. ■

Example 7.24. m persons $P_1, \ldots, P_m$ are passing a ball around. Each time the ball is passed to one of the other $m - 1$ players with equal probability. Suppose that p_1 initially has the ball which is passed n times. What is the probability p_n that the ball is at the hand of p_1 in the nth pass?

Solution: Let

$$q_n = P(\{P_2, \ldots, or P_m \text{ has the ball}\}).$$

Since everyone is equally likely to have the ball at any one time, we have

$$p_n + (m - 1)q_n = 1. \tag{7.8}$$

A necessary and sufficient condition for P_1 to be passed the ball in the nth pass is that, in the $(n - 1)$th pass, $P_2, \ldots, or P_m$ must have the ball who then passes the ball to P_1. We have

$$P(\{P_2, \ldots, or\ P_m \text{ has the ball in the } (n-1)\text{th pass}\}) = (m-1)q_{n-1},$$

$$P(\{P_1 \text{ is passed the ball by } P_2, \ldots, or P_m \text{ in the } (n-1)\text{th pass}\})$$
$$= \tfrac{1}{m-1},$$

implying

$$p_n = (m - 1)q_{n-1} \cdot \frac{1}{m - 1} = q_{n-1}.$$

By (7.8), we have $p_{n-1} + (m - 1)q_{n-1} = 1$. Then,

$$p_n = q_{n-1} = \frac{1 - p_{n-1}}{m - 1},$$

implying

$$p_n = \frac{1}{m-1} - \frac{1}{m-1}p_{n-1}$$

$$= \frac{1}{m-1} - \left(\frac{1}{m-1}\right)^2 + \left(\frac{1}{m-1}\right)^2 p_{n-2} = \cdots$$

$$= -\sum_{i=1}^{n}\left(\frac{-1}{m-1}\right)^i + \left(\frac{-1}{m-1}\right)^n p_0.$$

Since $p_0 = 1$, we find

$$p_n = \left(\frac{1}{1-m}\right)^n - \sum_{i-1}^{n}\left(\frac{1}{1-m}\right)^i$$

$$= \left(\frac{1}{1-m}\right)^n - \frac{\frac{1}{1-m} - \left(\frac{1}{1-m}\right)^{n+1}}{1 - \frac{1}{1-m}}$$

$$= \frac{1}{m}\left[1 - \left(\frac{1}{1-m}\right)^{n-1}\right].$$

This implies that, if n is large enough, we have $p_n \approx 1/m$, meaning that everyone has the same chance of being passed the ball in the nth pass, irrespective of who initially has the ball. ∎

Example 7.25. Consider a shooting game and event $A = \{$the target is hit$\}$, with $p = P(A) > 0$. n shots are fired. An event is called an m-success if the target is hit m times consecutively. Derive the probability p_n of $A_n = \{$there is an m-success in n shots$\}$.

Solution: Event A_{n+1} can be divided into two independent events: A_n and

$$B_n = \{\text{an } m\text{-success appears only after } n+1 \text{ shots,} \\ \text{but not in } n \text{ shots}\}.$$

B_n is an intersection of the following events:

$C_1 = A^c_{n-m}$,
$C_2 = \{$miss the target in the $(n-m+1)$th shots$\}$,
$C_3 = \{$the target is hit in the remaining m shots$\}$.

We obviously have

$$P(C_1) = 1 - p_{n-m}, \quad P(C_2) = 1 - p, \quad P(C_3) = p^m.$$

Hence,

$$p_{n+1} = p_n + (1 - p_{n-m})(1 - p)p^m. \tag{7.9}$$

The initial values are:

$$p_0 = p_1 = \cdots = p_{m-1} = 0, \quad p_m = p^m.$$

Given these initial values, we can find any p_n iteratively from (7.9). ■

3. Random Variables

We use an example to motivate random variables.

Example 7.26. Consider the travel cost of a person arriving in Hong Kong from Beijing. The vehicle the person uses for the trip is a random event. Denote

$$\omega_1 = \text{by air}, \quad \omega_2 = \text{by train}, \quad \omega_3 = \text{by boat}.$$

The travel cost is dependent on the vehicle of travel and can be denoted by $x(\omega)$. We can alternatively denote the travel cost by $\tilde{x}$, which we call a random variable. That is, a random variable is a real-valued function of outcomes. ■

Definition 7.3. Given a probability space $(\Omega, \mathcal{F}, P)$, a real-valued function $x : \Omega \to \mathbb{R}$ is called a random variables if, for any real value x, the set $\{\omega | x(\omega \leq x)\}$ is an event. ■

In a special case, if $\mathcal{F}$ contains all subsets of Ω, then any real-valued function on Ω is a random variable. If Ω has countable points, then the σ-algebra $\mathcal{F}$ that we typically use to define a probability space consists of all subsets of Ω.

For any function $g(x)$ defined on $(-\infty, \infty)$, denote

$$g(-\infty) \equiv \lim_{x \to -\infty} g(x), \qquad g(\infty) \equiv \lim_{x \to \infty} g(x),$$

$$g(a^-) \equiv \lim_{x \to a^-} g(x), \qquad g(a^+) \equiv \lim_{x \to a^+} g(x),$$

where "$x \to a^-$" and "$x \to a^+$" mean that x converges to a from left and right, respectively.

Given a random variable $\tilde{x}$, we can define a distribution function $F_{\tilde{x}} : \mathbb{R} \to [0,1]$ by

$$F_{\tilde{x}}(x) = P(\{\omega | x(\omega) \le x\}), \quad \text{for } x \in \mathbb{R}.$$

Theorem 7.7. *Distribution function $F_{\tilde{x}}(x)$ has the following properties:*

- $F_{\tilde{x}}(x)$ *is increasing.*
- $F_{\tilde{x}}(x)$ *is right-continuous:* $F_{\tilde{x}}(x^+) = F_{\tilde{x}}(x)$ *for any $x \in \mathbb{R}$.*
- $F_{\tilde{x}}(-\infty) = 0$ *and* $F_{\tilde{x}}(\infty) = 1$. ∎

The three properties in Theorem 7.7 are fundamental properties. This means that a real-valued function is a distribution function iff it has these three properties.

Corollary 7.1. *Some useful properties of a distribution function:*

- $P(a < \tilde{x} \le b) = F_{\tilde{x}}(b) - F_{\tilde{x}}(a)$, *for any $ab \in \mathbb{R}$ with $a < b$.*
- $P(\tilde{x} = a) = F_{\tilde{x}}(a) - F_{\tilde{x}}(a^-)$.
- $P(\tilde{x} < a) = F_{\tilde{x}}(a^-)$. ∎

To transform a random variable y to another x, assuming a strict monotonic relationship between the two variables, we use the formula

$$f_{\tilde{x}}(x)|dx| = f_{\tilde{y}}(y)|dy|. \tag{7.10}$$

This formula simply means $P(\tilde{x} = x) = P(\tilde{y} = y)$. For example, suppose $\tilde{y} = \phi(\tilde{x})$ and $\phi(\cdot)$ is strictly monotonic. If we want to deal with

x, using formula (7.10) and since

$$f_{\tilde{y}}(y)|dy| = f_{\tilde{y}}[\phi(x)]|\phi'(x)||dx|,$$

we have

$$f_{\tilde{x}}(x) = f_{\tilde{y}}[\phi(x)]|\phi'(x)|. \tag{7.11}$$

That is, given the density function of $\tilde{y}$, if $\tilde{y} = \phi(\tilde{x})$, the density function of $\tilde{x}$ will be as defined in (7.11). If we want to deal instead with y, using formula (7.10) again, we have

$$f_{\tilde{x}}[\phi^{-1}(y)]\left|\frac{1}{\phi'[\phi^{-1}(y)]}\right||dy| = f_{\tilde{y}}(y)|dy|,$$

implying

$$f_{\tilde{y}}(y) = f_{\tilde{x}}[\phi^{-1}(y)]\left|\frac{1}{\phi'[\phi^{-1}(y)]}\right|.$$

That is, given the density function of $\tilde{x}$, if $\tilde{y} = \phi(\tilde{x})$ we can find the density function of $\tilde{y}$. In general, we can transform n random variables to n other random variables. The following theorem offers the formula.

Theorem 7.8. *There are n random variables $\tilde{x}_1, \ldots, \tilde{x}_n$ with density function $f_{\tilde{x}}(x_1, \ldots, x_n)$. There are another n random variables $\tilde{y}_1, \ldots, \tilde{y}_n$ defined by*

$$\tilde{y}_i = u_i(\tilde{x}_1, \ldots, \tilde{x}_n), \quad i = 1, \ldots, n. \tag{7.12}$$

Suppose that the n-equation system (7.12) has a unique solution $\tilde{x}_i = v_i(\tilde{y}_1, \ldots, \tilde{y}_n)$, $i = 1, \ldots, n$. Suppose that the v_i's are continuously differentiable. Let J be the Jacobi matrix defined by

$$J \equiv \frac{\partial(x_1, \ldots, x_n)}{\partial(y_1, \ldots, y_n)} \equiv \begin{vmatrix} \frac{\partial v_1}{\partial y_1} & \cdots & \frac{\partial v_1}{\partial y_n} \\ \vdots & & \vdots \\ \frac{\partial v_n}{\partial y_1} & \cdots & \frac{\partial v_n}{\partial y_n} \end{vmatrix}.$$

Then, $(\tilde{y}_1, \ldots, \tilde{y}_n)$'s density function is

$$f_{\tilde{y}}(y_1, \ldots, y_n) = f_{\tilde{x}}[v_1(y_1, \ldots, y_n), \ldots, v_n(y_1, \ldots, y_n)]|J|,$$

where $|\cdot|$ means the absolute value. ∎

Theorem 7.9. *Suppose that $(\tilde{x}, \tilde{y})$ is normally distributed, $g'(\tilde{y})$ has expected value, and $\lim_{y \to -\infty} g(y) f_{\tilde{y}}(y) = \lim_{y \to \infty} g(y) f_{\tilde{y}}(y) = 0$, where $f_{\tilde{y}}$ is the density function of $\tilde{y}$. Then,*

$$\text{cov}[\tilde{x}, g(\tilde{y})] = E[g'(\tilde{y})]\text{cov}(\tilde{x}, \tilde{y}). \quad \blacksquare$$

4. Distribution Functions

In the above, we have defined a distribution function for a given random variable. It turns out that we can also define a distribution function without referring to a random variable.

Definition 7.4. A real-valued function $F(x)$ is called a distribution function if it has the three properties in Theorem 7.7.

Theorem 7.10. *For any distribution function $F(x)$, there exists a probability space $(\Omega, \mathcal{F}, P)$ and a random variable $\tilde{x}$ defined on it such that $\tilde{x}$'s distribution function $F_{\tilde{x}}(\cdot)$ is exactly $F(\cdot)$.* $\quad \blacksquare$

Proposition 7.2. *The number of a distribution function's discontinuous points is countable.* $\quad \blacksquare$

Proof. A distribution function $F(x)$ either moves up continuously or jumps up. Since $F(x) \leq 1$, the number of points where $F(x) - F(x^-) > 1/2^n$ must be less than 2^n. As n takes integers from 1 to ∞, all jump points with $F(x) - F(x^-) > 0$ are taken into account. These points are countable.

Two types of distribution functions are common in practice: discrete and continuous distribution functions. For a distribution function $F(x)$, if there is a matrix

$$P \equiv \begin{pmatrix} a_1 & a_2 & a_3 & \cdots \\ p_1 & p_2 & p_3 & \cdots \end{pmatrix},$$

where $p_i \geq 0$ and $\sum_{i=1}^{\infty} p_i = 1$, such that

$$F(x) = \sum_{i : a_i \leq x} p_i,$$

then $F(x)$ is called a discrete distribution function, where the a_i's may be any of a finite or infinite set of values. If there is no i such that $a_i \leq x$, set $F(x) = 0$. We call P the density matrix or density.

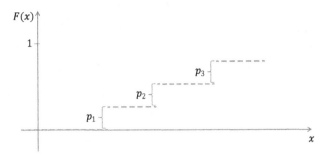

For a distribution function $F(x)$, if there is a positive real-valued function $f(x)$ such that, for any x,

$$F(x) = \int_{-\infty}^{x} f(t)dt, \tag{7.13}$$

then $F(x)$ is called a continuous distribution function. We call $f(x)$ the density function or density. Given any positive real-valued function $f(x)$, if $\int_{\infty}^{\infty} f(x)dx = 1$, we can define a continuous distribution function $F(x)$ by (7.13). Note that a continuous distribution function $F(x)$ must be continuous. In fact, it must be absolutely continuous.

Example 7.27. For a positive function:

$$f(x) = \begin{cases} 1 & \text{if } x \in [0,1] \\ 0 & \text{if not,} \end{cases}$$

since $\int_{\infty}^{\infty} f(x)\,dx = 1$, we can define a continuous distribution function $F(x)$ using (7.13). We find

$$F(x) = \begin{cases} 1 & \text{if } x > 1, \\ x & \text{if } x \in [0,1], \\ 0 & \text{if } x < 0. \end{cases} \qquad \blacksquare$$

Since a probability distribution function F is monotonic, its derivative $f(x)$ — the density function — exists almost everywhere, but may not be Lebesgue integrable. Since $f(x)$ may not be Lebesgue integrable, we do not necessarily have $F(x) = \int_{-\infty}^{x} f(t)dt$. In fact, this is true iff F is absolutely continuous. A bounded-variation function g is differentiable almost everywhere. But the derivative g' is Lebesgue integrable iff g is absolutely continuous. See Jiang and Wu (1978, p. 124).

For n random variables $\tilde{x}_1, \tilde{x}_2, \ldots, \tilde{x}_n$ defined on a probability space (Ω, F, P) let $\tilde{x} = (\tilde{x}_1, \tilde{x}_2, \ldots, \tilde{x}_n)$ and define its distribution function as

$$F_{\tilde{x}}(x_1, x_2, \ldots, x_n) \equiv P(\tilde{x}_1 \leq x_1, \tilde{x}_2 \leq x_2, \ldots, \tilde{x}_n \leq x_n).$$

We call $F_{\tilde{x}}$ the distribution function of $\tilde{x}$ or the joint distribution function of $\tilde{x}_1, \tilde{x}_2, \ldots, \tilde{x}_n$. We call $F_{\tilde{x}}(x_1, \ldots, x_k, \infty, \ldots, \infty)$ the marginal distribution function of $\tilde{x}_1, \tilde{x}_2, \ldots, \tilde{x}_k$, which is the distribution function of $\tilde{x}_1, \tilde{x}_2, \ldots, \tilde{x}_k$.

For n random variables $\tilde{x}_1, \tilde{x}_2, \ldots, \tilde{x}_n$, if

$$F_{(\tilde{x}_1, \ldots, \tilde{x}_n)}(x_1, x_2, \ldots, x_n) = F_{\tilde{x}_1}(x_1) F_{\tilde{x}_2}(x_2) \cdots F_{\tilde{x}_n}(x_n),$$

for all $(x_1, x_2, \ldots, x_n)$, we say that the random variables are independent.

Proposition 7.3. *Given arbitrary continuous functions $f_1(x), \ldots, f_n(x)$, if random variables $\tilde{x}_1, \tilde{x}_2, \ldots, \tilde{x}_n$ are independent, then $f_1(\tilde{x}_1), f_2(\tilde{x}_2), \ldots, f_n(\tilde{x}_n)$ are independent random variables.* ∎

Proposition 7.4. *For discrete random variables $\tilde{x}_1, \tilde{x}_2, \ldots, \tilde{x}_n$, suppose $\tilde{x}_i$ takes values in A_i. If*

$$P(\tilde{x}_1 = a_1, \cdots, \tilde{x}_n = a_n) = \prod_{i=1}^{n} P(\tilde{x}_i = a_i),$$

for all $a_i \in A_i$ and $i = 1, \ldots, n$, then $\tilde{x}_1, \tilde{x}_2, \ldots, \tilde{x}_n$ are independent. ∎

Proposition 7.5. *For continuous random variables $\tilde{x}_1, \tilde{x}_2, \ldots, \tilde{x}_n$, let $f(x_1, \ldots, x_n)$ be the density function of $(\tilde{x}_1, \tilde{x}_2, \ldots, \tilde{x}_n)$ and $f_{\tilde{x}_i}(x_i)$ be the marginal density function of $\tilde{x}_i$. If*

$$f(x_1, x_2, \ldots, x_n) = f_{\tilde{x}_1}(x_1) f_{\tilde{x}_2}(x_2) \cdots f_{\tilde{x}_n}(x_n), \quad a.s.$$

then $\tilde{x}_1, \tilde{x}_2, \ldots, \tilde{x}_n$ are independent. ∎

Proposition 7.6. $(\tilde{x}_1, \ldots, \tilde{x}_n)$ *is normally distributed iff any of its liner combination* $\tilde{y} = \alpha_0 + \sum_{i=1}^{n} \alpha_i \tilde{x}_i$ *is normally distributed.* ∎

Proposition 7.7. *If the sum of two independent random variables is normally distributed, then both random variables are normally distributed. It is the same for poisson distributions.* ∎

A distribution function $F(x)$ is singular if function $F(x)$ is continuous and has zero derivative almost everywhere (in terms of Lesbegue measure).

Theorem 7.11. *Any distribution function can be written in the following form:*

$$F(x) = \alpha_1 F_1(x) + \alpha_2 F_2(x) + \alpha_3 F_3(x),$$

where $F_1(x)$ is a continuous distribution (i.e., $F_1(x)$ is absolutely continuous), $F_2(x)$ is a discrete distribution, $F_3(x)$ is a singular distribution, and α_i's are constants with $\alpha_i \geq 0$ and $\alpha_1 + \alpha_2 + \alpha_3 = 1$.
∎

Tables 7.1 and 7.2 give popular distribution functions.

Proposition 7.8. *For a sequence $\{p_n\}$ of real numbers, if*

$$\lim_{n \to \infty} n p_n = \lambda,$$

for some $\lambda > 0$, then for any integer k we have

$$\lim_{n \to \infty} C_n^k p_n^k (1 - p_n)^{n-k} = \frac{\lambda^k}{k!} e^{-\lambda}.$$

That is, a Binomial distribution converges to a Poisson distribution under certain conditions. ∎

Using Proposition 7.8, we can find an approximate probability of an event occurring k times.

Example 7.28. Suppose that we have n machines and each machine has probability p of breaking down in each hour. If we want to keep the probability of more than one machine breaking down in each hour to less then 1%, how many machine do we actually need?

Table 7.1. Discrete Distributions

Distribution	Domain	Density	Mean	Variance	Parameter Domain
Poisson $P(\lambda)$	$i = 0, 1, 2, \ldots$	$\dfrac{\lambda^i e^{-\lambda}}{i!}$	λ	λ	$\lambda > 0$
Geometric $G(p)$	$i = 1, 2, 3, \ldots$	pq^{i-1}	$\dfrac{1}{p}$	$\dfrac{q}{p^2}$	$0 < p < 1, \quad q = 1 - p$
Super Geometric $H(n, M, N)$	$i = max\{0, n - N + M\},$ $\ldots, min\{n, M\}$	$\dfrac{C_{N-M}^{n-i} C_M^i}{C_N^n}$	$n \dfrac{M}{N}$	$n \dfrac{N-n}{N-1} \dfrac{M(N-M)}{N^2}$	N, M, n positive integers
Binomial $B(n, p)$	$i = 0, 1, 2, \ldots$	$C_n^i p^i q^{n-i}$	np	npq	$0 < p < 1, \quad q = 1 - p$
Negative Binomial $B^-(\alpha, p)$	$i = 0, 1, 2, \ldots$	$C_{\alpha+i-1}^i p^\alpha q^i$	$\alpha \dfrac{q}{p}$	$\alpha \dfrac{q}{p^2}$	$0 < p < 1, \quad q = 1 - p, \quad \alpha > 0$
Log $L(p)$	$i = 1, 2, 3, \ldots$	$-\dfrac{1}{lnp} \dfrac{q^i}{i}$	$-\dfrac{q}{plnp}$	$-\dfrac{q\left(1 + \frac{q}{lnp}\right)}{p^2 lnp}$	$0 < p < 1, \quad q = 1 - p$
Two Point	$i = 0, 1$	$p^i q^{1-i}$	p	pq	$0 \leq p \leq 1, \quad q = 1 - p$

Table 7.2. Continuous Distributions

Distribution	Domain	Density	Mean	Variance	Parameters
Normal $N(\mu\sigma^2)$	$\mathbb{R}$	$\frac{1}{\sqrt{2\pi}\sigma}e^{-\frac{(x-\mu)^2}{2\sigma^2}}$	μ	σ^2	$\mu\in\mathbb{R},\ \sigma>0$
Uniform $u(a,b)$	$[a,b]$	$\frac{1}{b-a}$	$\frac{a+b}{2}$	$\frac{(b-a)^2}{12}$	$a,b\in\mathbb{R}$
Exponential $e(\mu,\sigma)$	$[\mu,\infty)$	$\frac{1}{\sigma}e^{-\frac{x-\mu}{\sigma}}$	$\mu+\sigma$	σ^2	$\mu\in\mathbb{R},\ \sigma>0$
Gamma $\Gamma(\alpha\sigma)$	$[c,\infty)$	$\frac{1}{\Gamma(\alpha)\sigma^\alpha}(x-c)^{\alpha-1}e^{-\frac{x-c}{\sigma}}$	$\alpha\sigma+c$	$\alpha\sigma^2$	$\alpha,\sigma>0,\ c\in\mathbb{R}$
Log-normal $\ln(\mu\sigma^2)$	$\mathbb{R}_+$	$\frac{1}{\sqrt{2\pi}\sigma x}e^{-\frac{(\ln x-\mu)^2}{2\sigma^2}}$	$e^{\mu+\frac{\sigma^2}{2}}$	$e^{2\mu+\sigma^2}(e^{\sigma^2}-1)$	$\mu\in\mathbb{R},\ \sigma>0$
Rene $R(\mu)$	$\mathbb{R}_+$	$\frac{x}{\mu^2}e^{-\frac{x^2}{2\mu^2}}$	$\sqrt{\frac{\pi}{2}}\mu$	$\frac{4-\pi}{2}\mu^2$	$\mu>0$
$\chi^2(n)$	$\mathbb{R}_+$	$\frac{1}{2^{n/2}\Gamma\left(\frac{n}{2}\right)}x^{\frac{n}{2}-1}e^{-\frac{x}{2}}$	n	$2n$	$n\in N,\ n>0$
Student $t(n)$	$\mathbb{R}$	$\frac{\Gamma\left(\frac{n+1}{2}\right)}{\sqrt{n\pi}\Gamma\left(\frac{n}{2}\right)}\left(1+\frac{x^2}{n}\right)^{-\frac{n+1}{2}}$	0	$\frac{n}{n-2}$	$n>2$

(Continued)

Table 7.2. (*Continued*)

Distribution	Domain	Density	Mean	Variance	Parameters
$F(m,n)$	$\mathbb{R}_+$	$\dfrac{x^{\frac{m}{2}-1}}{B\left(\frac{m}{2},\frac{n}{2}\right)}\left(\dfrac{m}{n}\right)^{\frac{m}{2}}\left(1+\dfrac{mx}{n}\right)^{-\frac{m+n}{2}}$	$\dfrac{n}{n-2}$	$\dfrac{2n^2(m+n-2)}{m(n-2)^2(n-4)}$	$n>4$
William $W(m,\alpha)$	$[\gamma,\infty)$	$\dfrac{m}{\alpha}(x-\gamma)^{m-1}e^{-\frac{(x-\gamma)^m}{\alpha}}$	$\alpha^{\frac{1}{m}}\Gamma\left(1+\dfrac{1}{m}\right)+\gamma$	$\alpha^{\frac{2}{m}}\left[\Gamma\left(1+\dfrac{2}{m}\right)\right.$ $\left.-\Gamma^2\left(1+\dfrac{1}{m}\right)\right]$	$m,\alpha>0$
Cauchy $C(\mu,\alpha)$	$\mathbb{R}$	$\dfrac{\alpha}{\pi}\dfrac{1}{\alpha^2+(x-\mu)^2}$	NA	NA	$\alpha>0,\quad \mu\in\mathbb{R}$
Poisson	$\mathbb{R}$	$\dfrac{a^x e^{-a}}{\Gamma(1+x)}$	a	a	$a>0$
Beta	$[0,1]$	$\dfrac{\Gamma(p+q)}{\Gamma(p)\Gamma(q)}x^{p-1}(1-x)^{q-1}$	$\dfrac{p}{p+q}$	$\dfrac{pq}{(p+q)^2(p+q+1)}$	$p>0,\quad q>0$
Laplace	$\mathbb{R}$	$\dfrac{1}{2\lambda}e^{-\frac{|x-\mu|}{\lambda}}$	μ	$2\lambda^2$	$\lambda>0,\quad \mu\in\mathbb{R}$

Solution: Let

$$\tilde{x} = \text{the number of machines breaking down in an}$$
$$\text{hour given } n \text{ machines.}$$

We have

$$P(\tilde{x} = k) = C_n^k p^k (1 - p)^{n-k}.$$

Then,

$$P(\tilde{x} > 1) = 1 - P(\tilde{x} = 0) - P(\tilde{x} = 1) = 1 - (1 - p)^n - np(1 - p)^{n-1}.$$

Then, the number of machines that we actually need is the integer solution of the following problem:

$$\max_{n} \quad 1 - (1 - p)^n - np(1 - p)^{n-1}$$
$$\text{s.t.} \quad 1 - (1 - p)^n - np(1 - p)^{n-1} \leq 1\%. \quad \blacksquare$$

Example 7.29. A book seller sells books from two bags with n books in each bag. The seller picks a book randomly from the two bags every time he sells a book. Consider event

$$A = \{\text{all books in one bag are sold, while the other bag}$$
$$\text{still has m books}\}.$$

Solution: $2n - m$ books are sold, and among them n books are from one of the bags. Hence, the probability is

$$P(A) = C_{2n-m}^n \left(\frac{1}{2}\right)^n \left(\frac{1}{2}\right)^{n-m} = C_{2n-m}^n \left(\frac{1}{2}\right)^{2n-m}. \quad \blacksquare$$

5. Conditional Distributions and Expectations

For a random variable $\tilde{x}$, if $\int_{-\infty}^{\infty} x dF_{\tilde{x}}(x)$ is absolutely convergent, i.e., $\int_{-\infty}^{\infty} |x| dF_{\tilde{x}}(x) < \infty$, define the expectation of $\tilde{x}$ as

$$E(\tilde{x}) \equiv \int_{-\infty}^{\infty} x dF_{\tilde{x}}(x).$$

Generally, for a continuous function $g(\cdot)$, if $\int_{-\infty}^{\infty} g(x) dF_{\tilde{x}}(x)$ is absolutely convergent, i.e., $\int_{-\infty}^{\infty} |g(x)| dF_{\tilde{x}}(x) < \infty$, define the expectation of $g(\tilde{x})$ as

$$E[g(\tilde{x})] \equiv \int_{-\infty}^{\infty} g(x)dF_{\tilde{x}}(x).$$

More generally, for random variables $\tilde{x}_1, \tilde{x}_2, \ldots, \tilde{x}_n$ and a continuous function $g(x_1, \ldots, x_n)$, if $\int_{-\infty}^{\infty} g(x_1, \ldots, x_n)dF_{(\tilde{x}_1,\ldots,\tilde{x}_n)}t(x_1, \ldots, x_n)$ is absolutely convergent, define

$$E[g(\tilde{x}_1, \ldots, \tilde{x}_n)] \equiv \int_{-\infty}^{\infty} g(x_1, \ldots, x_n)dF_{(\tilde{x}_1,\ldots,\tilde{x}_n)}(x_1, \ldots, x_n).$$

Proposition 7.9. *If $\tilde{x}_1, \tilde{x}_2, \ldots, \tilde{x}_n$, are independent, then*

$$E(\tilde{x}_1\tilde{x}_2\cdots\tilde{x}_n) = E(\tilde{x}_1)E(\tilde{x}_2)\cdots E(\tilde{x}_n). \quad \blacksquare$$

For a random variable $\tilde{x}$, for any event A with $P(A) > 0$, let

$$F_{\tilde{x}}(x|A) \equiv \frac{P(\tilde{x} \leq x, A)}{P(A)},$$

and call it the conditional distribution function of $\tilde{x}$ under event A. If $\int_{-\infty}^{\infty} xdF_{\tilde{x}}(x|A)$ is absolutely convergent, then call this integral the conditional expectation of $\tilde{x}$ under event A and denote it by $E(\tilde{x}|A)$, i.e.,

$$E(\tilde{x}|A) = \int_{-\infty}^{\infty} xdF_{\tilde{x}}(x|A).$$

We say that a random variable $\tilde{x}$ and an event A are independent if

$$P(\{\tilde{x} \leq x\}\bigcap A) = P(\tilde{x} \leq x)P(A).$$

This means $F(x|A) = F(x)$. Then,

$$E(\tilde{x}|A) = \int_{-\infty}^{\infty} xdF(x|A) = \int_{-\infty}^{\infty} xdF(x) = E(\tilde{x}).$$

Proposition 7.10 (Complete Expectation Formula). *Let $\{H_i\}_{i=1}^{n}$ be a partition of a probability space (Ω, F, P), where n can be finite or infinite. Then, for any random variables $\tilde{x}$,*

$$E(\tilde{x}) = \sum_{i=1}^{n} E(\tilde{x}|H_i)P(H_i). \quad \blacksquare \qquad (7.14)$$

For two random variables $\tilde{x}$ and $\tilde{y}$, define the distribution function of $\tilde{x}|\tilde{y}$ as

$$F_{\tilde{x}|\tilde{y}}(x|y) \equiv P(\tilde{x} \le x|\tilde{y} = y),$$

and denote the density function by $f_{\tilde{x}|\tilde{y}}(x|y)$. Then, for a continuous function g, define

$$E[g(\tilde{x})|\tilde{y} = y] \equiv \int_{-\infty}^{\infty} g(x)dF(x|y), \qquad (7.15)$$

assuming that the interval is convergent (i.e., the expectation is well defined). We have

$$f_{\tilde{y}|x}(y)dy = P\{\tilde{y} = y|\tilde{x} = x\} = \frac{P\{\tilde{y} = y, \tilde{x} = x\}}{P\{\tilde{x} = x\}} = \frac{f_{\tilde{x},\tilde{y}}(x, y)dxdy}{f(x)dx}.$$

Hence, we define

$$f_{\tilde{y}|x}(y) \equiv \frac{f_{\tilde{x},\tilde{y}}(x, y)}{f_{\tilde{x}}(x)},$$

and more generally,

$$f_{\tilde{x},\tilde{y}|z}(x, y) = \frac{f_{\tilde{x},\tilde{y},\tilde{z}}(x, y, z)}{f_{\tilde{z}}(z)}.$$

We call $f_{\tilde{y}|x}(y)$ the conditional density function of $\tilde{y}$ given $\tilde{x} = x$.

Proposition 7.11. *For any two random variables $\tilde{x}$ and $\tilde{y}$ and a continuous function g, assuming that the following expectations are well defined, we have*

$$E\{E[g(\tilde{x})|\tilde{y}]\} = E[g(\tilde{x})]. \qquad (7.16)$$

Proof. We have

$$
\begin{aligned}
E\{E[g(\tilde{x})|\tilde{y}]\} &= \int_{-\infty}^{\infty} E[g(x)|y] f_{\tilde{y}}(y) dy \\
&= \int_{-\infty}^{\infty} \int_{-\infty}^{\infty} g(x) f_{\tilde{x}|\tilde{y}}(x|y) dx f_{\tilde{y}}(y) dy \\
&= \int_{-\infty}^{\infty} \int_{-\infty}^{\infty} g(x) f_{(\tilde{x},\tilde{y})}(x,y) dx dy \\
&= \int_{-\infty}^{\infty} g(x) f_{\tilde{x}}(x) dx = E[g(\tilde{x})]. \quad \blacksquare
\end{aligned}
$$

The formula in (7.6) is similar to the complete expectation formula in (7.14). If $\tilde{x}$ and $\tilde{y}$ are independent, then by the definition in (7.15) we have $E[g(\tilde{x})|\tilde{y}] = E[g(\tilde{x})]$.

For a random variable $\tilde{x}$, let $\tilde{y} = g(\tilde{x})$ for some continuous function g. We have

$$
E(\tilde{y}) = \int_{-\infty}^{\infty} x dF_{\tilde{y}}(x) \quad \text{and} \quad E[g(\tilde{x})] = \int_{-\infty}^{\infty} g(x) dF_{\tilde{x}}(x).
$$

We must have

$$
\int_{-\infty}^{\infty} x dF_{g(\tilde{x})}(x) = \int_{-\infty}^{\infty} g(x) dF_{\tilde{x}}(x), \tag{7.17}
$$

otherwise we would have a contradiction. Fortunately, this identity holds.

Proposition 7.12. *If one of the integrals in (7.17) exists, then the other must also exist and (7.17) holds. Generally, (7.17) holds when $\tilde{x}$ is vector of random variables.* $\blacksquare$

Proposition 7.13 (Filtering Property[1]). *Let $\tilde{x}$ be a random variables defined on a probability space $(\Omega, \mathcal{F}, P)$. Then, for any σ-algebras F_1 and F_2, $F_1, F_2 \subset F$, we have*

$$
E[E(\tilde{x}|F_1)|F_2] = E(\tilde{x}|F_1 \cap F_2). \quad \blacksquare
$$

---

[1]See Miermont (2006, p. 10).

Proposition 7.14 (Markov Inequality). *For a random variables $\tilde{x}$, if for $r > 0$ we have $E|\tilde{x}|^r < \infty$, then for any $\varepsilon > 0$ we have*

$$P(|\tilde{x}| \geq \varepsilon) \leq \frac{E|\tilde{x}|^r}{\varepsilon^r}. \quad \blacksquare$$

Proposition 7.15 (Chebyshev inequality). *Let $\tilde{x}$ be a random variable with mean μ and variance σ^2. For any $\varepsilon > 0$, we have*

$$P(|\tilde{x} - \mu| \geq \varepsilon) \leq \frac{\sigma^2}{\varepsilon^2}. \quad \blacksquare$$

The Chebyshev inequality is a special case of the Markov inequality.

Proposition 7.16. *For a random variables $\tilde{x}$, $\tilde{x} = a$ constant a.s. iff $var(\tilde{x}) = 0$.* $\quad \blacksquare$

Define the correlation coefficient of two random variables $\tilde{x}_1$ and $\tilde{x}_2$ as

$$\rho \equiv \frac{E[(\tilde{x}_1 - E\tilde{x}_1)(\tilde{x}_2 - E\tilde{x}_2)]}{\sqrt{E[(\tilde{x}_1 - E\tilde{x}_1)^2]E[(\tilde{x}_2 - E\tilde{x}_2)^2]}}$$

When $\rho = 0$, we say that $\tilde{x}_1$ and $\tilde{x}_2$ are uncorrelated .

Proposition 7.17.

- $\rho \in [0, 1]$.
- *If $\tilde{x}_1$ and $\tilde{x}_2$ are independent, then $\rho = 0$.*
- *$|\rho| = 1$ iff $\tilde{x}_1$ and $\tilde{x}_2$ have a linear relationship almost surely, i.e., there exist constants $a \neq 0$ and b such that*

$$\tilde{x}_1 = a\tilde{x}_2 + b, \quad a.s. \quad \blacksquare$$

6. Convergence

In probability theory, there are four types of convergence.

Let $\{\tilde{x}_n\}$ be a sequence of random variables and $\tilde{x}$ be a random variable. We say that $\tilde{x}_n$ converges to $\tilde{x}$ in probability and denote

$$\tilde{x}_n \xrightarrow{P} \tilde{x},$$

if $\forall \varepsilon > 0$, we have

$$\lim_{n \to \infty} P(|\tilde{x}_n - \tilde{x}| < \varepsilon) = 1.$$

We say that $\tilde{x}_n$ converges to $\tilde{x}$ almost surely and denote

$$\tilde{x}_n \xrightarrow{a.s.} \tilde{x},$$

if

$$P\{\omega| \lim_{n \to \infty} \tilde{x}_n(\omega) = \tilde{x}(\omega)\} = 1.$$

Let $\{F_n(x)\}$ be a sequence of distribution functions and F be a distribution function. We say that F_n converges weakly to F and denote

$$F_n \xrightarrow{w} F,$$

if at any continuous point x of F, we have

$$\lim_{n \to \infty} F_n(x) = F(x).$$

We say that $\tilde{x}_n$ converges weakly to $\tilde{x}$ and denote

$$\tilde{x}_n \xrightarrow{w} \tilde{x},$$

if the distribution of $\tilde{x}_n$ converges weakly to the distribution function of $\tilde{x}$.

We say that $\tilde{x}_n$ converges to $\tilde{x}$ in rank r and denote

$$\tilde{x}_n \xrightarrow{r} \tilde{x},$$

if

$$\lim_{n \to \infty} E|\tilde{x}_n - \tilde{x}|^r = 0.$$

Theorem 7.12.

- $\tilde{x}_n \xrightarrow{r} \tilde{x} \Rightarrow \tilde{x}_n \xrightarrow{p} \tilde{x} \Rightarrow \tilde{x}_n \xrightarrow{w} \tilde{x}.$
- $\tilde{x}_n \xrightarrow{a.s.} \tilde{x} \Rightarrow \tilde{x}_n \xrightarrow{p} \tilde{x}.$ ∎

Theorem 7.13 (Strong Law of Large Numbers). *If $\{\tilde{x}_n\}$ are identically distributed with mean μ, then the sample average $\bar{x}_n \equiv (\tilde{x}_1 + \cdots + \tilde{x}_n)/n$ converges almost surely to expected value:*

$$\bar{x}_n \xrightarrow{a.s.} \mu \quad as \quad n \to \infty, \quad or \quad P\left(\lim_{n \to \infty} \bar{x}_n = \mu\right) = 1. \quad ∎$$

Theorem 7.14 (Weak Law of Large Numbers). *If $\{\tilde{x}_n\}$ are identically distributed with mean μ, the sample average $\tilde{x}_n$ converges in probability to the expected value: for any $\varepsilon > 0$,*

$$\bar{x}_n \xrightarrow{p} \mu \quad as \quad n \to \infty, \quad or \quad \lim_{n\to\infty} P(|\bar{x}_n - \mu| < \varepsilon) = 1. \quad \blacksquare$$

Theorem 7.15 (Central Limit Theorem). *If $\{\tilde{x}_n\}$ are identically distributed with mean μ and variance σ^2, where $0 < \sigma < \infty$, then the following limit holds uniformly for all $x \in \mathbb{R}$:*

$$\lim_{n\to\infty} P\left(\frac{1}{\sigma\sqrt{n}} \sum_{i=1}^{n}(\tilde{x}_i - \mu) \leq x\right) = \frac{1}{\sqrt{2\pi}} \int_{-\infty}^{x} e^{-\frac{t^2}{2}}\, dt. \quad \blacksquare$$

Notes

A good reference is Ross (2010). Many examples in this chapter are from Wang (1976).

References

[1] Afriat, S.N. (1971). Theory of Maxima and the Method of Lagrange. *SIAM Journal of Applied Mathematics,* 20, 343–357.

[2] Arrow, K.J.; Enthoven, A.C. (1961). Quasi-Concave Programming. *Econometrica,* 29(4), 779–800.

[3] Blanchard, O.J.; Fischer, S. (1989). *Lectures on Macroeconomics.* MIT Press, London.

[4] Chiang, A.C. (1984). *Fundamental Methods of Mathematical Economics,* 3rd edition. McGraw-Hill, New York.

[5] Chiang, A.C. (1992). *Elements of Dynamic Optimization.* McGraw-Hill, New York.

[6] Chiang, A.C.; Wainwright, K. (2005). *Fundamental Methods of Mathematical Economics,* 4th edition. McGraw-Hill, New York.

[7] Greene, W.H. (1993). *Econometric Analysis.* Maxwell Macmillan, London.

[8] Jiang, Z.J.; Wu, Z.Q. (1978). *Real Analysis.* People's Education Publisher, Beijing.

[9] Kamien, M.I.; Schwartz, N.L. (1981). *Dynamic Optimization: The Calculus of Variations and Optimal Control in Economics and Management,* North Holland, New York.

[10] Kamien, M.I.; Schwartz, N.L. (1991). *Dynamic Optimization: The Calculus of Variations and Optimal Control in Economics and Management.* 2nd edition. North Holland, New York.

[11] Leitmann, G. (1981). *The Calculus of Variations and Optimal Control.* Plenum Press, New York.

[12] Matthews, K.R. (1998). *Elementary Linear Algebra,* free.

[13] Miermont, G. (2006). *Advanced Probability.* University of Cambridge, Cambridge.

[14] Ross, S. (2010). *A First Course in Probability*, 8th edition. Prentice Hall, New Jersey.

[15] Samuelson, P.A. (1947). *Foundations of Economics Analysis.* Harvard University Press, Cambridge, MA.

[16] Sargent, T.J. (1987). *Dynamic Macroeconomic Theory.* Harvard University Press, Cambridge, MA.

[17] Stokey, N.L.; Lucas, R.E. (1989). *Recursive Methods in Economic Dynamics.* Harvard University Press, Cambridge, MA.

[18] Sydsæter, K.; Hammond, P.; Seierstad, A.; Strøm, A. (2005). *Further Mathematics for Economic Analysis.* McGraw-Hill, New York.

[19] Takayama, A. (1993). *Analytical Methods in Economics.* University of Michigan Press, Ann Arbor, Michigan.

[20] Turnovsky, S.T. (1986). Short-Term and Long-Term Interest Rates in a Monetary Model of a Small Open Economy. *Journal of International Economics*, 291–311.

[21] Varian, H.R. (1984). *Microeconomic Analysis*, 2nd edition. Norton, New York.

[22] Varian, H.R. (1992). *Microeconomic Analysis*, 3rd edition. Norton, New York.

[23] Wang, S. (1986). The Convex Vector Programming on an Order Complete Ordered Topological Vector Space. *Chinese Annals of Mathematics* (English Edition), 111–123, Vol. 7.

[24] Wang, Z.K. (1976). *Elementary Probability Theory and Its Applications.* Xinhua Publisher, Beijing. (in Chinese)

Index

Printed in the United States
By Bookmasters